The High Ministry
of Government:
The Political Career of
Frank Murphy

by Richard D. Lunt
Rochester Institute of Technology

Detroit   Wayne State University Press
1965

We wish to thank the Michigan
Historical Commission which has
generously granted permission to
reprint a part of Chapter IV, the
earlier version of which originally
appeared as "Frank Murphy's Decision to Enter the 1936 Gubernatorial Race," in *Michigan History,* XLVII, No. 4 (December,
1963), 327-34.

The High Ministry of Government

Frank Murphy, 1935

to Ruth

Contents

Illustrations

Preface

Frank Murphy (1890-1949) was a political leader and a jurist. Until 1940, when Murphy was appointed to the Supreme Court, his career was essentially political. It is this portion of Murphy's life that is treated in this study.

Because this is a biography, Frank Murphy remains the central figure throughout. However, Murphy was intimately associated with the New Deal, and his contribution to it—politically, administratively, and ideologically—is also a major theme. While his contribution is evaluated, there is no attempt to evaluate the New Deal as a whole.

I wish to acknowledge the cooperation and assistance of the following archival institutions: the Burton Historical Collection of the Detroit Public Library, the Labor History Archives of Wayne State University, the Michigan Historical Collections of the University of Michigan, the National Archives, and the Franklin D. Roosevelt Library. (The Franklin D. Roosevelt Library has given special permission to quote from material in its collection.) The *Detroit News* generously permitted me to use its clipping file and those of the *Detroit Times* and the *Detroit Saturday Night*. Mrs. Ruth P. Braun, chief librarian of the *Detroit News,* was most patient in meeting my requests. In addition, I have relied heavily on the *New York Times,* the *Manila Daily Bulletin,* the *Manila Tribune,* and the *Philippines Herald.* I have not footnoted newspaper sources unless I considered my statement open to serious dispute.

The following individuals, all associated with Frank Murphy, were interviewed by me, and their commentary, criticism, and encouragement are much appreciated: Irene Ellis Murphy and Brigid Murphy, Frank Murphy's sisters-in-law; Sharon Murphy, his niece; the late Judge George Murphy, his brother; Russell Barnes, Martin S. Hayden, and Carl Muller, newspaper reporters who followed Murphy's Michigan career; Eleanor Bumgardner, Murphy's personal secretary (1933-49); the late Lawrence P. Fisher who, as a director of General Motors, met with Murphy frequently; Josephine Gomon, Murphy's executive secretary during his mayoralty period; Eugene Gressman, Murphy's law clerk during Murphy's tenure on the Supreme Court; Charles Hedetniemi, his speech writer (1937-39); Norman H. Hill, his secretary and confidant from the mayoralty period to the end of his career; J. Weldon Jones, insular auditor of the Philippines while Murphy was high commissioner of the islands; Edward G. Kemp, his friend and adviser from 1920 until Murphy's death; Edward Williams, caretaker of Frank Murphy's birthplace.

In order to protect the confidence of these individuals I have decided to omit citations of interviews. In any case, I have incorporated the information gathered from these individuals into my own interpretation of Frank Murphy's life and career. I naturally assume full responsibility for this interpretation. (This assumption of responsibility applies as well to the others who have helped me in the preparation of this book.) Scholars who wish to know how interviews have affected my thinking may use my dissertation deposited at the University of New Mexico under the same title as this book.

My adviser at the University of New Mexico, Professor Frank

D. Reeve, has given me much sound advice and encouragement. J. Weldon Jones has read Chapter III, and I have profited greatly from his criticism. Mrs. Gene Tendler has given me valuable editorial assistance.

Rochester Institute of Technology has made every reasonable effort to assist me in the preparation of my manuscript. Mrs. Corrine Goff and Mrs. Alzire Kemp have helped by typing the manuscript.

My wife, Ruth B. Lunt, has provided assistance in many ways, but most helpful have been her suggestions in matters of style.

R. D. L.

Political meeting in June 1931 between New York Governor Franklin D. Roosevelt and Mayor Murphy with G. Hall Roosevelt (left), the governor's cousin and the mayor's aide, joining in. *Courtesy Michigan Historical Collections, University of Michigan.*

Hunger marchers cross Rouge River on the way to Ford Motor Plant in Dearborn, March 7, 1932. Photo by *Detroit News.*

Introduction

*The enlightened administrator must . . . act;
and his acts must be written into the statutes
in the form of old age pensions, better factory laws and general social legislation; they
must be in brick and stone in the shape of
hospitals for children; they must be in dollars and cents and bread and butter in the
form of relief and succor for the helpless
victims of an unemployment they did not
create.*

*It is high ministry, that of government.
It is putting Christianity to work, and by
that standard its success or failure will be
measured.[1]*
—Frank Murphy (1890-1949)

When, on January 18, 1940, Frank Murphy took his oath of office
as associate justice of the Supreme Court, he closed the door on
one phase of his life, and began another. That first phase, his
political career, is the subject of this book.

Above all Frank Murphy was a political leader. He made the
people's hopes his own and tried to realize them by seeking out
and wielding political power. This necessarily involved Murphy
himself holding political office. He thereby served his own ambition, which was not inconsiderable.

Frank Murphy's parents schooled him to the responsibilities and
qualities that greatness requires—particularly singlemindness in
purpose. Persuaded by his parents of his potential greatness, he

13

used all legitimate means to achieve this goal—even to the extent of employing Irish superstition. When his father warned he knew of no great men with middle names, the son shortened his baptismal name, William Francis Murphy, to Frank Murphy. He also lopped three years off his age.[2]

Many considered Frank Murphy to be an enigma. In part this was because the mystery and foreignness of his Irish ways made him unfathomable to many Americans. Another clouding factor was Murphy's obvious ambition which appeared to predominate at the expense of humility. Thus Secretary of the Interior Harold L. Ickes noted his relief at finding Murphy, on one rare occasion, undiverted by pretty ladies and uninterested in talking about himself.[3] But a balanced portrait would also note that Murphy consciously strove for humility by denying himself many—although not all—of the amenities and privileges of his official positions. His close advisers found he could joke about himself. When a woman, who had read accounts of Murphy—then governor of Michigan—picturing him as a saint, rushed up to him and congratulated him on his purity, Murphy pulled away from her and wryly observed to his secretary: "St. Francis, the Virgin Governor!"[4]

Although Murphy didn't become the first Catholic President of the United States as he had hoped, he attained several high posts during the 1930's in which he served his state and his country as mayor of Detroit, governor-general of the Philippine Islands, U.S. high commissioner to the Philippines, governor of Michigan, and U.S. attorney general. The attainment of these positions in itself demonstrated his skill as a politician.

Murphy's particular contribution to American government was his unusually strong faith in American democratic values. To understand this faith it is necessary to understand Murphy's political philosophy. Murphy was a Roman Catholic and a deeply religious person, although he was not punctilious in all the church practices and was anti-clerical. He studied Catholic writers, particularly Thomas Aquinas and his twentieth century adherent, Jacques Maritain. Murphy accepted their thesis that man's reasoning power was a tool for making temporal law conform to divine law. To Murphy, politics and economics were branches of ethics—not independent sciences.

Jacques Maritain used the concept of the individual as opposed to the person when he spoke of man's role in political society. According to Maritain, the individual is but a small part of the political community and is therefore inferior to it; hence the community can justly impose restraints and sacrifices on him. On the other hand the person, which Maritain equated with the soul, is an end in himself. In this case society is subordinate, for the God-given soul transcends the things of this world. The rights of the person, or soul, must be assured by the state. Maritain found these rights defined in writings such as the Magna Carta and the Declaration of Independence.[5]

Murphy accepted the essence of Maritain's theory and blended it with the American political tradition, which, as expressed in the Constitution and its amendments, is distinctly secular. It declares man has natural rights, which have been discovered through man's wisdom; their validity lies not in their moral worth but in their being immutable. Murphy grafted the moral injunction in Maritain's thought onto the American secular tradition. The result was a highly personal political theory. Since Murphy was not a political theorist, this was not necessarily a conscious act, but the results were evident in his words. He believed individual rights—free speech, free assembly, due process—were inalienable because they were God-given. Moreover, one is tempted to suggest that in his mind the saints might just as well have preached from the Bill of Rights as from the Sermon on the Mount. Murphy's speeches often referred to the common goals of Christianity and democracy:

> The essential faith of Christianity and the essential faith of democracy are one and the same. It is the faith that the human personality is inherently free; that every man is endowed with certain rights founded in the very nature of human living; and that there is a code of justice—of wrong-doing and right-doing—that is not subject to change by the law of man.[6]

Murphy advocated nothing new and revolutionary, but rather an adherence to the most fundamental of divine ordinances. He was not a visionary or radical who would wipe out the present society in order to start afresh with a new order. In the basic sense of the word, he was a conservative. His conservatism was often evident, as in his fiscal policies which were based on the balanced-budget principle. Ickes sensed Murphy's essential conservative spirit but mistook it for a latent right-wing tendency and accordingly bet President Franklin Delano Roosevelt that Murphy would be the first of F.D.R.'s Supreme Court appointees to oppose the New Deal.[7]

But Ickes' fear was unwarranted. Murphy was very much a New Dealer. He was convinced the country's troubles fundamentally lay in its refusal to guarantee basic rights. He reasoned that once all men became really free—politically and economically —the injustice of the depression would disappear. Murphy's crucial extension was to include economic well-being in his list of basic individual rights.

This extension was again a product of both Catholic and American traditional thought. Murphy adopted the doctrine of social justice from the labor encyclicals of Popes Leo XIII and Pius XI in which were expressed the church's concern for the unjust conditions of the laboring man in industrialized countries. From the American tradition Murphy adopted the demand of the Progressives for governmental intervention in the economy on behalf of the people. In an address entitled "The Right Use of Democracy" he described how the two traditions reinforced each other in his mind. Expounding on the theme of the expansion of the general welfare clause in the Constitution, Murphy credited the Progressives with "bringing about an understanding of the new, positive role of government," which had been adopted by the New Deal. Then he cited the "Bishops' Program of Social Reconstruction" which fourteen years prior to the New Deal had advocated many of the reforms brought about by F.D.R.[8]

If the bulwark that sustained Murphy was his faith in the rightness of assuring individual freedoms, the implementation of this faith depended on his intuitive sensitivity. He developed this gift in part from learning to understand and help his own family. But this sensitivity was also an inherited part of his constitution as an Irishman—he personally suffered with the past generations of his people. Without this sensitivity he could not have understood, for example, the Filipinos and their need for saving face; neither could he have appreciated the suffering the depression brought. He once declared, as quoted by the *Detroit News* (August 10, 1936): "I believe I am orthodox in my religion, but honestly I believe there would be comparatively little use in trying to inculcate spiritual understanding in a man or woman hungry, cold or destitute in the matter of clothing."

When Murphy took his oath as associate justice, a picture of the frigate *Constitution* hung on the wall behind him. President Roosevelt saw the import of the coincidence and joked: "Frank— you will do a good job for there is the Bible before you and the *Constitution* behind you."[9] This jest, which Murphy had F.D.R. record on a photograph of the ceremony, revealed the essence of Murphy's political faith. This faith gave him a sense of history that guided his actions and enabled him, in many instances, to reach out ahead of his time.

Murphy's political faith was flexible; he adhered to no dogma—religious, economic, or social. He could explore new ideas without hindrance. This helps to explain how he could be both a conservative in fiscal policy and a liberal in public welfare matters. Any seeming contradiction he explained by his belief that an administration can both "be sound and meet its certain obligations of social responsibility for the same reason that . . . a man can be [both] scientific and spiritual."[10]

Like others who have wrestled with seemingly insoluble problems, Murphy developed an attitude of cautious optimism which enabled him to continue striving in spite of major discouragements. He came into prominence at a time when the American social system was challenged, and he demonstrated that the American tradition could be brought up to date to meet the economic problems of the depression. He believed the rights of man included a chance to earn a living and that it was as much the government's job to assure this right as it was the government's job to protect free speech and association. In the automobile sit-down strikes of 1937 Murphy acutely sensed the significance of the crisis—he saw that mass industry crushed the individual and that the workers were demanding the right to protect themselves. He facilitated a peaceful change in the status quo that eventually won for the workers their rights as human beings.

In the Philippines Murphy faced quite a different task, but the same principle, the protection of the rights of individuals, was at stake. While encouraging Philippine independence, he insisted on a carefully controlled transition period in which the Filipinos would learn the privileges and burdens of freedom. He also insisted the United States must continue its responsibility for maintaining a stable Philippine economy during the transition period.

As attorney general, Murphy allowed some infringement on the right of free speech and thought, but he also contributed toward the protection of civil liberties by creating in the Justice Department a civil liberties unit to protect individual rights and by speaking out against abridgment of these rights.

These are not the accomplishments of a great man, for that tribute must be reserved for those few who are ultimately responsible for bringing about major changes. Murphy was one of many who assisted President Roosevelt in directing the social revolution of the New Deal whereby the government assumed fuller responsibility for the economic security of the individual. For all his own ambition, Murphy was able to help F.D.R. without rancor or jealousy; he could follow as well as lead.

Murphy's political career demonstrated the vitality of the American democratic tradition; his faith in this tradition is an inspiration. In his creed there was room for discouragement, but not for loss of hope or inaction. He believed Americans have an obligation to face and solve the problems of an imperfect world. In Frank Murphy's words: "'Faith without works is dead.' So it is with democracy."[11]

Workers inside Fisher Body Plant no. 1 during the early days of the 1937 sit-down strike. The headline reads: "STRIKE SPREADS / MEN ARE FIRED." Photo by *Detroit News*.

President Roosevelt jests with Murphy, taking oath as attorney general, January 2, 1939: "Frank, you will do a good job for there is the Bible before you and the *Constitution* [frigate] behind you." *Courtesy Michigan Historical Collections, University of Michigan, and United Press International.*

Chapter I

Initiation into Politics

The Murphy family home, which is still in Harbor Beach, Michigan, was Frank Murphy's residence throughout his life. It is an attractive, white frame Victorian house, immediately projecting warmth and friendliness. In contrast is Frank Murphy's own room. Left as it was when he used it, its meager dimensions easily accommodate its sparse furnishings. There are a small bureau and an iron frame bed that lacks the modern comfort of box springs and an innerspring mattress. On a bedside table are a few of his books, among them works by Jacques Maritain and Reinhold Niebuhr, which he was reading at the time of his death in 1949 at the age of fifty-nine. The room has no radiator to counter the severe cold of Michigan winters.

The austerity of Frank Murphy's living quarters reflects the self-discipline he imposed on his life. He did not drink alcoholic beverages, coffee, or tea. Neither did he smoke. This asceticism was his way of preparing himself—both spiritually and physically—to wrestle with the political tasks he chose to undertake. However, Murphy did not permit these denials to interfere with other pleasures. He enjoyed parties and the company of pretty women in particular. His winning sense of humor was widely known, making him a popular figure at social functions.

Frank Murphy was a handsome figure. He was of more than medium height, inclined toward slenderness, and good-looking.

His head was finely modeled. Both sensitivity and ambition were revealed in his demeanor. Harold Ickes, secretary of the interior under Franklin D. Roosevelt, commented on first meeting him, "He has the look of a fanatic mixed with a tinge of melancholy." Later Ickes observed that if Murphy "had turned to the Church instead of the law he would have been a man like the early Jesuit fathers who would have been willing to undergo any hardship or subject himself to any danger in order to carry forward his cause."[1]

Murphy's personality was full of contradictions—introspection and action, pugnaciousness and pacifism, generosity and niggardliness, athletic prowess and hypochrondria, reason and superstition. But underlying them all was a fierce consciousness of being Irish. One evening in 1941, as the United States was preparing for war, a friend mistakenly asked him, "Governor, when are the blessed Irish going to get their backs up and let our convoys land in Ireland?" The reply, explaining the historical reason for Irish hatred of the British, lasted until 2:00 A.M.[2] Murphy's relatives had participated in the struggle for Irish independence, and his father had continued revolutionary activity while he resided in Canada. Murphy believed these trials had been the making of the Irish. They had suffered and lived; therefore they had a special mission to help the oppressed:

> Every Irishman who catches a vision of his heritage well knows that he has an errand here, knows that he has a mission on this earth. That mission . . . is to enrich life, to lift the weak, to put them in the way of hope and strength; to take the old folks, to comfort them; to take the sick and heal them . . . , and any one Irishman who ever forgets that mission, he impoverishes himself upon this earth.[3]

His father, John Murphy, was a lawyer and politician. He reared his sons, Harold, Frank, and George (and to a lesser extent his daughter, Marguerite) in the skills and values of his profession—public speaking, obedience to law, individual liberty, and independent thought. Although John Murphy taught his family to believe in the teachings of the Roman Catholic Church, in particular those requiring love and charity, he instructed it to accept the church conditionally, as an institution whose merits were derived from individual priests. This skepticism was enriched by the tolerant attitude the family adopted toward the Protestant majority in Harbor Beach. To attest to its liberal attitude the family participated occasionally in Protestant social functions.

The mother, Mary Brennan Murphy, equally influenced her children. She was unusually close to them and anxious for their well-being—wanting them to win recognition in the world as well as make a contribution to it. Her special care was for the family's spiritual growth, which she demonstrated by leading the family in the rosary daily. For the rest of his life Frank Murphy lived by this spiritual training, reading his Bible daily and freely offering assistance to his church in carrying out its charitable tasks.

By the time Frank Murphy entered manhood he was certain his destiny was to be a leader of men. Fittingly he chose his father's profession, that of law and politics, as his own. To assure professional success he imposed the severest discipline on himself. It was this zeal which led him to abstain from stimulants. As one would temper steel for a sword, he forged his life. Years later he advised a class of students: "Plan your future. Set yourselves definite objectives and strive for them mightily. If you care enough, you will work hard enough to achieve the goal."[4]

Believing he would be a great politician as well as a successful one, Frank Murphy was not above spreading this news among his associates, thereby earning considerable enmity for himself. But his ambition was to achieve greatness by doing what he called the "right thing"—by leading a discouraged citizenry into a world where social justice would replace exploitation and security would replace fear.[5] An associate of his advised that one must take time to understand him in order to appreciate the strengths amidst his failings.[6] There were two kinds of people in the world, Murphy observed: those who believed in "things" and those who believed in the "imperishable splendors of man and life," by which he meant both spiritual and humanistic qualities.[7] His Irish heritage alone endowed him with enough sensitivity to be counted among the latter. This sensitivity was nourished further in the climate of inseparable ties which bound the Murphy family together. Each member shared the hopes, the joys, and the sorrows of the others. It is perhaps indicative that Frank Murphy never left the family through marriage, and his brothers postponed marriage until their forties. In any case his close family life helped to develop in him an intuitive sense for understanding the needs and sufferings of man.

Frank Murphy had been educated in the Harbor Beach public schools and at the University of Michigan, which had awarded him both a bachelor's and a law degree. When the United States entered World War I, he resigned from private law practice in Detroit and served as an officer in the army overseas. After the war he remained in Europe to do graduate work at Lincoln's Inn, London and Trinity College, Dublin. Returning from abroad, he was appointed a U.S. assistant district attorney for eastern Michigan in 1919. The appointment lasted until 1921, when a change in administration removed him from office, and he returned to private law practice.

In 1920 Murphy ran unsuccessfully for Congress on the Democratic ticket. He described himself as a Progressive in the tradition

of Theodore Roosevelt. The Progressive label was a comfortable
one, for Progressivism had brought distinguished leaders to Michigan, among them Governors Chase S. Osborn and Woodbridge
N. Ferris. Equally important, Michigan traditionally had been
cool to the Democratic party; political dissenters could find their
niche only in the Progressive movement. But 1920 was an unfavorable year for both Democrats and Progressives in Michigan.

Fortune favored Murphy's next political effort. In 1923 Joseph
S. Mulcahy, editor of the *Detroit Times,* was searching for a
popular issue to boost circulation. William Randolph Hearst had
recently purchased the *Times* and had commissioned Mulcahy to
transform the newspaper into a successful venture. The editor
shrewdly calculated Murphy's exceptional political talents and
encouraged him to run for a position on the Detroit Recorder's
Court.

Four of the seven judges then on the court formed a bloc that
once had been dedicated to reform. However, an attitude of com-
placency had succeeded reform, making the four vulnerable to
attacks by an aspiring attorney. Murphy had trained himself to be
a good orator, believing this skill was essential if he were to
succeed as a political leader.[8] Employing his skill, he lashed out
at the bloc, saying, according to the *Times* (March 29, 1923), it
was time to fight a judicial tyranny "that is invisible, that is of
the star chamber method." Assisted by banner headlines in the
Times, Murphy easily won his court position.[9] He made a com-
mendable record during his seven years on the bench. He established a sentencing board, consisting of a psychiatrist and probation
officer, to guide him in his decisions. Angered because a clique of
bondsmen was monopolozing the sale of court bonds, he stopped
the practice, and one bondsman was sent to prison.

In 1926 while he was on Recorder's Court, the controversial
murder trial of Dr. Ossian Sweet, a Negro physician, came before

Murphy. Dr. Sweet had bought a house in a white neighborhood. Shortly after he moved in, a white mob formed outside his home and made threatening advances. In panic, a Negro companion of Dr. Sweet fired a shot from within the house, killing one of the mob participants. Clarence Darrow defended, and ultimately won freedom for, Sweet and his companion.

Murphy presided over the case with dignity. Darrow wrote, "When I went to court to arrange for the trial, I found a judge who not only seemed human, but who proved to be the kindliest and most understanding man I have ever happened to meet on the bench. . . ."[10] Murphy likewise was impressed by Darrow's handling of the imponderables of racial prejudice. The sole issue, pleaded Darrow, was whether a Negro had the same right as a white man to defend his home. In an emotional appeal to the jury he challenged it to seize this opportunity to reduce the prejudice and hatred affecting Negro-white relations. " 'To me this case is a cross section of human history,' " said Darrow. " 'It involves the future and the hope of some of us that the future shall be better than the past.' "[11] Murphy was so moved by Darrow's oratory he was shaking when he returned to his office at the end of the trial, and he later confided to a friend that it was the most intense emotional experience of his life.

In the 1928 presidential race Murphy campaigned for Al Smith, asserting the New York governor was in the Progressive tradition of Theodore Roosevelt, Wilson, and La Follette. He also dallied with the idea of running for the U.S. Senate that year and even officially entered the campaign, but then withdrew his name. In Detroit Murphy's ambition was no secret; indeed he told his friends and associates he hoped to become the first Catholic President of the United States.[12]

In July 1930 an unusual opportunity occurred for Murphy. An unpopular mayor, Charles Bowles, was removed from office in a recall election brought about by his failure to stem a rising crime rate stimulated by prohibition. He was also a political casualty of the depression which struck Detroit sooner than most cities.

Sniffing victory and a chance to further his political aspirations, Murphy entered the race to complete the unexpired term due to end December 31, 1931. The field soon became crowded with a total of seven candidates, including the recalled mayor. The recall committee panicked, fearing Bowles might be reelected, and tried to persuade the anti-Bowles candidates to agree on one man to remain in the campaign. (Under a faulty provision in the city charter, no primary was provided for in the event of a recall.) Sensing he might not be chosen as the single anti-Bowles candidate, Murphy boycotted the fusion session. The final list was only reduced to five candidates.

Murphy had begun his campaign with a public relations stunt. He inveigled a committee of American Legion veterans to ask him publicly to run. The gist of the Legionnaires' request was that Murphy should be self-sacrificing and enlist as a candidate for mayor, just as he had enlisted as a soldier in war time. In his reply, reported in the *Detroit News* (August 10, 1930), Murphy said he was "very touched" to have his old buddies make this petition, and without further ado he launched into his acceptance speech before them. With revealing candor he commented, "Everybody who aspires to public office does it because he wants the job, or there is a career ahead of him, or fame, or something else that is personally desirable to him."

As in 1923, the judge was strongly supported by Hearst's *Times*. Again, expediency rather than conviction probably motivated the newspaper—an expediency which could have arisen only in the fantastic world of Hearst journalism. The *Times* had given mild support to Bowles in the past and had opposed the recall election. Then, on the night of the election an idolized, liberal-posing radio announcer, Jerry Buckley, was murdered. The *Times* rushed out a morning edition with a headline associating Buckley with the underworld. It was clearly implied Buckley had double-crossed criminal friends who now paid him back. The outraged public refused to buy the *Times;* circulation plummeted. By championing Murphy, the *Times* saw an opportunity to beat the drum of virtue and win back its readers.[13]

In his campaign speeches Murphy promised reform and relief. By reform he meant getting politics out of government and putting civil service into government. Public works employees, he declared, should be secure in their jobs and not subject to the whim and caprice of politicians. It was an old Progressive cry but an effective one in a city dedicated to nonpartisan government. He promised both to humanize the Police Department and at the same time restore its morale. He termed Detroit's debt "staggering" and pledged he would put a stop to extravagant public improvements. As for the needs of the unemployed and the aged, he said they should be met through unemployment insurance, public works projects, and old-age pensions. But while he believed the ultimate success of this program depended on federal and state aid, he also declared that the city should on its own take the first step—by establishing employment agencies, using existing social agencies more efficiently, and making unemployment studies for future use. He reminded his listeners that Hazen Pingree, a fore-runner to the Progressive movement and a mayor of Detroit, had faced a similar unemployment crisis in the depression of 1893 and assured them that he, like Pingree, accepted the principle of municipal responsibility for unemployment.

Murphy won with a plurality of over 13,000 votes. On September 23, 1930 he was inaugurated mayor of one of the largest and potentially richest cities in the United States. Detroit had become so through the miracle of mass production and the automobile industry. Attracted by Henry Ford's fabled five-dollar day, immigrants from the East and poor whites and Negroes from the South had migrated to the automobile capital. From a population of 400,000 in 1907, Detroit had grown to 1,500,000 in 1930. This rapid growth resulted in a belief that the economy would expand indefinitely. Speculators hurriedly bought up the countryside; normally conservative city fathers willingly put the city into debt to provide the newly developed areas with schools, sewers, and other necessary public utilities. Detroit proudly was a leader in the expansion of the twenties. But in 1930 it led the downspin into depression.

Soon the commonplace newspaper picture in Detroit was one of men standing in lines before employment bureaus or the Welfare Department. Statistics tell why. A study of a representative district in Detroit found the work week dropped from a median of 46 hours in 1929 to 23 hours in 1932. Hourly earnings, meanwhile, dropped from a median of 67 cents in 1929 to 44 cents in 1932. The shrinkage in both hours of work and hourly earnings amounted to a 67 percent loss in weekly wages. Nine individuals out of the 1400 families sampled were unemployed in 1929, as compared to 353 individuals out of 1400 families in 1932.[14]

On first becoming mayor, Murphy fully expected to be able to cope with the problem of unemployment within a few months, whereupon he could begin effecting reforms within the government. In his inaugural address he said work-relief projects would be the core of his welfare program for the unemployed. Citing the example of Pingree, he urged using jobless men as an army to demolish antiquated buildings to make room for new highways, buildings, parks, and schools. He planned to ask each city department to submit plans for using the unemployed. Meanwhile, to satisfy immediate relief needs, he asked the city council for

$25,000, emphasizing that the crisis was temporary and that this modest appropriation should meet the emergency.

Mayor Murphy likened his efforts to a war and attempted to bring the idealism of Wilson's war to end all wars into his own battle. The *Times* (November 12, 1930) reported him as saying: "Let those of us who caught the spirit of brotherhood in the days of the World War bring to the solutions of our problems today that same spirit of devotion to the needy." Alleviating the hardships of men was always Murphy's first concern.

The mayor was not alone in his approach. Throughout the country many others, among them future members of the Franklin Roosevelt administration, shared his views. They, like Murphy, had been reared on Progressivism and its successor—the New Freedom—which had culminated in a total war to free men of tyranny. Murphy's work-relief proposals were not unique, but he showed courage in suggesting them at a time when they were unpopular with Michigan's political leaders and not yet endorsed by a national administration.

Soon after his inauguration Murphy formed a Mayor's Unemployment Committee to spearhead the attack on unemployment and relief. This was made up of private citizens who reflected both liberal and conservative elements. He appointed G. Hall Roosevelt, brother-in-law and distant cousin of New York Governor Franklin D. Roosevelt, as chairman of the committee. Not unaware of Hall's connections with Hyde Park, the mayor shrewdly asked him to obtain information on unemployment relief organizations from Governor Roosevelt.[15]

The unemployment committee's first project was to register the unemployed. This begun, the committee set up a free Municipal Employment Bureau to place the unemployed with city departments and private concerns. The hope was to provide work for those in greatest need first. When the registration of the unemployed revealed that many lacked clothing and shoes, the mayor issued a special appeal through the news media for these items on their behalf. Using the prestige of his office, he also made pleas to public utilities to keep the homes of the unemployed supplied with gas and light. To maintain local jobs Murphy encouraged awarding municipal contracts to city concerns regardless of whether or not they submitted the lowest bid.

But with the coming of winter, the undertaking slackened as the city began to suffer financially, and in December the mayor announced all work-relief projects except those on which public welfare labor could be used would be deferred. At the same time the Department of Public Works reached its seasonal depression on paving and sidewalk construction jobs. Reports from the employment bureau meanwhile indicated private companies had stopped hiring men. Murphy's critics took devilish delight in reminding him of his failure to get "the unemployed in the trenches before Christmas."[16]

Murphy's assault had indeed failed. With the depression ever deepening, the city was in no position to finance work-relief projects on the scale needed to absorb all the unemployed. Other projects similarly found themselves undone by the extent of the need. Since the enemy could not be conquered, Murphy's strategy became defensive. Only a few months after coming to office, he was forced to limit his activities to providing food and shelter for the restive victims of unemployment. He gave up trying to find them jobs.

Murphy had campaigned on a platform upholding financial integrity. He believed in a balanced budget; this was his goal as an administrator. Therefore it was something of a shock to discover that his goal could not be achieved. Unemployment relief was not the only drain on the budget. Rapid expansion of public services in the twenties to accommodate a growing population had put Detroit precariously into a debt totaling $378,000,000. The interest and retirement charges on this debt were an enormous burden.

Faced with a full-blown financial crisis in January 1931, Murphy had no alternative but to pare expenses. In February he appointed a committee of Detroit bankers to assist the city in cutting costs. Its efforts resulted in a $24,000,000 saving over normal operating expenses for the next fiscal year. For his part, Murphy warned department heads to cease immediately any deficit-making or juggling of funds.[17] Committees of three were organized in every department to campaign against waste. Yet these efforts were not enough. In April the city borrowed $5,000,-000 to meet regular expenses. The next month it announced the suspension of all public improvement projects, except those already contracted for. By the end of the fiscal year in June, Detroit had again run out of cash and was forced to depend on a $5,000,000 loan from the Ford Motor Company to meet payrolls and emergencies.

Detroit's Common Council thereupon issued a policy statement declaring that during the 1931-32 fiscal year the city would have to live within its income regardless of what that income might be.[18] To carry out this pledge the council adopted a report of a citizens' finance committee which had been organized early in 1930. In accordance with this report the council cut the Welfare Department budget in half, stopped all local improvements in districts which had substantial tax delinquencies, and established a quarterly accounting system. Although hampered by state legislation limiting its borrowing power, the city set out to refinance its notes falling due through long-term loans with a New York banking syndicate. All these efforts were designed to reduce the drain on Detroit's ready cash.

If Murphy lacked the money to undo the depression through

massive public works projects, he at least was determined to provide the unemployed and their families with the minimum necessities of life. His relief organization was two-pronged. He relied on both the Welfare Department and the citizen-run Mayor's Unemployment Committee. The Welfare Department dispensed relief funds; the committee organized community aid projects, drawing on private contributions to pay its expenses.[19] Although the activities of the two organizations were basically different, their programs frequently overlapped.

Aside from registering the unemployed and establishing the free employment bureau, the unemployment committee directed activities such as creative work projects for selling apples. In general it tried to undertake projects which could not be handled by other public or private agencies. When city employees' pay was delayed, the committee provided food on credit until the wages were paid. On other occasions the committee provided lunches for school children of destitute parents. It also served as a clearinghouse for the administration of private relief.[20]

Hundreds of single men who had left their homes in other states to work in the automobile factories were without funds to return to their homes and without relatives in the city to provide for them and were dependent on the city for food and a place to sleep. The Fisher brothers and Studebaker Corporation donated factory buildings to house these men, and the unemployment committee maintained them for about a year before turning them over to the Welfare Department. The cost to the city—most of which went for food—was about eighteen cents per day per man. The men clothed themselves by cutting firewood and selling it to the public.[21]

To assist families the unemployment committee sponsored the thrift garden project. Many Detroiters were skeptical of it—how could assembly line workers be transformed into gardeners? But the project was carried out successfully. Vacant land was donated, the state tested it for fertility, and city tractors plowed it. Classes on gardening were taught in high schools. The unemployment committee bought fertilizers, tools, and seeds and assigned the individual gardens. Plots cultivated improperly were transferred to someone else on a waiting list. Temporary canneries were set up at which the gardeners preserved food for winter use. In some areas a vital community spirit was created by the gardens, with weekly open-air meetings held to discuss agricultural problems. In 1931 over twenty thousand people were supplied with food from forty-three hundred gardens; the next year sixty-two hundred gardens were planted and harvested.[22]

When Murphy came into office the Welfare Department's activities increased measurably. Its staff swelled; it distributed $14,000,000 in assistance—not all of it wisely, however. The unemployment committee asked citizens to request relief en masse before the criteria for judging cases was properly established. Consequently many hundreds of persons received relief who did not need it. Carried through the winter, by spring they were dependent on the city and unwilling to be removed from the welfare rolls.[23]

To give the men on relief a feeling of purpose, a wage-work plan was instituted. The men were paid forty cents an hour in cash and worked enough hours to earn their weekly welfare allotment. This spared them humiliation and kept them physically strong as well. They actually worked for a department of the city, though at a job which did not compete with a full-time city employee. Although much of the work was "made" work, much of it was important and saved the city money. Some relief workers, for example, shoveled snow for the Department of Public Works. Others worked as field overseers in the thrift garden project.[24]

In small ways the mayor's office tried to supplement the task

of the Welfare Department and unemployment committee. It
wrote letters of introduction to employers for unemployed workers
and gave out information on such matters as how to obtain shoes
and clothing for school children.[25] Murphy ordered a half ton of
coal be delivered to anyone who asked his office for it, with the
investigation of need to be made later. He knew this wasn't the
way to save money, but he was far more concerned that no one
suffer from the cold.

In June 1931, at the end of Murphy's first fiscal year, his welfare program came under sharp attack. Harry Bennett, director of
personnel for the Ford Motor Company, led the way, charging the
Welfare Department with tolerating fraudulent claims. The company was particularly sensitive because Murphy asserted 20 percent of the city's relief budget went to workers laid off by Ford
while the company itself resided comfortably outside the city
limits and refused to contribute to the welfare budget. (This
situation was true as well for other manufacturing concerns.) Bennett contested Murphy's percentage figure and attacked the dole
system as a whole, asserting it took no administrative genius to
scatter $2,000,000 a month. Much to Murphy's embarrassment, a
$207,000 theft by a welfare clerk was discovered in the midst of
the Ford squabble. A subsequent investigation of the department
by an accounting firm revealed an "utter lack of internal check"
on funds. Murphy assumed full responsibility and announced that
in the future every welfare worker would be bonded. Further, the
city agreed to institute the changes recommended by the accounting firm.[26]

Murphy's critics continued to probe for weak spots in his
welfare program. The large relief budgets were said to be driving
the city into bankruptcy. Murphy argued this assertion was unfair, since relief was paid for through reductions in other city expenses.[27] Other detractors charged his dole system was politically

motivated. It appeared to be more than a coincidence that the city wards where Murphy received most of his votes were the same ones receiving the greater part of welfare assistance.[28] While Murphy was not unaware of the political value of relief, there was no reason to believe the program was distorted into primarily a political tool. Immediately after his first inauguration this was made clear. At that time many applicants at the employment bureau sought preference on the basis of having supported him in the campaign. The chairman of the unemployment committee condemned their attempt and announced on Murphy's behalf that anyone trying to secure preference would have his name dropped to the foot of the list.

The Mayor's Unemployment Committee early was the object of criticism. The Common Council claimed it committed the council to projects without first coming to the council to find out if money was available. There was friction among the committee members themselves when labor representatives opposed shortening the work week and business representatives advocated it to meet depression conditions. With some justification critics cited the ineffectiveness of the committee's employment bureau. After seven months of operation 112,282 families were registered, but only 23,926 persons had been given work and in more than half of these instances the positions were temporary. Nonetheless the bureau did a far better job in placing workers than the state employment offices. Between three hundred and four hundred persons passed through the bureau daily. To thousands this was the last opportunity to secure a job, as the men in greatest need were without fees to pay private agencies. Men lined up as early as 10:00 P.M. to be the first on hand for the next morning.[29]

A particularly unpopular undertaking of the unemployment committee was its lodges for homeless men. Expressing the Common Council view was John C. Nagel who termed them flophouses and said they would bring into the city hundreds of itinerants from all over the nation.[30] Nagel's view was common in Detroit. It was generally believed drifters would come into the city to take advantage not only of the free lodges but of the whole city welfare program. This belief was unfounded. No person was given relief without a certificate from a taxpayer indicating he had lived in Detroit for at least a year. Indeed the median residence time for relief recipients was almost fourteen years.[31]

In July the council slashed the relief budget in half to $7,000,000 for the next fiscal year. In part this reflected public criticism, although it was required as well by financial necessity. Under the circumstances Murphy had no choice but to accept the council's decision. One consequence was the reduction of individual welfare allotments to the minimally safe level. A family of two had its aid cut to $3.50 a week; a family of five was cut to $37.50 a month. The council's decision also meant closing the lodges for homeless men.

To help fill the relief void, Senator James Couzens, former mayor and once a wealthy partner of Henry Ford, offered $1,000,-000 for relief if other wealthy citizens would pledge a combined $9,000,000 more. On behalf of Couzens, Murphy arranged a meeting of potential contributors to discuss the proposal. In his invitation he reminded them that "the present business depression has drifted . . . close to the edge of a real calamity, threatening not only the poor but the prosperous as well."[32] But Murphy's plea was to no avail. Those invited rejected the proposal, letting it be known, moreover, they disapproved of Couzens' "embarrassing offer."[33] Nonetheless a contribution from Couzens formed the nucleus of an emergency relief fund which carried Detroit through the winter of 1931-32.[34] With this assistance even the lodges for homeless men were reopened.

Reform was a second goal for Murphy. He strove for good

government with the same fervor that made the muckrakers famous in the early years of the century.[35] Detroit was ready for reform. Under his immediate predecessor, Charles Bowles, the city had succumbed to the practices of corruption and inaction. However, the impact of the depression was too great in 1931 to allow time or money for reforming efforts. Relief and financial solvency absorbed all the energies of the municipal leaders. Although blocked from any large-scale reform, Murphy restored a high sense of morality and public duty to the more routine administrative duties of the mayor's office.

He started slowly. By his own admission, few changes took place in his first ninety days as mayor. "During this interval," he told the council, "I have attempted to acquire a working knowledge of the city's needs. . . ."[36] When he made changes in personnel, his policy was to insist on ability first. His appointments generally adhered to the principle of nonpartisan selection, in that his appointees represented all the differing shades of public opinion in Detroit. Yet Murphy also met the demands of good politics by giving occasional posts in recognition of political support.

To please conservatives, Murphy appointed two men who had worked for private business: Joseph E. Mills, formerly a purchasing agent for an automobile company, who served Murphy in several capacities, and James K. Watkins, a corporation lawyer, who became Murphy's chief of police. In recognition of labor's support in his campaign, he chose the former president of the Detroit and Wayne County Federation of Labor, John Taylor, to be his personal secretary and appointed the head of an electrical workers' union, William P. Frost, to the public lighting commission. To demonstrate his strong belief in municipally owned transportation he appointed two friends of municipal ownership to the Detroit Street Railway Commission, one of whom was

Frank Couzens, the son of James Couzens who had created the public railway system. James Couzens had great influence in Detroit because of his wealth and his earlier term as mayor. Murphy especially wanted the elder Couzens as an ally because his political views—even though he was a Republican—were close to Murphy's own. To further curry his favor, Murphy retained Couzens' lawyer as corporation counsel.[37]

Murphy had no magic formula for running his administration. He felt the most important thing was "getting things done,— getting things started and getting them done."[38] He likewise approved of subordinates who had this ability and was quick to capitalize upon their gifts. Joseph Mills, whom he first appointed as commissioner of purchases and supplies, proved to be such a person. When Mills achieved economies in the purchasing department, Murphy moved him to the Public Works Department and later to the Detroit surface railway system. In one year Mills reduced the public works budget from $17,000,000 to less than $6,000,000. Mills could not have accomplished these economies without support from Murphy. When Frank X. Martel, the president of the Detroit and Wayne County Federation of Labor, pressed his influence with Murphy and demanded that truck drivers hired by the city be unionized, the mayor stuck by Mills who opposed the union.

James Watkins, chief of police, belonged to Detroit's high society and had been a Rhodes scholar after graduating from the University of Michigan. Murphy gave Watkins complete control of the department; no political appointees were forced on him, and no grafters were protected. Watkins instituted schools in which patrolmen were trained in police technique, laws and ordinances, court procedure, and courtesy. Excesses of the previous administration were curbed. Property-destroying raids on speakeasies were prohibited, and the practice of overlooking search warrants in search and seizure operations was halted.[39]

Murphy's administrative technique appeared untidy. His office was open to almost everyone and without appointment. Even discounting this policy, the corridors of City Hall were invariably crowded, and one had to push through the milling people to reach his office.[40] He loved to court new acquaintances and renew old friendships. Wanting to be everywhere at once, he flitted about City Hall and all of Detroit. The *Detroit Saturday Night* (November 29, 1930), a persistent Murphy critic, observed that the mayor constantly appeared at luncheons or dinners "shaking hands at every opportunity with the lowly and the mighty, expostulating at great length on how he hopes to save the city." When a problem arose, he appointed a committee to advise him. The Common Council lost patience with this procedure because, as a matter of courtesy, it had to wade through the lengthy committee reports.

By temperament Murphy needed to be the center of attention. One way of achieving this was to arrive late for engagements. He confided to his friends he didn't like being told what to do and showing up late was his way of letting people know it. In his meanderings he was followed by a retinue of hangers-on and friends. While all other chief executives of Detroit had reportedly had only one police officer detailed as a bodyguard, Murphy was surrounded by no less than four—two in uniform and two in plain clothes.[41] A regular member of Murphy's evening entourage was a former boxer, Samuel Ozadowsky, affectionately nicknamed Patsy O'Toole. Patsy was full of joviality and provided Murphy with light diversion. His nightly appearances with Murphy earned him the appellation of Night Mayor.

This unreal night life combined with concern for social justice by day made the handsome mayor a charmer with the ladies. His radical politics were a little frightening to the fair sex, but for that very reason he was also more exciting company. He remained an eligible bachelor all his life, twitting the hearts of many romantically inclined young women, as well as their matchmaking mothers. Growing fame turned high society his way— and he was not unmindful of this interest. Always ready to join the glittering world of the rich, Murphy felt that membership in high society was as much a measure of success as the attainment of important public office.

After burning up the evening hours and flitting through the business day, the mayor had only the early morning hours for hard work. From 2:00 to 6:00 A.M. much of Murphy's basic study and decision-making took place. Free from the interruptions of the telephone and visitors, the mayor read reports prepared by advisers. After a few hours of sleep Murphy went to City Hall about 10:00 or 10:30 A.M. This pace periodically laid him low. Only three weeks after taking office he announced that under doctor's orders he was obliged to budget his time more carefully. "I don't like to complain," the *News* reporter quoted him as saying (October 15, 1930), "but really I am working too hard."

Actually, Murphy did work hard. He brought to government a dedication and conviction which were felt in many small ways. When all his efforts are added up, they total a dignity and stature which transcend the facade of showmanship that often surrounded his administration. Expecting the best from all government employees, he demonstrated this by disapproving his sister-in-law's scheduled salary increase. She was a city social worker whose raise had been recommended before Murphy took office. In denying the increase he said simply that a member of his family should be expected to do more for less money than other city employees.

Murphy involved himself in a variety of liberal, and sometimes odd, causes when he was mayor. Since he believed all of these causes would better the world, he would not turn his back on the strange ones; indeed, perhaps their very strangeness appealed to his own desire to be different. In collaboration with members of the Fellowship of Reconciliation, a national Christian organization dedicated to pacifism and furthering liberal causes generally, he founded the American League for India's Freedom.[42] As an Irishman undoubtedly he was delighted to support a movement which had as its objective the breakup of the British Empire. At Clarence Darrow's request he served on the advisory council of the American League to Abolish Capital Punishment.[43] He had strong convictions as to the debasing influence of capital punishment. He observed: "When an execution . . . takes place, it is not the victim alone who is killed; something fine and decent is killed in all who in any manner participate, and in the people of the community who acquiesce in it."[44]

More unusual was Murphy's support of Detroit's Fellowship of Faiths. This organization, of which Murphy was vice-president, was dedicated to achieving peace and brotherhood among people of all races, religions, and cultures. It held that all the problems of the world, whatever they might be, would be solved if man would believe in what it termed "real religion" or a "Soul Force." Among the members were Protestants, Jews, Catholics, Moham-medans, Hindus, Negroes, and whites.[45]

Before he was mayor, Murphy had ardently supported the National Association for the Advancement of Colored People, both with financial contributions and by serving on its board of directors.[46] As mayor he continued to work for the cause of Negro rights. When white unemployed workers requested Negroes be released as garbage collectors to make room for whites, he refused, reminding the petitioners that in good times only Negroes would

42

take the jobs. The Negroes' consolation was the city's promise of security, and he was not going to take their security away from them. Similarly, he reacted vigorously when he was told a district office of the Welfare Department treated Negroes discourteously. The district supervisor was replaced, and case workers were warned their promotions would be endangered if they developed a "sense of contempt or condescension" toward any clients.[47] Once Murphy intervened on behalf of two Negro medical students to assure consideration of their applications for internship at the city Receiving Hospital. To Murphy's knowledge, Negro applicants had always been rejected in the past on the grounds that the quota of interns had been filled.[48] Negroes were not fully satisfied with Murphy's administration. Depression-caused layoffs of Negro city employees frequently were interpreted by them as racially motivated.[49] They were unhappy too with the administration's failure to promote Negroes to higher ranking city jobs. Here Murphy was hindered by civil service regulations which favored the better-educated and longer-employed white employees.[50]

Murphy was as devoted to the principle of individual liberty as to that of racial equality. His predecessor had not shared this conviction. When in March 1930 Mayor Bowles's police force had attempted to break up a Communist demonstration, what had been an orderly gathering became disorderly and violent. In October 1930—a month after Murphy took office—the Communists called for another demonstration, and, three thousand strong, they gathered in Grand Circus Park. There the unsuccessful Communist candidate for mayor, Philip J. Raymond, debated with Murphy, complaining of arrests and interference. Murphy assured Raymond interference would not occur as long as his meetings were as orderly as the current demonstration. His policy was tested in July 1931 when Communist leaders harangued six hundred followers outside City Hall, agitating the crowd until it jammed the front door and made entrance impossible. Although this might have been sufficient cause for breaking up the demonstration, Murphy refused to intervene. These favorable incidents aside, Communists and other radicals were by no means satisfied with his policy of free speech and assembly. They continued to complain of unjust police harassment.[51]

Actually Murphy went a step beyond tolerating free speech, he promoted it. He asked the council to establish places like Hyde Park in London, where soapbox orators could hold forth without interference. The irritated council responded by designating the space beneath his City Hall window as one such site—their idea being to give the mayor an earful, seeing that he wanted to let radicals have free speech.[52]

Through letters Murphy patiently explained his philosophy of free speech and assembly to his fellow citizens. To a merchant who complained about demonstrations in Grand Circus Park, he advised: "We all must appreciate that wherever these gatherings are held someone will be disturbed. . . . Yet it is highly desirable that full opportunity for protest and assembly be given the victims of unemployment."[53] He was convinced civil liberties had to be maintained in Detroit's time of troubles if violence were to be averted. Providing relief for the destitute allays hunger in their stomachs and shelters their bodies, but it does not satisfy their compulsion to cry out their grievances.

Chapter II

Crisis Government

The foremost task of a politician is to win his office and hold it. Since Murphy was originally elected to complete an unexpired term, he was obliged to seek reelection in the fall of 1931, this time for a full two-year term. His platform consisted virtually of one plank, that the people in the "common misfortune" of depression should have a government which would be "an agency of service. . . . This hunger within our hearts to do the right and tolerant and neighborly thing," he said, "is the way out for you and for me."[1]

His strategy was to work harder than his opponents—to build a good record to run on and to execute a tireless campaign to publicize it. Detroit had tried to take politics out of politics by making the mayoralty elections nonpartisan. To the extent that this arrangement prevented party machines from organizing, the city was successful; consequently each candidate was left to his own resources for soliciting support from various economic, ethnic, and social groups in the community.

Lacking the bonds of party patronage to motivate support, Murphy solicited votes on the higher plane of personal allegiance. He did this by making himself into an image of the public servant who is resolved to use the power of government to help the people. While in concrete terms the "people" often were organizations such as the AF of L, Detroit Teachers' Association,

45

or city employees, in 1931 the term "people" likewise meant the unemployed, the hungry, and the cold. These also were invariably the minorities: Negroes, Irish, Germans, Jews, Poles, Italians, and Hungarians. If these disparate peoples could be united, Murphy would command a majority. Among these groups Murphy volunteer committees were formed.[2]

Money was not easy to come by in 1931, and, as much as possible, free services were solicited for the campaign. Handbills were sponsored by such diverse organizations and businesses as the Greek American Political Association, French Cleaners and Dyers, and People's Political & Industrial Association. A radio station volunteered time for a short political talk, and a newspaper publisher printed an advertisement—gambling that he might be paid later.[3]

Aware that constant exposure was necessary, Murphy went through the political ritual of attending every possible meeting. He welcomed the American Ornithologists' Union to Detroit and attended the dedication of the Charity Crucifixion Tower at Father Charles E. Coughlin's church. The Detroit branch of the National Singing Federation invited him to the Serbian Eastern Orthodox Church for a social hour, assuring him he would thereby "cover" the Serbian vote.[4]

Sometimes support came from unsuspected quarters. The manager of Detroit Kresge stores arranged for Murphy to visit the company and be presented with a large cake, which in turn the mayor was to give to a charitable institution. In addition, the manager advised all his storekeepers to favor Murphy. Since there were 550 Kresge stores in Detroit, the impact should have been sizable.[5]

But while organizations helped, Murphy's public appeals won him the most votes. Most of his speeches were extemporaneous and unsophisticated. As the *Detroit Saturday Night* (December

28, 1930) reported, his reference to the present "dew" that would be followed by the "sunshine" of tomorrow, had earned him the appellation of the "dew and sunshine" mayor.

Critics accused him of appealing to the fears and prejudices of the masses in the same way the Hearst press played on emotions. The fact that the Hearst press in Detroit backed Murphy seemingly strengthened the critics' charge.[6] But it did not take much to arouse the people. Times were bad. Hope and belief in freedom, self-sufficiency, and opportunity had been shaken. Murphy now proposed a new economic order in which the government would assure a minimum standard of living for all. He was a leader offering hope, and the crowds cheered.

Newspaper accounts tell the story of his campaign.[7] The mayor's days were long. One typical day was divided among twenty-eight meetings. He was met everywhere with wild and frenzied applause. Men and women followed him into the street, climbed onto the automobile running boards, and shouted, "Good luck, Frank." Topics of his speeches varied—from city finances, to efficiency in the public works department, to civil rights. When his major opponent, Harold Emmons, tried to capitalize on his association with the Republican party, Murphy chided him for violating the city charter and introducing party politics into a nonpartisan election. Always Murphy returned, and each time with increasing fervor, to the woes of the suffering. "My people," he called them. "How do you want it this winter?" he was quoted by the *News* (October 20, 1931) as saying. "Do you want to turn your government over to those who have never raised their voices above a whisper in defense of the unfortunate, but whose only audible cry has been one of bitter criticism and vituperation. . . ."

The campaign was drawn out, involving both a primary and an election runoff between the top two contenders. Although

Murphy received more than a majority of the votes cast in the primary, he did not diminish his efforts. Senator Couzens aided the mayor's cause by publicly offering his good wishes to the candidate. In a desperate move, Murphy's opponent raised the religious question. The Ku Klux Klan had been active in Michigan throughout the twenties, and the Emmons' camp published a pamphlet reviving this latent bigotry.[8]

In a last effort Murphy asked fifteen hundred volunteer workers to go out to the homes and solicit votes. He addressed them in the rich tradition of Progressivism:

> Before the war America was on the progressive road. Teddy Roosevelt and other great leaders were concerning themselves and the people with problems of hours of labor, workmen's compensation and the other issues of that day.
>
> Today we have social and economic problems far more devastating and perplexing. Today we have sufferings and want and distress more than ever before. And I want to ask you, where do you think the Teddy Roosevelts and Wilsons of the 1912 or 1914 era would be today?
>
> Would they be among those who so smugly say that the way to prosperity is to cut wages? Would they be among those who oppose the redistribution of wealth and restoring power to the masses?
>
> Would they sit in the councils of those who say that the poor are "bums"—

There was no need for an answer to the rhetorical question, but the audience cried, "No! No! No!"[9]

Harold Emmons' religious-hate campaign did not help him. Murphy won the election by a margin of nearly two to one. In the districts in which racial and ethnic minorities were predominant Murphy obtained huge majorities. His prize was a Negro ward where he received 377 votes and Emmons only five. Furthermore, the conservative majority of the Common Council, which had strongly criticized Murphy during his first term, was turned out. The voters unquestionably endorsed Murphy's plea for governmental responsibility in times of economic crisis.

In his 1932 annual message, delivered before the council on January 12, Murphy called uncompromisingly for a balanced budget: "It no longer matters what standard of municipal life Detroit desires . . . departmental red ink is at an end." However, the flow of red ink could not be stopped due to the rapid and unforeseen rise in tax delinquency. While in the fiscal year 1929-30 tax delinquency was $1,354,466, in the next year (Murphy's first in office) it rose to $11,404,970, and in the current fiscal year (1931-32) it was to soar to $18,993,519.[10] The current tax delinquency was the ruination of the refunding and retrenchment program of the previous summer. Although it was not yet fully perceived, Detroit was entering a new period of crisis—a crisis which was to pale the 1931 financial setback by comparison.

Shortly before the new year James Couzens had eased the city's financial plight by buying a $1,000,000 share of the Detroit Street Railways bond issue. (The previous year he had donated a like amount to the emergency relief fund to assist the unemployed.) But only drastic expense cutting could permanently alleviate the pressure of decreasing city income. As much as he disliked doing it, Murphy was forced to reduce city salaries. In January all wages up to $4000 were cut 10 percent, and wages over $4000 were trimmed an additional 10 percent; Murphy's own wage thereby received the largest reduction, a total of 17.5 percent. Murphy tried to mollify city employees with the fact that Detroit had suffered a 40 percent drop in the cost of living—highest of any city in the nation—thus enabling them to buy still more than ever before. As part of the same economy move, five hundred public works employees were laid off, and the art commissioner's payroll was reduced by nearly $80,000, stripping the Institute of Arts of all its curators and experts.[11]

City officials did not fully accept Murphy's economy order. They were especially opposed to laying off personnel in critical areas. The commissioner of health warned Murphy that the current reduction in his department of a hundred employees was maximal. Further cuts in personnel, he predicted, would endanger the public health of the city by eliminating medical control over the spread of diphtheria, scarlet fever, tuberculosis, and other communicable diseases.[12]

In February 1932 the radio commentator from the public affairs bureau of the Detroit Board of Commerce spoke excitedly of reaching the economic " 'corner' we have all been seeking." The event causing his enthusiasm was Henry Ford's announcement about his new model cars. The commentator continued: "Thousands of people have been waiting for 'something to happen' so they can start new projects, quit hoarding and generally add to the improvement of business. . . . If you have been waiting for that 'something' here it is. It should be a distinct signal for any timid soul who has heretofore been hesitant. Let's get busy."[13]

The commentator's confidence was not shared by the New York banking syndicate carrying the city under the terms of the August 1931 agreement to refinance Detroit's short-term loans. The syndicate announced in February it would not continue its loans unless Detroit eliminated $6,000,000 from its current expenses. Ralph Stone, who, as chairman of the board of the Detroit Trust Company, was chosen by the syndicate to be its spokesman in Detroit, suggested the present situation could have been avoided had the city adopted a sound economy plan a year before. He added that influential politicians afraid of losing their jobs—among them he undoubtedly counted Murphy—were responsible.[14] A volatile member of the Common Council retorted the city could go it alone and use money designated for interest payments to meet payrolls if the bankers refused to lend their money. But Murphy saw no alternative and announced the city would meet the bankers' demand for a $6,000,000 reduction. The syndicate thereupon agreed to continue its loans—at the going rate of 6 percent, the maximum permitted by law.

During February and March the city tried various schemes for increasing revenues. Murphy asked citizens to make a community effort to pay delinquent taxes in order to prevent a crumbling of essential governmental functions. He saw to it that his own taxes, some of which had been delinquent since 1921, were paid before the drive was launched.[15] The council announced plans to force the sale of $500,000,000 worth of property unless its owners paid the city $14,600,000 in overdue taxes. The hope was to win co-operation from speculators who in flush times had invested in subdivision property. Struggling homeowners who could prove inability to pay were to be exempt.

Murphy ordered an end to all unnecessary spending by the city. Departments which leased space from private owners were told to move into city-owned buildings. Night shifts replaced overtime. The recreation department cancelled its boys' hikes, and Murphy himself gave up his privately assigned automobile. He even ordered the replacing of burnt-out light bulbs with the next smaller size to save electricity.[16]

And yet it was impossible to pare expenses enough. Not only did the rate of tax delinquency continue to rise, but the burden of fixed interest and principal payments on past indebtedness left little leeway for cutting the budget. Out of a budget of $76,000,000 the city owed over $27,000,000 to banks.[17] When bank payments were added to the current tax delinquency of nearly $19,000,000, only $20,000,000 was left for running the government. The New York bankers managing the city's debt grew increasingly nervous, fearing Detroit might default on its payments. When rumors to this effect reached the newspapers, Murphy attempted to allay the bankers' concern by telegramming his pledge: "DETROIT WILL BALANCE ITS BUDGET AND LIVE WITHIN ITS CASH INCOME. . . ."[18]

Two weeks later this pledge was exposed as premature. The city comptroller reported the city was about to default in payments on special assessment bonds. This would wreck Detroit's credit. Since the bond-buying public would no longer trust the city, it would be impossible for Detroit to borrow funds for the next fiscal year—an absolute necessity under the circumstance of depression.[19]

At this point the New York banking syndicate refused to aid the city through additional loans; instead, it demanded all salaries be cut one-third for April, May, and June. Murphy supported the reduction in a secret session before the council, but when the council passed the effecting ordinance, he publicly reversed himself and vetoed it. Perhaps his political instinct told him the council would override his veto, thus enabling him to pose as the champion of the working man while still achieving the desired economy. Or perhaps he was stalling for time, hoping he could work out a compromise with the bankers under which they would loan Detroit additional funds. At any rate, the council was dumbfounded by Murphy's veto and refused to override it. A month passed before Murphy capitulated to the syndicate—at which time the council passed an ordinance reducing employees' salaries 50 percent for May and June.

Adherence to the bankers' demands that spending be curtailed necessitated a slash in Welfare Department expenditures as well. The department was already operating under a retrenchment policy whereby couples were moved in with other families, but now it ceased paying rents altogether. Evictions increased to 150 daily.

Having no place to go, evicted families moved into tent colonies set up in the parks. Likewise the wage-work plan was suspended. Had grocers not been willing to wait until the next fiscal year to be paid, food would not have been provided at all. As it was, the only food distributed was bread and flour. Moreover, the total number of families on relief was cut to 21,500, the lowest figure thus far during Murphy's administration.[20]

What personal hardship the crisis must have caused! A woman asks the mayor what she is to do about having her baby, since the city has discontinued sending maternity cases to the hospital.[21] A high school principal reports a threefold increase in the number of tuberculosis cases among his students over the past two years. In his civics classes students question the social and economic system under which they were brought up.[22] Hundreds of men and women, to whom Murphy must send negative replies, ask him for jobs. Pathetic in its honesty is a letter from a young man who writes: "I am 22 yrs. old and I love good times. I can't have none if I don't get a job."[23] For Murphy, the 1932 crisis led him "to realize anew that man is petty; his power futile."[24]

With city government near cessation, Murphy searched diligently for financial relief. One possibility was a reduction in utility bills, which was justified by the increased value of the depression dollar. In April he initiated negotiations with the Detroit City Gas Company, and by June agreement was reached on a schedule of moderately reduced rates. However, the reduction was far from what the city wanted, and the Common Council angrily legislated an ordinance, of doubtful legality, charging the gas company an expensive license fee for the use of city streets. The company took the issue to the courts, thereby avoiding payment of the additional levy. Detroit likewise attempted to win rate reductions from the telephone and electric utilities. Success depended on prompt action from the Public Utilities Commission, but the conservative commission was in no hurry.[25]

A logical source of assistance was the state. In March Murphy wrote Governor Wilber M. Brucker, (later President Dwight Eisenhower's secretary of the army), a plea to turn over a larger percentage of state tax money to the cities. He urged using revenue from the weight and gas taxes to meet school expenses and to pay for local road maintenance.[26] These suggestions, as well as others made by Murphy, were pigeonholed.

Although neither the banking syndicate nor Murphy intended it, by April 1932 events had built up to a point where bitterness replaced understanding. At the showdown the syndicate had won; it had thwarted city government and proclaimed the financial irresponsibility of the mayor. There was no doubt Murphy had contributed to the breakdown with self-righteous public utterances directed against the financial world. During the fall election campaign, as reported by the *News* (September 30, 1931), he had emphasized the niggardliness of his fiscal opponents, saying: "We spent $14,000,000 in caring for the distressed and I haven't any apology to make to property interests, to the moneyed people." In his 1932 annual message to the council he had made the fiscally heretical statement that he was "more disposed to hear the present cry for elemental social justice even above the loud demand for the traditional sanctity of contract." And ever since January, from the viewpoint of the bankers, he had done just that, squandering tax money on relief and expendable governmental services when city debts needed to be paid.

The denouement was a verbal duel between Ralph Stone, the syndicate's spokesman, and Murphy on the occasion of the syndicate's order for a one-third cut in city wages. Although their personal relations were pleasant, their diamentrically opposed views led to heated exchange. Stone charged Murphy's moralisms about putting social justice before sanctity of contract were a verbal ruse designed to hide his failure to balance the budget. Stone added—contrary to Murphy's assertion—that bankers and industrialists felt a great sense of social responsibility, as was indicated by their lending $40,000,000 to the city during the past year.

In a lengthy statement to the press Murphy disputed Stone's contention.[27] The mayor lost patience with the bankers; he despised them for their moral incompetence—their failure to see the worthlessness of their god of the balanced budget and the safe return. Murphy began with restraint by announcing the banking syndicate had refused Detroit additional credit enabling it to meet the current expenses of government; instead, the syndicate had ordered the salary cut. His words hardened as he observed how easy it was for the financial world to reduce expenditures when it "ruthlessly concentrated upon labor . . . its principal economies."

The charge against Murphy that had hurt most was that of financial irresponsibility. Shrewdly he directed it back at the bankers by exposing the role they had played in the extravagant expansion of the twenties. He described how they had profited twice, first by financing the schemes of real estate operators for speculating in suburban home sites, and second by selling public improvement bonds for building roads, schools, and other facilities in these tracts. And all the while, "the bankers themselves were best entitled to know [the tracts] might never be built up. . . . In the boom years," Murpy went on, "all was grist that passed through the bankers' mill. Let the people recognize that despite the foolishness of many an executive and many a legislative body there was always behind the scenes the American banker, approving wild extravagances to create a surplus of tax exempt bonds for a thirsty market." Only when the depression came did the banking community demand economy in government.

55

Murphy then expounded his central argument. In contrast to what bankers may believe, government, he said, must live by different values from the material ones upheld by the banking world:

> The whole question between the administration of the City of Detroit and the bankers is a question of point of view.
>
> There is an automaton that can stand behind the wicker cage of a bank and under instruction loan money in good times on substantial blue chip securities. No genius is needed.
>
> There is also the American banker who can concentrate his financial operations on cold-blooded statistical data which will automatically insure a profit every time a dollar turns over. This likewise demands no genius.
>
> But in the art of government a broader policy must prevail. There must be a deep understanding of the functions of government and a recognition that government exists for the protection of all its citizens.
>
> The City of Detroit is content to send its Police Department to guard the transfer of every dollar going from Detroit to New York [banks].
>
> The full acumen of its detective force will be employed to search out any embezzler, and check kyter {sic} or any forger. . . .
>
> But there are other duties of government not so closely associated with banking.
>
> The health of the people must be maintained to a high degree. The helpless child and the hopeless aged must be our tender care. We watch the mortality rate of infants. Pure food, particularly pure milk, education, recreation, the care of the sick and the indigent infirm, the transporation of a people to and from their homes, the maintenance of courts, the care of the delinquent and the criminal. These are only part of

the functions of government that distinguish the great organization of government from private business. . . .

In his closing plea Murphy urged the bankers to reconsider their decision not to lend additional funds to Detroit. He emphasized the city would always stand by its obligations to the financial world, and he hoped they would discover an obligation of a new sort, the obligation to aid human beings in trouble:

> It is time, it is the opportunity for the banks to lend, not for the profit of some wild extension of the City's activities— not for expansion that will supply tax exempt bonds for their customers—but because a people is burdened and suffering.
>
> On our part the debt will be repaid. The security is ample. We have abided in principle by our contract—we have done our best to live within our income. . . .
>
> I suggest to the bankers that they recognize the dawning fact that government is to be distinguished from cold statistical, analytical, impersonal type of business that banking seemingly must be, and that it has broad humanitarian aspects, and that the credit of the people . . . is good and will be kept sound even in the midst of a deep depression as it was in the heyday of banking prosperity when the City's business was so welcome to banks and their wealthy customers.[28]

While Murphy disagreed with the bankers on the worth of a balanced budget—being willing to unbalance it when human beings needed succor—he was much closer to their conservative view than they sometimes realized. It was part of his credo that government should be clean, honest, and efficient. An unjustifiable imbalance in a budget was untidy and wasteful. Moreover, he held government was like a business enterprise in that it must account to the people just as a corporation must account to its stockholders—a government that became bankrupt was one that had betrayed the trust of its constituents. Accordingly it was consistent for Murphy both to chastise the financial world for its myopic social vision and to serve on the state advisory committee of the National Economy League, an organization dedicated to shrinking government expenses. Among the sponsors of this body were dependable conservatives such as Calvin Coolidge and Elihu Root.[29]

Murphy became convinced Detroit's solvency could be maintained only if federal aid were forthcoming. President Herbert Hoover's administration thus far had offered no help to cities, although it had assisted private corporations through the Reconstruction Finance Corporation. At the suggestion of Dr. Frank Adams, a member of the Mayor's Unemployment Committee, Murphy called a conference of Michigan mayors to discuss ways of persuading Congress to enact legislation providing for unemployment relief, the refunding of municipal debts, and a federal public works program modeled after William Randolph Hearst's $5,000,000,000 prosperity-loan proposal. The mayor was not concerned about what specific legislation was endorsed; the important thing was to arouse public opinion for federal relief of some kind.[30]

The conference of Michigan mayors met at City Hall, Detroit on May 18, 1932. The eighteen attending mayors were in a serious mood. Murphy set the tone in his assertion it was "folly to go along [any further] on the theory that there would be . . . a sudden return to prosperity."[31] One after another the chief executives stood up to echo or expand upon this theme. George Welsh of Grand Rapids described his fruitless days attending the special session of the Michigan legislature, which had voted $20,000,000 for state highways but nothing for cities, although the cities paid the greater share of the taxes. In summary he warned: "If we cannot borrow or obtain money, if our people are not fed, Communism and Bolshevism, working at top speed will undermine the morale of our people."[32] Another chief executive put caution aside and demanded the prosperity-loan proposal be amended to eliminate the loan feature and permit the distribution of the $5,000,000,000 in greenbacks.[33] At its conclusion the conference urged passage of a federal assistance program and called also for a national conference of mayors to meet in Detroit June 1, 1932.

Murphy invited to the national conference mayors of all cities with populations over 100,000. Considering the short notice on which the conference was called, the response was impressive. Among the cities represented were Cleveland, Minneapolis, New Orleans, New York, Milwaukee, Denver, Boston, and Indianapolis.[34] Not all the participants shared the extreme concern of some of their colleagues. J. Fulmer Bright of Richmond believed the depression would end by the next winter and, in any case, that every city in the nation had sufficient resources to meet its needs. Mayor Walmsley of New Orleans promptly begged to differ, asking, if Mayor Bright is right, "Why are we here today discussing this?" Taking the floor from Walmsley was Mayor Jimmie Walker from New York City who proceeded to instruct Bright in the realities of the depression, declaring, "This country is on the verge of destruction." More tactfully, Murphy joined the challenge: "Now, the Mayor of Richmond I regard as my personal friend, but we are here to say to him that something worse than a cyclone or an earthquake has hit the large American cities—our people are hungry."[35]

If not unanimously, the conference near-unanimously called for congressional passage of the $5,000,000,000 prosperity loan and for an amendment to the RFC act enabling the corporation to refund municipal debts. In language typical of Murphy, and common for the times, the preamble of the adopted resolutions asserted: "The world and the nation are at war. The enemy is hunger. . . . Such a situation calls for the prompt vigorous and intelligent measures which war always makes imperative."[36] Father Coughlin, radio priest for millions of Americans and Murphy's personal friend, closed the conference with a flourish:

> This meeting would never have been called . . . had not there been hypocrisy enunciated from the rostrums of our nation; had not there been greed and avarice proposed in place of justice and charity. . . .
>
> Money, millions and billions for foreigners. Last week the Berengaria carried out of Mayor Walker's port one hundred and nineteen million dollars of gold for foreigners who refused to pay us the debts they already owe us and we can't get one million for the starving people of the United States.

The transcript of the conference reported prolonged applause with all delegates standing.[37]

A committee of the conference, headed by Murphy, went to Washington to press the proposals on President Hoover. He told them he preferred to handle relief by letting the RFC lend modest sums to the states for distribution. Accordingly, in July Hoover vetoed a bill providing for large-scale public works and direct relief. Later he signed an act authorizing the RFC to lend $300,-000,000 for relief and another $1,500,000,000 for self-liquidating public works.[38]

Ralph Stone had opposed Murphy's effort to obtain federal assistance, believing it was wrong for the United States government to rescue cities that lacked the discipline to keep expenses down to a level they could afford. He conceded this reduction in expenses would mean "very much less police and fire protection, school service, recreation and all the rest of the multitude of services." But he was confident people were willing to submit to this in order to free business from its heavy tax burden. Then business would prosper, and the depression would disappear.[39]

When the budget for the new fiscal year (1932-33) was drawn up in June 1932, Stone's view prevailed. It was a mark of Murphy's political skill that he accepted this without rancor. He proposed a so-called five-year financial plan, implying the ambitious hope of permanently solving the city's financial plight. The key was to pay off enough of the city's indebtedness to appreciably diminish the burdensome principal and interest payments. If five years of austere government living were maintained, the city would be over the worst in terms of debt payments.[40] As drawn up, the plan included a saving of $5,400,000 achieved by a permanent salary reduction of 14.5 percent and an additional saving of $1,500,000 gained by curtailing departmental expenses. The larger taxpayers were to make advance tax payments to take care of overdue bills. An expected tax delinquency of 25 percent on the $72,000,000 budget was to be covered by the sale of $20,000,000 in emergency bonds. Authority to issue them was to be sought from the state legislature in January. Welfare expenses were to be covered by RFC loans.[41]

Since the cooperation of the city's larger taxpayers and creditors was essential, Murphy presented the proposed budget to them in a private meeting on July 5 prior to consideration by the council.[42] The five-year financial plan won their immediate favorable response, and Murphy was credited with great statesmanship. The Detroit Board of Commerce went on the air July 13 to praise the plan, stating it had "met the approval of practically all competent students of municipal and financial affairs."[43] With Murphy temporarily in the conservative camp, liberals grumbled. Councilman Edward J. Jeffries, Jr., (later mayor of Detroit), who had voted in vain against the budget, complained that the plan legislated the desire of the bankers and industrialists to slash Detroit's living standards.

No sooner was the new budget approved in July than a group of real estate operators protested and called for a limitation on it. Organized into the Associations for Tax Reductions, Inc., they proposed a charter amendment to be voted on by the citizens in August limiting the budget of the current fiscal year (planned for $72,000,000) to $61,000,000, that of the next year to $60,000,-000 and so on until a limit of $57,000,000 was reached. This amounted to a tax strike by realtors who were unwilling or unable to pay city assessments. These men had speculated in housing lots on the outskirts of Detroit during the twenties. When the 1929 crash came, they found themselves with vast amounts of property on their hands and no money for paying taxes. For example, Louis G. Palmer, the president of Associations for Tax Reductions, had subdivided the northwestern part of Detroit and currently owed the city $150,000 in delinquent taxes.[45]

Advocates of the $61,000,000 plan presented it several times to the Common Council. On each occasion they were told to come back with a more constructive, workable proposal, which they were unable to do to the council's satisfaction. But the proponents of the plan complained the council didn't want to listen to them, preferring to dismiss them with the reprobate name of anarchists. Murphy's administration found many flaws in the plan, among them that it ignored the problem of tax delinquency and debt payments. Moreover, the proposal would affect the legal commitments of the city, such as its pension plan. Murphy soon was convinced the real estate operators' objective was to tie the whole tax question into a legal tangle giving them a de facto moratorium on taxes for several years. They hoped, and admitted privately, if they could achieve this, by the time the question was settled perhaps prosperity would have returned and they could recoup their losses.[46]

Because of its natural appeal the $61,000,000 plan was a serious political threat. What voter wouldn't have been for reducing taxes? Murphy's corporation counsel, Clarence Wilcox, readily admitted the plan was the only way taxpayers could get taxes cut.[47] As the August 9 date for the special election on the plan drew near, friends of the charter amendment intensified their campaign. They asked voters to approve the $61,000,000 plan and "Pull Detroit out of the 'MURPHY MUDDLE.' "[48] One of their circulars pictured the mayor and other city officials as Indians doing a war dance around the helpless citizen tied to a stake over a fire. The caption read:

> "Yes, the Citizen has a Stake in the Community—but the Officials are trying to make it pretty Hot for him. . . ."

> The Mayor knows that his administration is on trial. He knows that adoption of this amendment will constitute repudiation of his administration of wastefulness. His POLITICAL CAREER IS IN JEOPARDY. He CAN'T AFFORD TO LOSE. . . .[49]

Murphy took up the challenge. A campaign of broad proportions was begun. Every newspaper in the city and all the leading business firms and industrialists were lined up to oppose the amendment.[50] The Committee on City Finances, which had often attacked Murphy for extravagant spending, issued a public statement condemning the $61,000,000 proposal, although its real estate board member voted against it.[51] Symbolic of the unity Murphy achieved was Ralph Stone's support. He even wrote the mayor a personal note of praise and encouragement.[52]

Pro-Murphy handbills called attention to the illegality and unworkable elements in the amendment proposal. They termed it

"A DESPERATE DODGE" and asked for a vote against "Chaos and Disaster." The real estate men behind the proposal were described in one leaflet as "the fellows who sold you a jerry-built house . . . for twice what it is worth." The literature also emphasized that the proposed tax reduction would mean an end to, or a strict curtailment of, schools, sanitation, and police and fire protection.[53]

On election eve Murphy spoke on the radio against the amendment. The issue, as he saw it, was whether the voters had the wisdom to understand the difficult question placed before them:

> Our decision at the polls tomorrow will be a rare test of democratic government. Are we a vigilant, lively-minded and discriminate electorate which can choose between an alluring but deceptive proposal and the hard and inescapable facts of a definite condition, or are we not?
>
> Can we take a highly involved, abstract problem of government and decide it on its merits. . . . I am confident we can.[54]

The next day the voters supported his position by a margin of three to one.

In the midst of its financial struggle, Detroit found itself with yet another emergency. Early in March 1932, circulars were passed announcing a hunger march on the Ford Motor Company, located in neighboring Dearborn. The unemployed had resolved to dramatize their plight at an employer's door, in accordance with the Communist party's assertion that the bosses were to blame for the closing down of the factories.[55] Although no permit for the demonstration was requested, the Detroit police were prepared. On March 7, with law enforcement officers present, the march formed in Detroit, and an orderly walk to Dearborn began.

Throughout the march the Detroit police treated the demonstrators good-humoredly.[56]

At the boundary between the two cities, Dearborn police commanded the marchers to stop. Despite the order they advanced, and Dearborn enforcement officers launched tear gas grenades. Returning the attack with stones, the marchers pressed on up the half-mile stretch to the Ford company gates. Here the police leveled their guns at the marchers and fired—killing four, wounding a score more—with all wounds in the backs and sides of the frightened, fleeing workers. Meanwhile, Detroit police, requested by Dearborn authorities, had arrived on the scene.[57]

A few days later the workers held a funeral march of huge proportions. The route stretched for seven miles, from the Detroit Institute of Arts to Grand Circus Park and on to the cemetery. There were ten thousand marchers. Spectators four-deep lined the route from the institute to the park. At the park itself thirty thousand people watched the demonstrators. While foot policemen, under orders to dispense with their clubs, guarded the seven-mile route, motorcycle policemen led the cortege itself. There was no disorder of any kind.[58]

After the hunger march, Murphy issued a statement reiterating his administration's position on demonstrations: "The policy of the government has been one giving full and complete expression to principles of free speech and free assemblage. Mass meetings and parades are held as a matter of right—police merely supervise and regulate them." He added that Detroit police were not involved in the Dearborn shootings and that he would make no investigation of possible wrongdoing, since Dearborn was outside his jurisdiction.[59]

While the hunger marchers accepted Murphy's statement that he could not investigate the actions of Dearborn police, they were not convinced Detroit police had not themselves participated in the firing on the marchers. At a mass meeting in the Arena Gardens they called for the prosecution of all those responsible for the shooting, including Murphy. In addition they accused Murphy of ordering police to raid the offices of the Communist party, the Unemployed Council, and the United Auto Workers union in an effort to throw his own "guilt for the dastardly murders onto the shoulders of the working class leaders."[60]

With Roger Baldwin, the national head of the American Civil Liberties Union, Murphy discussed these accusations in a long series of communications beginning the day after the shooting and lasting into June. Baldwin pressed Murphy on every detail of the affair. Throughout Murphy was cooperative; he appeared to welcome the opportunity to open his administration to Baldwin's scrutiny.

Baldwin determined as false the accusation that Detroit police had participated in the shooting, after Murphy provided an accounting of all the activities of the Detroit police in Dearborn. In fact, the Detroit police had arrived after the shooting was over and only in time to assist in directing traffic and restoring order. The second accusation, that Detroit police had conducted a roundup of Communists following the hunger march, turned out to be partially true. While Murphy had no need to throw guilt for the slain onto radical leaders, the Dearborn police had good reason to do so. They requested and, according to Baldwin, won cooperation from the Detroit police in conducting the raids. James Watkins, Detroit's police commissioner, denied Baldwin's charge; but Baldwin stuck to it. Moreover, Communist leaders verified Baldwin's statement in Murphy's presence. Probably Watkins was right that the Detroit police had not conducted a roundup as such. However, Detroit police customarily were zealous in their harassment of radicals, and when the Dearborn police asked for assistance, they undoubtedly quietly cooperated.[61] Discouraged about the whole affair, Murphy wrote Baldwin: "There will be no lawless policy on the part of the Detroit police *that I can control.*"[62] [Emphasis added.]

Equally condemning was Baldwin's discovery that a few of the wounded demonstrators taken to Receiving Hospital were chained to their beds by Detroit police. In an explosive letter to the hospital superintendent in which he termed the chaining a "brutal practice," Murphy demanded a full explanation of the alleged threats supposedly justifying the action.[63]

A minor incident connected with the hunger march—a sequel to the good samaritan parable with a twentieth century ending—exemplified the problem Murphy faced. On the afternoon of March 7 three women driving toward Dearborn learned of the shooting at the Ford plant and turned toward home. On the way they encountered two wounded men and "in mere decent humanity" took them to Detroit's Receiving Hospital. The women waited there a few minutes, thinking they might be of further service. As they were about to leave, a Detroit officer arrested them and took them to a police station. Later Detroit police drove them to Dearborn police headquarters. Dearborn police held them for several hours and finally fingerprinted and questioned them. Eventually they were released by Dearborn authorities, but only because a prominent citizen intervened.[64]

Three months after the Ford hunger march, violence broke out again—this time in Detroit proper. On June 6 a column of unemployed workers marched under the supervision of Detroit police to a vacant lot opposite the Briggs manufacturing plant. After arriving, the workers asked for a conference with Briggs representatives, but the company turned down their request, whereupon the workers moved across the street and demanded entrance to the plant. When the police blocked their way, a demonstration leader struck the commanding officer in the mouth, knocking out two of his teeth. This began a general melee. The police guarding the plant charged and, by Murphy's admission, indulged in indiscriminate clubbing, seriously injuring several persons. Baldwin, who was still keeping his eye on Detroit police, asked for an explanation of the police brutality. When Murphy described the reason for the police assault, Baldwin replied that under the circumstances "there is certainly nothing for us to discuss." He added, "I know what the Communist tactics are on such occasions. They regard police refusal of what they conceive to be their rights as warrant for the use of force."[65]

After the Briggs riot Murphy found it increasingly difficult to maintain community support for his free speech and assembly policy. Too often these rights were abused by radicals, conservatives reminded him. The Wayne County American Legion Council asked him to stop communist abuse of the American flag and high government officials, demanding "these people" be "taught to respect the Flag for which we and our forefathers fought."[66] Complaints from ordinary citizens increased too; one citizen asserted the free assembly policy interfered with business, for timid customers were hesitant to come downtown for fear of getting " 'caught' in a parade, demonstration or riot."[67] Murphy believed the time had come for more cooperation from radicals in maintaining the rights of free speech and assembly. He confided to Baldwin:

> There has been so much abuse of the free speech policy . . . that is, interference by groups refusing to recognize the rights of free speech and assemblage of others, . . . that the public generally is being educated up to a more conservative view. . . . The crystalized judgment of the dominant groups in the City is now demanding vigorous police action. . . . Our problem now is not one of educating the conservatives to the necessity for free speech and assemblage, demonstra-

68

tions and the like, but to gain or compel, in some manner, the cooperation of small vocal minority groups who do not share views on these questions.[68]

Baldwin sympathized with Murphy's position and said he would ask Communist leaders to refrain from premeditated acts of violence.[69]

In Washington the federal government evidenced less concern for protecting civil liberties. In July President Hoover ordered the army to drive out the bonus marchers encamped on the mud flats of the Anacostia River where they were residing while they petitioned Congress for payment of the veterans' bonus. General Douglas MacArthur commanded the troops and carried out the mission with dispatch, using tanks and infantry. When asked to comment on the President's action, Murphy replied it was "without justification or excuse." He spoke from experience of the past spring when he had struggled under the most unfavorable conditions to maintain civil liberties. In elaborating on his statement he said:

> In these anxious and unhappy days for so many of our people, careless officials and governments are often tempted to do what appears to be the easy and safe thing, that is exercise with violence the police force. Such a policy is a perilous one. It is an example of recklessness unbecoming the government. It demonstrates weakness rather than strength and does not reveal the qualities of character in government essential to maintain leadership at a time when patience and a broad understanding should mark the conduct of those in authority. There is not a city in the land but would be almost open warfare by now if it adopted such a policy.[70] [Punctuation added.]

The 1932 financial crisis led Detroit again to examine its welfare policy. As of July 1931 the welfare budget was cut in half. But was even the authorized $7,000,000 too much to spend? Was it really necessary? If it was necessary, should relief needs have taken precedence over the principle of a balanced budget or the property rights of taxpayers?

The pressure of drawing up a budget for the next fiscal year required immediate answers to these questions. In late June the Public Welfare Commission reported the $3,000,000 tentatively allocated for relief during the next year already had a $2,200,000 obligation for deficits previously incurred. Under the circumstances the commission felt obligated to reduce the case load from the current figure of twenty-four thousand to sixty-two hundred families. It realized this meant "chaos and violence," but it saw no alternative.[71] Murphy, who was attending the Democratic national convention in Chicago, was shocked by the news and rushed back to Detroit to countermand the action. The welfare commission members, as the *News* (July 3, 1932) reported, did not appreciate this "grandstand play" which put them in the embarrassing position of having to perform a financial miracle with an empty bank account.

The soul-searching that Detroit went through was revealed in two studies of the Welfare Department. One was by the auditors of Wayne County prepared for the Welfare Department, and the other was a confidential analysis made by the Citizen's Committee, a self-appointed body. Since the city's Welfare Department handled welfare cases for the county and in turn the county reimbursed the city, the county had a legitimate concern as to how its money was spent. The Citizen's Committee was a businessmen's organization which was concerned with how efficiently tax dollars were spent, in this instance, by the Welfare Department. The two studies were initiated on the assumption welfare expenditures could be cut, and their goal was to make recommendations both for administrative savings and for savings in the actual amount of relief distributed.[72]

The county auditors' report was especially keen in discovering instances of waste in administration. There was no doubt the Welfare Department was guilty of administrative inefficiency; this had been revealed during the welfare controversy of 1931. Even the mayor's office had difficulty occasionally with the Welfare Department. In exasperation a secretary testily wrote a district supervisor, "There are times . . . the [social] Workers do not seem to understand our desire to cooperate and be helpful to them."[73]

John F. Ballenger, the welfare director, accepted the charge of inefficiency made by the county auditors and instituted some of their recommendations. These included establishing uniform employment conditions for all employees, reducing the number of district offices and transferring them to city-owned buildings, instituting standard operating procedures for all district offices, consolidating bureaus under the Welfare Department, and studying alternative plans for distributing relief more economically.[74] These changes did save money, but because the administrative share of the welfare budget was small, the total saved was small as well.

In suggesting means for cutting welfare relief itself, the studies floundered. The Citizen's Committee report had a special proclivity in this regard.[75] Prepared by eighty-one persons, it was bound to reflect differing views. At one extreme were the reactionaries whose premise was that many unworthy people were receiving relief, although they conceded this could not be substantiated with figures. Their main concern was to suggest ways of catching misrepresentations and frauds. To counter assumed softness in social workers they would require that all new workers have a business background as well as sociological training. In addition, they proposed that social workers be trained in detective skills, believing, for example, that welfare recipients should be fingerprinted and required to thus identify themselves when they received relief checks. Likewise, punctuality in calling for relief checks should be insisted upon—"while this is a small thing, . . . as a reflection of discipline . . . it is extremely desirable." They were sure, too, the "peculiar characteristics and temperaments of the colored people" made them lazy and content to live forever off welfare aid. To their surprise they discovered little radical sentiment among relief recipients. All this indicated "too generous an attitude on the part of the Welfare Department." Their suggestion for both eliminating generosity and saving money was to divide a fixed sum for food among as many people as possible instead of guaranteeing a minimal nutritional level for an individual on relief, as was currently done.

If the reactionaries were convinced relief expenditures could be cut, J. W. Scoville, in a sole dissenting opinion, was equally convinced they could not. He made a statistical analysis of the welfare cases investigated by the committee and found little evidence indicating fraud by applicants or gross negligence by welfare workers. In only thirty-six instances out of a total of 174 cases were changes recommended, and most of these were minor. That this statistical evidence had been a blow to the reactionaries was seen in their attempt to discredit the interviewers (all businessmen), of whom they said not half "got into this work and did the type of job which we expected would be done."

Moreover, Scoville made cogent observations about the value of the committee's investigations. He doubted whether a layman could enter a household and determine by a casual study whether the food allowance was sufficient: "That the allowance prevents starvation is evident if the members of the family are alive." Instead, what the records did show was a large amount of sickness. Also, Scoville observed, the study did not discuss the number of needy families not yet on the relief rolls. Likewise, it neglected to point out the study was made in summer, not in winter when the relief load was the heaviest.

Between Scoville and the reactionaries were the moderates. They accepted as necessary the welfare program and saw no way of appreciably reducing welfare costs, as much as they would have liked to. Indeed, the final recommendations of the Citizen's Committee, which were written by the moderates, accepted as "not unduly high" the Welfare Department's request of $10,000,000 for the next fiscal year.

Thus, as these investigations of the Welfare Department indicated, after the crisis of 1932, Detroiters, and responsible conservative opinion in particular, had come to recognize relief must be given to the unemployed. The need was legitimate, and the alternative to providing relief was to court violence. Remaining was the problem of obtaining money to pay for aid in the new budget. The budget for 1932-33 counted on receiving most of the money from RFC loans. While it was not difficult to justify the request to the RFC—the need was obvious enough—the state government's endorsement was necessary first. This was not easy to come by. In addition to the usual rural suspicion affecting the state's relationship with Detroit, there was the problem of politics. Governor Brucker, a Republican, viewed Murphy's request for RFC funds as a scheme to undo Democratic failure in Detroit, and Brucker wanted no part of it.

Murphy's administration began negotiations with Brucker on July 7, outlining in approximate figures the needs of the city Welfare Department. On July 27 Detroit sent a second letter to the governor, impressing on him the importance of prompt action. After the city wrote a third time, on September 8 it received a reply stating the governor's files did not possess Detroit's earlier correspondence. On September 12 copies of all previous correspondence were sent to the state capitol. Meanwhile, Detroit had lost a month of RFC welfare loans.[76] Brucker finally came to Detroit to discuss with Murphy and the council the city's request for loans. As Brucker's and Murphy's interpretations differed as to the extent of Detroit's need, their tempers flared. At the climax as Brucker rose to leave the council chamber, he snapped that Murphy obviously wanted to pull down a gift from a Christmas tree.[77] Murphy's response was to pursue his rotund opponent tenaciously until he won at least part of what he wanted.

After September virtually all of Detroit's welfare assistance was paid for by the RFC. This did not mean life was any easier for the relief recipient; if anything, his life became a little harder. To save money, the policy of issuing food orders was discontinued, and public cafeterias were set up. Each cafeteria was presided over by a hostess who looked after the children and saw to it that everyone was taken care of. Using cafeterias meant further disruption of family life, as meals were no longer prepared and eaten in the home. In addition an inescapable odium faced the families who walked twice a day to cafeterias; their poverty was displayed before the onlooking public. They were reduced to the humblest level of civilized existence—that of a municipal soup line.[78]

Having survived the spring crisis of 1932, Detroit looked confidently ahead to the new fiscal year. The state legislature was to meet in January and give Detroit authority to sell $20,000,000 in emergency bonds. This, it was expected, would more than cover the anticipated 25 percent tax delinquency. But by fall, as tax delinquency mounted to 36 percent, the hope of the previous summer was dissipated. On December 7 Murphy requested a special session of the legislature to authorize the $20,000,000 issue immediately. He believed a delay of even two or three weeks would lead to defaulting by the city on bank payments. Brucker—who had been defeated for reelection in November—complained the city should have foreseen the emergency more promptly; nonetheless he obliged Murphy, and before January 1, 1933 the emergency issue was authorized.[79]

In his January 1933 message to the Common Council Murphy was still confident Detroit would not be overwhelmed by the financial storm surrounding it. "There is fear and dread in the minds of the vast majority of our people," the *News* (January 11, 1933) quoted him as saying. "Yet I cannot share with my fellow man the pessimism of the hour." And perhaps Detroit could have ridden out the storm had not the Detroit banks, which had in the past saved the city from defaulting, themselves defaulted. On February 14 the governor closed the doors of Michigan's banks and thereby touched off a wave of bank holidays throughout the nation. Murphy's administration was helpless before the onslaught. The sale of the $20,000,000 tax anticipation bonds was stopped, and on February 15 Detroit defaulted on interest payments due. The only money that came into the city treasury following the bank closings was RFC relief funds. It was impossible for Detroit to pay its employees; but even if it could have, the banks could not have cashed the checks. By March currency circulation in Detroit dropped to 20 percent of normal.[80]

Immediately following the bank crash a food scare swept Detroit. Fearing they would run out of cash, many housewives laid in a ten-day to two-week supply of food. Since few retailers had reserve stocks, items became scarce, and prices rose sharply. Panic followed but passed as wholesalers brought supplies into the city.[81]

Tax delinquencies rose to a record 40 percent; no one knew how much further they would go. Under this circumstance the city could no longer depend upon high tax levies and payments by a few great industrial concerns to support its government. In rebellion industries began to demolish their buildings to save taxes. Unemployment continued to climb; it was now over 40 percent of the working force. Of this figure only 10 percent were being cared for by the city; the rest struggled as best they could.[82]

Although Michigan's new governor, William A. Comstock, was a Democrat, the mayor was no more successful in obtaining state aid from him than from his predecessor. Moreover, Comstock turned down repeated requests by Murphy for state cooperation in applying for RFC loans. In an effort to force the governor's hand, Murphy organized a gathering at the state capital of city welfare officials from all over Michigan. Acting more like former Governor Brucker every day, Comstock let loose a verbal volley at Murphy: "If Mayor Murphy wants to run the State," the *News* (March 26, 1933) quoted him as saying, "perhaps I'd better resign. Now Frank Murphy is a good friend of mine, but in all kindness, I advise him to keep his nose out of State affairs." Murphy remarked, according to the *News* (March 28, 1933): "Now Mr. Comstock seems to think my schnozzle is too long. Well, I intend to push my schnozzle into any affairs that have to do with obtaining relief for our destitute families."

In spite of the crisis and the failure to obtain state aid, Murphy resolved to keep city government going—the schools, police and fire departments—and to give a lift to the city's stymied economy. To accomplish this he asked the city to issue scrip. To prevent the scrip from depreciating, 90 percent of the issue was sold to business firms, which in turn used it to pay their taxes. The actual cash received from the sale of the scrip was paid to city employees as wages.[83] As wages were spent, the circulation of money in Detroit was to that extent renewed.

As he had many times in the past, on March 6, 1933 Murphy went on the air to reassure his people. But this time the optimism and confidence were missing. It was to stoic virtues that he appealed:

We need not worry so much about the complexity of the problem. We all can revive the old integrities and virtues and bring them to the forefront . . . .

We can all be honest with ourselves and with all of our following in every dealing and transaction.

We can all be industrious. Work, hard work will contribute as much to the solution of our problem as the finest and most careful planning of its details.

We can all be frugal—live within our means—be willing even eager to sacrifice for the common good.

We can all be kindly—be good neighbors—play our individual parts in harmony one with the other—be good friends and good citizens.

Murphy then asked citizens not to turn their wrath on the bankers for causing the present crisis:

It is easy to waste our gifts on abuse and denunciation of this group and that group—but that course is folly and besides it is futile and gets us nowhere. What energies and gifts a kind Providence has given us, let us exercise to mend and heal; to gather the threads that will weave our lives into the whole and healthy fabric they once were, and will be again.

In conclusion he reminded Detroiters of his faith in them:

I am confident that here in Detroit, we will do our part bravely and courageously and perhaps wage the battle just a little bit better than it is being waged elsewhere. We should, because we have been tempered to the struggle longer than our more fortunate neighbors. Our fibre has been toughened.

With all previous arrangements for refunding the city debt undone, Murphy worked again to find a way to restore Detroit's solvency. Ultimately the way was to be found through restora-

77

tion of national economic health, and he joined with city officials from all over the country in petitioning Congress for financial and relief legislation.[84] The New Deal Congress responded, and with the undergirding of federal legislation Murphy was able to achieve a sound financing of Detroit's debt. By June 1933 negotiations were completed with New York bankers, and the crisis began to ease.[85]

Despite the desperate situation, one group of workers was willing to risk more hardship by going out on strike. The Briggs manufacturing plants in Highland Park and Detroit had cut wages several times during 1932. Consequently, when in January 1933 Briggs reduced wages once again—to a high of 73 cents an hour and a low of 10 cents an hour—the workers rebelled and walked off their jobs.[86] At Highland Park State Police and local law enforcement officers supported the company by repeatedly breaking up picket lines. In Detroit, Murphy ordered the police to make no illegal arrests and to allow the establishment of picket lines. Nonetheless some police interference with picketing did occur.[87]

Murphy's authority for dealing with the strike was limited. Only the state could properly intervene to settle a strike involving two municipalities and one company. Nonetheless, Murphy appointed a Fact Finding Committee headed by Reverend H. Ralph Higgins to investigate the strike. It reported many of the workers' grievances were justified and criticized the company for not meeting with their spokesmen.[88] But, since the president of the company, Walter O. Briggs, had decided he would not negotiate with strike leaders who he believed were Communists, the committee's report was without effect. The strike lasted throughout the spring. It accomplished little and ended in failure.

The 1933 crisis was a strain on Murphy, which he showed in a loss of weight. His friends urged him to take better care of himself, but he did not give in to their pleas. Even seemingly unimportant details were not overlooked. He took time, for instance, to fill the request of a Catholic charity for 125 tons of coal.[89] He personally calmed down an irate matron who asked that Diego Rivera's recently painted fresco, which she called "hideously inappropriate," be removed from Detroit's Institute of Arts. Murphy tactfully explained art was something he knew little about, and since he did "not want to do anything but exactly the right thing," he thought it best to let the current excitement subside before making a decision.[90] Throughout the crisis, he held onto his sense of humor. On March 17 he addressed the Friendly Sons of St. Patrick in New York City. In his opening remarks he thanked the planning committee for "sending his carfare in advance," adding it was sent to him in the form of a check as if the committee believed "for a moment that a check might be cashed in the City of Detroit under present conditions."[91]

Not content with municipal prominence, Murphy strove to become a national figure as well. In the spring of 1931 he made a series of appearances outside Detroit. Speaking in Toledo, Ohio, he asked for immediate payment of the soldiers' bonus as an emergency anti-recession measure. He also spoke in Cleveland and Cincinnati and made journeys to New York, Indiana, and Illinois to introduce himself to new audiences.

In March he went to Washington to join in a public discussion with members of the Senate insurgent bloc and seventy others invited by Senator George W. Norris. Although the invitation stated the conference was not called to form a new party, Murphy volunteered that Norris was the best man in the U.S. Senate and if Norris were the presidential candidate on a third party ticket, he would gladly support him.[92]

In the summer of 1931 Murphy joined the People's Lobby,

chaired by John Dewey, in urging President Hoover to call a special session of Congress to enact federal aid for unemployment. The following January Murphy returned to Washington to appear before Senator Robert La Follette's Manufacturers' Committee to advocate federal relief aid for cities. In February 1933, as Detroit was defaulting on its debt payments, Murphy asked the National Conference of Mayors to reconvene at Washington. The previous resolutions of the conference were reapproved and presented to the Senate Committee on Banking and Currency. At this session, the conference was established on a permanent basis with Murphy its president and James Curley of Boston its vice-president.[93]

In 1932 Murphy plunged into the repeal issue. He was pledged to vote for a wet plank at the Democratic national convention, and in the fall campaign he continued to speak for repeal.[94] Although he was a total abstainer and believed in temperance for others, he was for repeal and was convinced that prohibition did more harm than good. Writing to a prohibitionist who criticized his support of a beer parade in Detroit, he said prohibition had struck a devastating blow to the "social order, good government, and standards of justice in large cities." He reminded his reader he was writing from seven years of experience on the bench and nearly two years more as mayor. Noting that "we both want the same thing—good government and, as a consequence, a well-governed and happy people," he concluded: "There will have to be correction in the prohibition law if this is to be brought about."[95]

At the insurgents' meeting called by Senator Norris in March 1931, Murphy had sounded very much like a maverick Democrat—for any flirtation with third party movements appeared to be a betrayal of party loyalty. However, in June he visited Governor Franklin D. Roosevelt in Hyde Park, and Roosevelt apparently had no difficulty persuading Murphy to give his full support to the Democrats. Murphy liked to consider himself a political independent in the Progressive tradition—knowing full well this was the basis for much of his appeal among liberals—but he always faithfully stood by his party in the final issue. G. Hall Roosevelt, a Murphy appointee, had introduced the two politicians. For the benefit of their mutual ambitions the two continued to keep in touch. In September 1931 Franklin Roosevelt's son, James, spoke at the American Legion convention in Detroit in place of his father.[96] Another Murphy visit with F.D.R. took place in January 1932. The mayor was now quietly pushing for Roosevelt's nomination among Michigan delegates to the Democratic convention, and in February Hall Roosevelt assured F.D.R. he would get a 100 percent delegation from Detroit.[97]

Murphy was the outstanding Democratic official in an intensely Republican state. However, this position did not make him a leader in the state Democratic party; the state organization men, who had labored through lean years, resented Murphy's intrusion, terming him a "fair weather Democrat." The Roosevelt camp did not at first realize Murphy's weak position. But when the state party convention almost refused to place Murphy among the accredited delegates, his true strength became apparent. From then on the Roosevelt forces worked with older Democrats. If, as reported, the mayor had vice-presidential aspirations, they necessarily were given up.[98]

After more correctly assessing Murphy's strength, F.D.R. strategists invited him to serve on the committee of the National Progressive League, a nonpartisan group organized to support Roosevelt for President.[99] With one foot in and one foot out of the Democratic Party, Murphy conducted a strong campaign for the New York governor. When industrialists threatened coercion to win employee votes for Hoover, the mayor shrewdly organized a Non-Coercion League in Detroit. Made up of clergy-men and non-partisan leaders of the city, the league condemned the practice and reminded workers of their right to a secret ballot.[100]

As in Murphy's campaign a year earlier, the issues of want and unemployment were the overriding ones. President Hoover was completely discredited. When Hoover appeared in Detroit, he was booed—something that rarely has happened to any President in office—and the Secret Service feared for his life.[101] Murphy toured the state for both the national and state tickets. His travel-ing companion was the Democratic candidate for governor, Wil-liam Comstock. Both men spoke to crowds that never before had turned out to hear Democrats. In Flint Murphy himself drew the largest crowd ever in the political history of the city.[102] As the oppressed in Michigan had looked to Murphy for leadership over the past two years, so now they looked to the Democratic party for guidance. On election day Michigan followed the national trend by voting Democrats into power in both Washington and the state capitol at Lansing.

When F.D.R.'s victory was announced, Murphy wired the President-elect: "The beauty of a democracy is that when a great leader arrives the people recognize him as they recognize you. God grant you strength in the huge task ahead."[103] Roosevelt's triumph became Frank Murphy's good fortune, for under presi-dential favor he was successively appointed to several administrative posts. Frank Murphy had become a lieutenant for the New Deal.

Chapter III

New Deal Colonialism

The game of guessing appointments began even before Roosevelt was inaugurated in March 1933. In early April, G. Hall Roosevelt wrote his brother-in-law: "Don't forget my friend Frank Murphy —he's valuable for you." Hall cited Murphy's qualifications: Catholic influence; forceful radio and public speaker; honest, obedient, and energetic; and a trained executive. "Unfortunately," Hall added, "he can hardly abandon his present job without the prospect of real responsibility and has his heart set on the Philippines."[1]

But Homer Cummings had been promised the governor-generalship of the Philippines.[2] Therefore, for a few months Murphy's future with the new administration remained unsettled, until fortune intervened. As Cummings was preparing to sail for the Philippines, F.D.R.'s appointee for attorney general, Senator Thomas J. Walsh, died. The President then asked Cummings to become attorney general; Cummings accepted, leaving the governor-generalship open for Murphy.

From Roosevelt's point of view the Murphy appointment was a shrewd one. He was confident of the mayor's ability. Further, he was anxious to bring into his administration an able politician from the normally Republican state of Michigan. He felt Murphy's future assistance in bringing that state into the Democratic column would be invaluable. However, Americans who were associated with the Philippines were less sure of the President's choice. Former Governor-General W. Cameron Forbes wrote F.D.R.: "I don't see how a man who has never had any training in that very difficult job is going to manage to swing it."[3] The outstanding American scholar on the Philippines, Joseph R. Hayden, confided to a friend: "It is an outrageous travesty upon every principle of good government and sound judgment that he should have been sent out there. However, there he is. . . ."[4] Washington officials connected with Philippine affairs were even more disturbed than Hayden. They felt the only qualities Murphy had demonstrated were those which would "militate against making [him] a good Governor-General."[5] Their only hope was that the President would appoint a vice-governor who could make up for Murphy's deficiencies.[6]

In early May 1933, after preparing an orderly transfer of administration to Frank Couzens, (who was acting mayor of Detroit until his election as mayor in November 1933), Murphy was sworn in as governor-general of the Philippines. He had already attended a series of briefing conferences in Washington, and with two of his Detroit aides, Joseph Mills and Norman Hill, he set sail for the Philippine Islands. The post was perhaps the most glamorous one the administration had to offer. The governor-general lived in a handsome residence, the Malacañang palace, and acted as chief executive for some 14,000,000 wards of the United States government. He was paid $18,000 a year and received a generous expense allowance in addition. Moreover, the governor-generalship of the Philippines had traditionally been a stepping stone for American politicians and statesmen—among them William Howard Taft and Henry L. Stimson.

After the islands had been won at the turn of the century as a prize of the Spanish-American War, much to the amazement of the Americans the Filipinos failed to distinguish between the motives of the new conquerors and the former ones. Instead, they fought the American liberators as valiantly as they had their Spanish rulers, though eventually they were forced to succumb. To the credit of the United States, upon quelling the rebellion it spared no energy in reconstructing the islands and in educating the Filipinos. The Americans made a supreme effort to train their wards in democratic government in anticipation of eventual independence.

At the time of Murphy's appointment it appeared that a definite date for independence would be proclaimed. Having had considerable experience in self-government, the Filipinos were anxious to free themselves from the United States. Moreover, Congress was willing, even eager, to grant independence to the islands in order to stop importation of Filipino agricultural products that were competing with those of continental farmers. Accordingly, it had passed the Hare-Hawes-Cutting independence bill, and when President Hoover vetoed it, Congress overrode his veto. When Murphy arrived in the Philippines in June 1933, the Philippine legislature was about to meet and decide whether it would accept the Hare act.

The new governor-general had to face typically colonial problems.[7] He was in the peculiar position of being the chief executive of the dependent nation as well as the chief representative of the sovereign power. Normal difficulties were heightened by racial feeling between the dark Filipinos and the white Americans. Although the islanders had some sense of unity through the predominance of Malayan stock and the English language, this unity was upset by several factors: the nation was made up of several large islands and a great many small ones, and English, imposed by the Americans, competed with twelve other distinct tongues, including Spanish and Chinese. While the majority of Filipinos were Roman Catholics, there was also an indigenous Catholic sect which had declared its independence from Rome. A sizable bloc of Moslem Moros in the south and another of animists in the north fragmented the islands even further.

The United States had invested heavily in the islands, principally in agriculture and with the intent of providing raw material imports for the States in exchange for manufactured goods. The Philippines became relatively prosperous under this arrangement, but only because it had a guaranteed market for its staple agricultural items. Once independence was won and the United States raised tariff walls against the islands, this assured market would be shut off, and other markets would be difficult to find. As the average Filipino in 1933 had a low standard of living, any anticipated drop in national income would surely bring great suffering.

The island nation's period of tutelage in democratic government had not been long enough to create a mature and vibrant democratic state. Not only were there economic limitations, but education was insufficient. In the 1930's only 40 percent of the population was literate. Not all the social classes were represented within the insular government. Overwhelmingly concerned with the independence issue, Filipino politicians had tended to forget domestic problems.

This situation also had discouraged the formation of a two-party system. No Filipino could campaign successfully against independence even if he were sincerely against it. Consequently, domestic politics became largely a contest among individuals vying for recognition as having done the most toward gaining Philippine self-rule. On this basis, by the end of 1933 Manuel Quezon had maneuvered himself into the position of being the number one Filipino politician. No one could successfully challenge his leadership.

All Murphy's predecessors had dealt with these problems, directly or indirectly, and with varying degrees of success. With independence clearly in the offing, the success or failure of the American trusteeship as a whole was now at stake. Previous administrations had laid the groundwork, but President Roosevelt and Murphy had to provide the wisdom to assure that transition to independence be smooth. The temptation was to sever the bonds with the young nation quickly and completely; Congress and many American citizens would have favored this course.

Murphy was aware his knowledge of the Philippines was limited when Roosevelt appointed him to the Manila post; consequently, he spent his first months of duty on background study. His cautiousness impressed the career personnel carried over from previous administrations. He listened to them and studied the subjects himself before making decisions.[8]

It took time for the details of the governor-general's policy to be formed. Until they were firmly set, he relied on his experience in government, his basic convictions, and his intuition. His approach was the same as it had been as mayor of Detroit—to have a simple, economically sound, and honest administration.

Murphy knew no government can be successful without the support of most groups within the area governed. As mayor, he had succeeded in winning strong support, but he had also aroused strong criticism. In the Philippines he was careful not to antagonize any portion of the populace unnecessarily. He accomplished this by convincing the Filipinos that the public welfare was his sole criterion for action.[9] It was easier for him to succeed in this endeavor when he did not have to face periodic elections.

Of considerable help in this regard was his good relationship with the press. He went out of his way to see that the newspapers understood what he was trying to do.[10] In particular, he courted the reporters; he liberally gave out confidential information as background to announced policies. Usually the newsmen were faithful in their trust, but on those few occasions when a reporter

did betray his confidence, the governor-general discouraged him
from doing it again by admonishing him in a manner reported by
the *Philippines Herald Mid-Week Magazine* (February 6, 1935):
"Perhaps, it was my fault for having revealed to you what you
published yesterday. I don't blame you, I blame myself for being
so indiscreet."

The chief executive took care to see that political allies in
Michigan and in the Roosevelt administration knew what he was
doing. Norman Hill, Murphy's secretary, constantly mailed clippings of the governor-general's accomplishments to the States.
Frank X. Martel, president of the Detroit Federation of Labor,
and William Green, president of the AF of L, were recipients, as
was the Bureau of Insular Affairs.[11]

As always, Murphy instinctively understood the feelings of the
people he governed and knew how he must deal with them. He
was one of the few Americans who could cross the racial barrier
and say, "You Filipinos," in a public address and not antagonize
his listeners. He identified with them: "'You Filipinos,'" he said
on one occasion, "'are a lot like us Irishmen. You love a good
fight.'"[12] Socially he was at ease with the Philippine people and
held more parties of an informal nature, where Filipinos were
made to feel at home, than any of his predecessors.[13]

He found the Philippine people to be proud and sensitive, not
unlike himself.[14] These traits could make for difficulties in dealing with them in an official capacity. But Murphy disarmed their
sensitivity by supporting their national aspirations. He tactfully
used the technique of government by indirection. Former Governors Davis and Stimson had employed this practice. It operated in
this fashion: when the governor wanted a particular thing done,
he would call in a responsible Filipino leader and suggest that he
assume the task. The Filipino did the work and got the credit.[15]

Murphy's religion was of help to him. Not only was he thereby superficially united to the majority of the Filipinos, but by conscientiously practicing the tenets of his faith he won the admiration of the islanders. The Filipinos were religious—a factor sometimes overlooked by Murphy's predecessors. Murphy, however, knew this and frequently brought his religious faith into his public addresses. A Protestant cleric described his reaction to one of Murphy's religiously oriented speeches: "Those of us who saw and heard him were carried away with his earnestness and with the feeling that this Roman Catholic has all the passion for the Christian religion that the most vociferous Evangelical Protestant could have."[16]

The governor-general was fortunate in having able aides in Malacañang palace. He had brought Hill and Mills with him from Detroit, and Secretary of War George H. Dern had sent J. Weldon Jones as insular auditor. He was also capably assisted by experienced American and Filipino officials. However, Murphy's most important single adviser was Vice-Governor Joseph Hayden who had been chosen because he could provide the expert knowledge which Murphy lacked. Unaware of Hayden's initial outrage over his own appointment, Murphy had urged that Hayden be made vice-governor when his name was suggested by the Bureau of Insular Affairs.[17]

The vice-governor's normal duties were limited to heading the Department of Public Instruction and acting as the governor's alternate. However, under Murphy, Hayden was expected to be cognizant of everything. The two men worked out an ideal relationship of scholar and administrator, and Hayden soon felt his doubts about coming to the Philippines as Murphy's aide had been unjustified. He came to admire Murphy, completely reversing his earlier opinion of the governor-general. In a letter describing this reversal Hayden gave a penetrating analysis of Murphy's success as an administrator:

> I want to emphasize that just one thing has made possible this rapid action and justified my expectation of good results: the confidence of the G-G and his determination to do absolutely anything that he believes to be for the best interests of this country,—and nothing but that. Frank Murphy has a devotion to his work that actually justifies the use of that much overworked word, passionate. Furthermore, government, not only government in the P.I., but government per se is his devouring interest in life. No political scientist ever thought more constantly upon this subject. . . . And while he may not be brilliant, he can see to the heart of a political or administrative problem as quickly as anyone I have ever known. . . . His mind is constructive and he is not satisfied with mere plans. He wants good plans, but he is not satisfied until he sees them being worked out.
>
> One of the most interesting things about the Murphy regime, all things considered, is the universal agreement that there has never been an occupant of Malacañang who has more finely upheld the dignity of his position and of the United States in these Islands. This is appreciated by both Americans and Filipinos. . . .
>
> From all of this (and I could write a great deal more of it) you must feel that I have "gone Murphy." I have! The time may come when the prediction that Frank made as a student [of becoming President] will be justified by the event. Should this happen, the country will be in safe hands.[18]

Thus Frank Murphy brought to the governor-generalship, not expert knowledge of the Philippines, but qualities equally as important—fundamental dedication to government, ambition to do a good job, and an intuitive understanding of the Filipinos as human beings. Having these gifts, he was able to shift from being mayor of Detroit to being governor-general of a foreign country with ease.

After several months of studying the Philippines, Murphy was ready to act. His twofold function, as both chief executive of the Philippines and representative of the United States, makes it logical to discuss separately each of these roles. As chief executive he undertook three tasks: first, to stop the three-year trend toward insolvency that was plaguing the insular government;[19] second, to further human rights by raising the standard of living of the poor and by striving to ensure justice for all; and third, to bring about Philippine independence in a wise fashion.

The depression did not affect the Philippines as severely as it did the United States. Nevertheless, it reduced the income of the islands, causing an insular government deficit. The govenor-general, insistent on reversing this trend, began by establishing a central budget control system. For the first time, monthly reports on the income and expenditures of the insular, provincial, and municipal governments came regularly to the chief executive's desk. Telegrams to local governments ordering cuts in expenditures or a speed-up in collecting taxes and accounts receivable often resulted from these reports. The financial-administrative system he established gave him more actual, immediate control over the government than any other governor-general had possessed.[20]

To dramatize his concern for a balanced budget, Murphy announced that, unlike past practice, he would not welcome the elaborate receptions accorded the governor-general on inspection trips through the islands. This order also made celar his disapproval of the insincere adulation which accompanied the extravagant welcomes to the governor-general. Murphy did not encourage inequality in any respect.

At Malacañang Murphy trimmed expenses in various ways. The insular government owned several enterprises, and, under Mills's careful management, all were turned into profit-making concerns; previously some of them had run deficits. The governor-general also made efforts to stop the practice of double compensation whereby an official received full pay for each of several positions he held in the government.

Since the Philippine legislature was the big spender, the governor-general determinedly stuck by the budget, not succumbing to the temptation of trading administration-sponsored bills for traditional pork barrel legislation. Often administration measures were not passed, but Murphy was willing to pay that price. Maintaining the yearly budget also meant defying the legislature through a liberal use of his veto power. In 1934 Murphy vetoed ₱4,000,000 in projects. (Two pesos equalled one United States dollar.) He conceded some of the vetoed projects were worthy, such as the legislature's proposal to develop national parks. But in his veto message on this particular bill, as on other such acts, he told the lawmakers this expenditure was in "the class of luxuries beyond our means either for the moment or in the immediate future."[21]

The insular auditor, Jones, planned Murphy's budget and suggested ways to cut expenses. Although the governor-general usually followed the suggestions, he did not always do so. Murphy seemed to know when to stop in order to forestall outright opposition to his economy moves. For example, Jones recommended that government employees no longer be allowed to use government gasoline for their private cars. At first Murphy went along with the proposal, but when it became evident that most employees would resent the removal of this time-honored privilege, he quietly shelved the proposal.

Murphy's program of fiscal responsibility was very successful.

While deficits in 1930, 1931, and 1932 totaled more than ₱20,000,000, by 1935 the trend had not only been stopped but was reversed with a surplus of ₱6,000,000. With evident pride the governor-general wrote Louis Howe, President Roosevelt's secretary, of this accomplishment. Still smarting from criticism incurred when he was mayor of Detroit, Murphy bemoaned the fact that similar efforts in Detroit had gone unknown because fixed debt charges and relief measures had more than used up any savings which he had effected.[22]

Once his program of financial integrity was underway, Murphy turned to the task of ensuring the human rights—economic, social, and political—of the Filipino. The core of this new policy was a broad sociological study made by Major George C. Dunham, medical adviser in public health, and Colonel Paulino Santos of the prison administration. On the basis of this study, recommendations were made in the areas of: recreation, crime and correction, labor and industry, child welfare, general relief and family welfare, health service, and community organization. While it was recognized it would take years to put some of the recommendations into operation, others were implemented right away. Murphy had in mind bringing to the Philippines the concept of the welfare state; for the first time the insular government was to assume full responsibility for relief of distress due to any cause.

In the islands the gap between the haves and have-nots was greater than in the United States of 1933.[23] The Philippine peasant, or *tao,* had been abused for generations by *caciques,* (local political bosses), landlords, and usurers. Many age-old habits of living were untouched by western concepts of diet, health, or education; further, the Oriental attitude toward the suffering of others, or of oneself, often discouraged western welfare measures. Unless the circle of low standards of living and physical lassitude could be broken, there would be no chance for national development.

In public health and welfare Murphy's predecessors had made great strides. However, Murphy extended this program. Puericulture centers, staffed by a nurse and a local health officer, had provided maternal and child care in the past but had served only a fifth of the municipalities and had failed to reach into the rural *barrios.* In 1934 the legislature appropriated ₱170,000 to expand this program. Community health-social centers, designed to deal with the family as a health-social unit, were established. Trained social workers based at these centers sought to improve conditions which exposed the individual to disease.

Surveys conducted prior to establishing such centers in Manila revealed altering the city slum environment to be essential. The 1934 legislature appropriated ₱250,000 to construct low-cost homes in these areas.

To aid workers, under Murphy's leadership a department of labor was created; a workmen's compensation act and a maximum-hours law were adopted. Unemployment was less severe than in the United States, but nevertheless the governor-general appointed a citizens unemployment committee to look into the problem. The committee, a copy of his Detroit unemployment committee, spurred public interest in colonization and thereby provided an end to unemployment and a new life for many. The legislature appropriated ₱1,000,000 to promote the settlement of unoccupied public lands on Mindanao. It was often difficult to persuade the Filipinos of the value of resettlement as they were wedded to their family, province, and *barrio.* But, like all people, the Filipinos would follow a road, and, using this lure, the government stimulated colonization by building roads into the jungles. The

94

unemployment committee also persuaded the legislature to appropriate funds for temporary assistance to the unemployed.[24]

The committee's studies culminated in the establishment of a National Emergency Relief Board which was made up of both government officials and officers of private relief agencies. In 1934 the effectiveness of the board was severely tested. Between October 16 and December 4, five unusually destructive typhoons and a flood ravaged the islands. By coordinating all relief activities, the distressed were quickly helped. Under orders from the relief board, fifteen rehabilitation units—each consisting of a doctor, three public health nurses, and an agronomist—were sent to the devastated areas. When private agency funds were exhausted, the government accepted full responsibility by providing ₱1,000,000 more for the relief work.

Committees on nutrition and rural development were appointed by the governor-general to appraise the problem of providing an adequate diet. On their initiative, units made up of a public health nurse and an agriculturalist were sent to show people in the *barrios* how to raise and cook vegetables.

Other programs undertaken during Murphy's term included the expansion of hospital facilities and playgrounds and the adoption of an improved leprosy control plan. Since only about 40 percent of the people in rural areas had access to toilets or latrines, a campaign was begun to build a latrine for each family; in three years, 557,609 were installed.

During 1934 and 1935 the legislature provided ₱1,469,582 in special appropriations for Murphy's welfare programs. (The largest amount legislated for similar services during any one year in the previous decade had been ₱530,000 in 1928). In addition, ₱1,000,-000 was granted for typhoon relief, and another ₱1,000,000 was allocated for colonization. Similar programs were continued by the Filipinos themselves after Murphy's return to the States.

But the assurance and extension of human rights required action on a broader front. One of the worst enemies of the *tao* was the usurer. Murphy once stated more than 80 percent of the rice farmers, for example, were hoplessly in debt from birth to death.[25] In an effort to ease this condition, he ordered the Philippine National Bank to reduce interest rates on all loans. He also urged the recently created anti-usury board to intensify its efforts. Similarly motivated was the installment sales law which protected the buyer from further liability if the mortgaged article was seized by the seller upon failure to pay the installments.

In an effort to make justice more corrective and less retributive, the governor-general persuaded the Filipinos to adopt the indeterminate-sentence system he had advocated as a Recorder's Court judge. He personally put into the bill a provision placing the administration of the indeterminate-sentence system in the hands of a board of experts composed of a sociologist, a psychiatrist, an educator or a clergyman, and a lay citizen. He further insisted that a woman be a member of the board. However, the Filipinos, not convinced of the merits of the measure, repealed it after Murphy left the islands.[26]

Murphy also opposed using the death penalty during his term in the Philippines. While there he commuted every death sentence to life imprisonment. His efforts were not in vain, for Manuel Quezon continued this policy when he became chief executive of the Commonwealth of the Philippines.[27]

Using his powers of appointment and dismissal, the governor-general improved the quality of both judges and administrative officials. Moreover, he ruled dismissed officials were not immune from subsequent criminal prosecution.

As always, Murphy insisted on the maintenance of civil rights. When he discovered third-degree methods were being used and special agents were employed by a provincial governor, he directed both practices be stopped.[28] A more difficult situation to solve was that of factional warfare between followers of Quezon and his opponents. Yet the governor-general managed to mollify the factions on one of his inspection trips to the southern provinces.

Part of Murphy's human rights creed was to adhere strictly to the doctrine of the separation of church and state. Three hundred years of Spanish rule in the Philippines had placed the Catholic Church in a position of special privilege. In many instances the church had served the islands well, but in others not as well. An example of the latter was its ownership of large estates. Under Governor-General Taft the insular government began a policy of purchasing these large estates, known as friar lands, and dividing them into small holdings for the former tenants. Murphy attempted to revive this program, but without much success.[29]

In another clash with the church Murphy urged the legislature to enact a divorce law. In a message to the legislature he declared that although divorce was repugnant to him on personal, ethical, and religious grounds—as it was to the majority of the Filipinos— it was unfair to the minority to deny them the legal procedure of divorce.[30]

But his sharpest brush with the church resulted from his handling of a celebrated criminal case. Here his anti-clerical upbringing came forward. A young woman of a prominent Catholic family was convicted of falsifying results in grading a bar examination. The case dragged through the higher courts for a number of years. Finally the Philippine Supreme Court upheld her conviction. Great pressure was put on Murphy to give the woman an executive pardon before she should begin serving her sentence. The priesthood asked that she be pardoned on the grounds she was a devout communicant. The governor-general rejected this argument, pointing out there was only one law for all Filipinos. Eventually the papal legate himself attempted to intercede; he indicated that unless clemency were exercised he would "reluctantly" be obliged to consider Murphy as less than a faithful son of the church. The governor-general replied: " 'And I am reluctantly obliged to remind you that I am in these Islands as the representative of the President of the United States and not of the Holy See.' "[31] The young woman went to prison. After she had served nine months of her term, the governor-general then made his act of mercy and pardoned her.

One especially difficult problem was the absorption of the Moros, an alien people, into Filipino society. The Moros were Mohammedans who lived primarily in the Sulu archipelago and on the island of Mindanao. Numbering 677,000 in 1939, they possessed a highly developed civilization very different from that of the Christianized Filipinos. Spain had, at best, nominally conquered the Moros, and consequently the task of formulating a successful Moro policy was left to United States and Filipino leaders. The official American policy became one of gradually preparing the non-Christians for equal citizenship in a democratic Filipino state.[32]

In the 1920's friction between Americans and Filipinos had developed over implementing this policy. Most Americans felt the Filipinos underestimated the political significance of the cultural gap and should have moved more slowly in integrating the Moros into the Filipino nation. The Filipinos, in turn, viewed this American criticism as an assertion that the Filipinos were incapable of governing the non-Christians. The Bacon bill, which was introduced in Congress in 1926, exacerbated this resentment by proposing to separate Sulu and Mindanao from the rest of the Philippines and permanently retain these provinces under American sovereignty. The bill only pressured the Filipinos into a more rapid attempt to assimilate the Moros. Complicating the matter further was the American belief that Filipino leaders had filled govern-

mental positions in Moro areas with incompetent political followers.[33]

Vice-Governor Hayden was deeply concerned about the Moro
situation. In an eighteen-month period beginning in 1932 between seventy and eighty Moros and twenty-seven Filipino constabulary soldiers were killed in guerrilla warfare clashes. Since
the Moslems believed in the righteousness of a holy war, they
did not hesitate to kill in order to defend their culture. In addition,
their cattle stealing had almost wiped out the animal on the island
of Jolo. In the face of this violence, Hayden sided with the
Americans as to how the insular government should treat the
problem.[34] Even before Murphy arrived in the Philippines, Hayden
had pressed the Moro situation on him.[35] Consequently, when
Hayden arrived at Malacañang, the governor-general made the
vice-governor his principal adviser on the problem.

Hayden evolved a plan which hinged on the reappointment of
James R. Fugate as governor of Sulu province. Fugate had been
successful in the past, but had been dismissed by Murphy's
predecessor in response to Filipino pressure.[36] The governor-
general diplomatically persuaded the responsible Filipino official,
the secretary of the interior, to approve Hayden's proposal. As a
result a new Moro policy was announced as the joint effort of the
Filipino secretary of the interior and the American governor-
general.[37] In addition to the reappointment of Fugate, this policy
envisioned that the Moros would eventually become patriotic
members of the Philippine nation, and definitely not part of the
United States and independent from the Philippines. Central to the
new policy was the maintenance of law and order and the un-
questioned recognition of the insular government by the Moros.
To achieve this end, the constabulary was to be strengthened.[38]

The new policy anticipated attraction would supplement firmness. This could be done only by respecting the culture and reli-

gion of the Moros and by promoting their social, political, and economic progress.[39] In the past funds had not been provided for public services in Sulu province because of its lack of political importance. To correct this the governor-general promised more funds for schools, roads, and other services.[40]

In March 1934 Murphy visited the Sulu archipelago and inaugurated the New Deal for the Moros. Fugate was installed as governor, and various other Filipino officials were replaced.[41] Whenever possible Moros were used as officials in their own communities. But over them was the strong hand of Governor Fugate. Previously, provincial heads of insular services had been responsible to their respective bureaus in the central government at Manila—making for inefficient and weak government.[42]

Six months after Fugate was appointed, a noticeable improvement was achieved. Conflicts between the constabulary and the Moro bands ceased; cattle stealing practically stopped. It was an uncertain calm, at best, but it was still an accomplishment.[43]

All of Murphy's actions were directed toward establishing a stable, democratic, and independent Philippines. But eventually he was obliged to deal directly with the problem of how independence was to be established. The Hare-Hawes-Cutting act, due for consideration by the Filipinos in the summer of 1933, provided for a ten-year transition period during which the Philippines would adjust as a commonwealth to the responsibilities of full nationhood. Murphy's task was to make the commonwealth stage meaningful without alienating sensitive Filipinos or abdicating American trusteeship responsibilities.

In facing this task he formed and carried out a colonial policy which met both requirements. Such a policy had always been a part of the so-called American experiment in the Philippines. But it is one thing to believe in the principle of trusteeship, and it is something else again to expound and act on it wisely in preparation for the precise moment of independence.

The first principle of Murphy's colonial policy was an unquestioning belief in the rightness of Philippine independence. Part of Murphy's talent lay in his ability to communicate his convictions, and in this instance the Filipinos were persuaded of his sincerity. A Filipino reporter wrote that Murphy's greatest accomplishment was his relentless but silent war against American imperialism. The governor-general put the cause of Philippine independence in the realm of highest idealism. He told Filipinos, as reported in the *Manila Tribune* (May 13, 1936): "There is something new, something different being attempted in the Philippines. . . . You see, we have attempted something here that will benefit not only the Philippines, not only America, but all mankind."

The second principle of Murphy's colonial policy was the conviction that America must maintain its influence during the commonwealth transition period. He believed it morally wrong for the United States to abdicate responsibility at this point, as this might allow the Filipinos to flounder. Moreover, to fail in the Philippines would damage United States world power and influence. As he said: "In this unprecedented venture in democratic rule, the prestige of American statesmanship is involved."[44] He envisioned the American government should continue to advise quietly, encourage, and, if necessary, reprimand:

> It should be our policy to avoid annoying and harassing intermeddling. As a matter of justice and good faith, we should give full recognition to the rights of the Philippine people and the dignity of their official representatives. By sturdy friendship and by tactful, wise and sympathetic administration, free from bias or intolerance, we should endeavor to make effective and successful the intention of

Congress to give to the Philippine people, in the way of preparation for complete independence, as large a measure of autonomy as circumstances justify and permit. It should be done, however, with an intelligent conception of *American interests and in a manner that will adequately safeguard them.*[45] [Emphasis added.]

The Hare-Hawes-Cutting act specified the Philippines must accept certain conditions before achieving independence. Since the terms were far from ideal to the Filipinos, the bill created a Philippine political controversy. Murphy carefully avoided choosing sides, only urging the Filipinos to decide quickly on acceptance or rejection.

The Filipinos objected in particular to the onerous economic provisions of the Hare act that provided for a rapid extension of tariffs to exclude the Philippines from the American market. However, Sergio Osmeña, who had lobbied for independence in Washington, defended the bill as the best one possible. His rival, Manuel Quezon, opposed the act. Quezon's followers supported him, and in the summer of 1933 the Philippine legislature rejected the independence act.

Quezon thereupon went to Washington and returned with a new bill, the Tydings-McDuffie act. This bill was exactly like the Hart act except for minor concessions on military bases and an accompanying promise from President Roosevelt to reconsider the economic provisions at a later date. It had been impressed on Quezon in Washington that the economic provisions of the Hare act were the best possible under the circumstances.[46] Murphy tried to assuage Philippine concern over the economic clauses in the independence bills. He described to the legislators the severity of the American depression and reminded them that if economic factors had entered and "played a part in the framing and adoption of the final act of liberation, this and the preparatory work that precedes it have been fundamentally conditioned and . . . inspired by the political idealism and altruism of the American people."[47]

Quezon's support guaranteed Philippine approval, and on May 1, 1934 the Philippine legislature accepted the Tydings act. Murphy continued his neutrality by refusing an invitation to preside at the constitutional convention. While some Filipinos took this as an affront, more thoughtful citizens appreciated his wisdom. The *Manila Daily Bulletin* commented that Murphy's conduct indicated Washington wanted the constitution to be a truly great Filipino achievement and wished to avoid bringing pressure at any point.[48]

Although he did not attend the constitutional convention, Murphy's influence was evident in the constitution. Basically, the constitution followed the United States model, but with Murphy's endorsement, the Filipinos experimented with a unicameral legislature. The governor-general assured the Philippine leaders that the President would not disapprove of their document because of this feature. Furthermore, he indicated that if the unicameral feature were to effect a genuine economy in government, it would be a contribution to good government. However, a few years later the Filipinos amended their constitution and reverted to the traditional two-house system.

The Philippine constitution also differed from that of the United States in specifically including economic security as part of its general welfare clause. Using Murphy's favorite phrase, "social justice," Article II, section 5 of the Philippine constitution states: "The promotion of social justice to insure the well being and economic security of all the people should be the concern of the State." Undoubtedly the development of the welfare state in the contemporary world scene had a great deal to do with this provision, but Murphy's personal concern for social justice, combined with the success of his welfare program, was the major influence on the Filipinos.[49]

Governor-General Murphy also persuaded the Filipinos to provide for women's suffrage in their constitution. He had created a stir by advocating women's suffrage in his first message to the legislature in 1933. To please the new governor-general legislators grudgingly passed a bill that session giving women the vote. However, women's suffrage violated Philippine tradition and was not popular with any group in the islands except the women. Reflecting this tradition, the delegates to the constitutional convention raised a hurdle to permanent women's suffrage by requiring 300,000 women's affirmative votes for it in a plebiscite. Apathy, coupled with pressure from political circles and from the Catholic Church, almost fulfilled the delegates' hopes. But Quezon, reversing his earlier stand, decided his friend Frank Murphy was right and urged the women to vote "yes" in the plebiscite. They did so and became the first women in the Orient to win equal suffrage.[50]

With the constitution written and 1946 set as the date for independence, rivalry among Philippine leaders ceased. The two most important opponents, Quezon and Osmeña, decided the difficulties of establishing a secure commonwealth necessitated a coalition government; they formed one party with Quezon as the presidential candidate and Osmeña as the vice-presidential candidate for the new commonwealth. Murphy viewed their agreement as the expression of national sentiment. Therefore, he broke with his tradition of neutrality in domestic politics and publicly endorsed the united front, despite his misgivings about one-party government.[51]

The difficulties facing the future commonwealth were dramatized shortly before the May 1935 plebiscite for the commonwealth constitution. On the nights of May 2 and 3 a dissident political group, *Sakdalistas,* staged an uprising. Leading armed mobs, they attempted to capture the municipal buildings of four-teen towns that lay in an arc around Manila. The constabulary headquarters was surprised by the suddenness and extent of the uprising. Murphy was in the United States on a mission, and acting Governor-General Hayden, the secretary of the interior, and other cabinet members were away on inspection trips. Even the chief of the constabulary had departed that very evening on an inter-island steamer which could not be reached by wireless. Further, communication between Manila and most of the territory in revolt was broken when telegraph and telephone wires were cut.[52]

In only three of the fourteen towns did the *Sakdalistas* succeed in seizing the government buildings. And, in these instances, the constabulary forces retook the buildings within a few hours. Fifty-nine *Sakdalistas* were killed and thirty-six were wounded in the encounters, with constabulary casualties numbering four killed and eleven wounded. But the end of fighting still left unanswered the question of why this political group had felt it necessary to attempt such a futile and desperate measure.

The coalition between Quezon and Osmeña on the eve of the commonwealth had removed almost all organized political opposi-tion. As a result, Filipino politicians did not have to compete for votes, and they forgot the needs of the inarticulate minority that suffered from various forms of oppression. Usually the individual in this minority was a *tao* who had never been able to escape the power of the *cacique.* Therefore the *tao* came to regard immediate independence from the United States as the way to free himself from oppression. To him, Quezon, Osmeña, and other Filipino leaders were puppets of the United States who wished to perpetuate American and *cacique* control in the guise of a commonwealth in order to enrich themselves at the hands of the poor. The specific purpose of the revolt—in which it failed—was to prevent the May 14 plebiscite on the constitution.

Besides holding a careful investigation to verify his suspicions, there was not much the governor-general could do, which he had not already done, to alleviate the underlying conditions that had created the *Sakdal* revolt. His human rights program had been directed toward helping the *tao* become a full-fledged citizen. As a sympathetic gesture he did pardon seventy-four of the eighty-seven *Sakdal* revolters convicted by the courts; Murphy declared they had been misled by agitators.

The *Sakdal* uprising inevitably raised doubts in the minds of many Americans as to the success of the Philippine independence experiment. But there was now no turning back. As Hayden had observed earlier: "It may as well be recognized and accepted that in establishing the Commonwealth, America had decided that the Filipino and not American ideas and ideals shall rule in this country without let or hindrance from us."[53] Under the circumstances all the United States representatives could do was to finish the job in the Philippines with the same vigor and imagination that had been used when the task began in 1900. This Murphy proceeded to do.

After the *Sakdal* uprising, Philippine discontent focused around two old revolutionary heroes of the struggles against Spain and the United States—General Emilio Aguinaldo, President of the first Philippine Republic, and Bishop Gregorio Aglipay, head of the Independent Church of the Philippines and former chaplain general of the insurrection army. General Aguinaldo, the more important of the two, probably had never ceased to regard himself as the natural choice of the people for the first position in the future republic. In establishing the date of independence as 1946, the Tydings act placed the presidency of the second republic beyond the probable life of the general who was sixty-six in 1935.[54]

Quezon and Osmeña had already announced their *Nacionalista* coalition ticket with themselves as candidates for President and Vice-President of the new commonwealth. Following the *Sakdal* uprising Aguinaldo and Aglipay entered the campaign, both as presidential candidates. The electorate for this first national election under the commonwealth constitution was so divided that Aquinaldo and Aglipay could not compete against each other. In reality, therefore, they presented a united front against the *Nacionalista* party. The platform of the revolutionary heroes was similar to that of the *Sakdal* movement. They accused Quezon and Osmeña of betraying the cause of independence and demanded a shortening of the transitional commonwealth period by three to five years. They also charged that the two *Nacionalista* leaders had exploited the common people for personal gain.

The veterans had no political experience, and no impartial observer expected them to win. Their effort was an expression of national discontent: it was an attempt to offer an alternative government to the Quezon-Osmeña coalition. To the political scientist their effort pointed up the special difficulty which faced the Philippines as a colonial nation. Since the Filipinos over the years had concentrated on the independence issue, there were no other real issues to divide men and around which parties could form. The climax to this development came with the Quezon-Osmeña coalition. While it would seem that the settling of the independence issue would encourage normal party formation, in reality the Philippines could not quickly rid itself of political habits learned during its dependent status.

At the polls in September 1935 the Filipinos elected Quezon and Osmeña, as had been expected. Surprisingly, however, one of every three voters cast his ballot for Aguinaldo or Aglipay. Thus one-third of the electorate felt itself not properly represented by the *Nacionalista* party and chose to protest by voting for a sure loser.

The election did not ease the tension that had been building up since the *Sakdal* uprising. During the campaign *Aguinaldistas* had predicted blood would flow if the general were defeated by fraud or intimidation. No sooner were the results announced than Aguinaldo publicly declared these means had been used to defeat him. At his residence crowds gathered to listen to seditious addresses by *Aguinaldista* leaders. Aguinaldo's aides pressed for an investigation of the alleged election fraud; they even indicated Murphy had permitted irregularities to take place.

Despite distrust of Murphy, Aguinaldo appealed to him for an investigation of the election. Murphy's course was determined by law and precedent; he turned over the request to the Philippine legislature and explained to Aguinaldo he could take independent action only if the regular authorities failed to perform their duties properly. The duly constituted Philippine authorities promptly referred the complaint to the committees on elections in the two houses of the legislature. But the general refused to deal with the committees and demanded his case be submitted to President Roosevelt.

The inauguration of the commonwealth was planned for November 15, 1935. It was feared that before then an attempt would be made on President-elect Quezon's life. Precautions to protect him became elaborate; a constabulary detachment was stationed on the grounds of his home, and his automobile was well guarded.

In a final effort Aguinaldo called for a demonstration on inauguration day, hoping for a crowd of fifty thousand to sixty thousand followers. At best a demonstration would have been embarrassing for both Filipinos and Americans, and at worst it could have led to bloodshed, if it had to be controlled by troups.

Murphy acted to prevent it. He invited Auginaldo to his office and, with diplomatic skill, presented arguments for calling off the planned action. He appealed to Aguinaldo's patriotism, asking him to reconsider his decision for the benefit of the Filipinos he had led in the past. Murphy then asked him to think about the embarrassment he would cause the United States, knowing Aguinaldo had been on friendly terms with Americans since the insurrection; to interfere with the inauguration would create a difficult situation for the American delegation of the Vice-President, secretary of war, and speaker of the House of Representatives. Murphy balanced his appeal to Aguinaldo with the promise that sufficient force would be used to prevent the demonstration. After the interview Aguinaldo called off the demonstration. In the opinion of his aides, Murphy had made a brilliant performance at a most crucial time. The end of the Aguinaldo affair came in December, when President Roosevelt tactfully denied the general's request for an investigation of the election.

Meanwhile, the inauguration of the commonwealth had taken place. It was a gala occasion, with balls given by all the dignitaries. As his last official duty as governor-general, Murphy freed sixty political prisoners. He discreetly declined a gratuity offered by the commonwealth government to all displaced insular officials, observing that his salary as governor-general had been quite adequate. Moreover, he was not out of a job, since F.D.R. had appointed him high commissioner of the Philippine Commonwealth. The new commonwealth was now self-governing with the exception of United States control over currency, foreign fiscal obligations, international affairs, tariff, and defense.

During Murphy's years in the Philippines, equally as important as his association with the Filipinos was his relationship with Washington officials. He considered himself above all else the representative of the President of the United States and of the Congress. His job was twofold in that he carried out present American policies and also advised the United States government as to future policies and actions.

President Roosevelt gave remarkable freedom to his plenipotentiary in the Far East. When asked on his arrival in Manila what the President's instructions were, Murphy replied the President let him shape his own policy. F.D.R. thereby not only expressed his faith in Murphy's abilities but, equally important, disclosed his own desire not to be concerned with Philippine affairs. The President was in the midst of reconstructing the national economy, and the demands on his energies were overwhelming. In August he confided to Murphy that the summer of 1933 was a "close parallel to the summers of '17 and '18" when the United States was in the throes of World War I. Murphy assured F.D.R., through Louis Howe, he was "putting every effort into the job here to the end that . . . the President, with all his colossal problems, will not have the added burden of worrying about the Philippines."[55]

When the Tydings independence act was accepted by the Filipinos, Murphy asked for permission to come to Washington in early 1935 for discussions on the future commonwealth. He wrote the President that, in particular, he had recommendations to make concerning Philippine-United States trade relations and the powers of the newly created office of high commissioner. F.D.R. readily agreed and passed word to Secretary of War George Dern to issue a formal invitation to Murphy for the visit.[56]

In March 1935 Murphy arrived in Washington. The President gave a luncheon in his honor and praised him at his news conference, telling the reporters Murphy had run the administration of the Philippines so well that "I haven't had to give a single worry or single care to [it]."[57] The governor-general immediately began a round of conferences within the administration to press his idea that a complete review of United States-Philippine relations should be made before the commonwealth was inaugurated in the fall. To this end he encouraged a coordination of Philippine and American policies through direct contact of members of both administrations. The 1935 visit was Murphy's single major effort at influencing policy coming from Washington. However, he constantly cabled the administration with pleas and advice throughout his term in the Philippines.

One of his concerns was the development of an independent economy for the Philippines. The United States had adopted a Philippine economic policy that conflicted with the stated promise of preparing the islands for independence. The tariff bills of 1909 and 1913 had established a free-trade relationship, making Philippine industries entirely dependent on the American market. Apparently United States officials gave no serious thought to the development of a truly independent Philippine economy. During the decade ending in 1937 the Philippines shipped between 75 and 80 percent of its annual exports to the United States and bought between 59 and 65 percent of its imports from the States. The major export item, sugar, accounted for 58 percent of all Philippine exports in 1936. Virtually none of this sugar could have been sold at a profit in the States except on a preferential basis, nor could any considerable portion of it be sold at a profit anywhere else. The other important island exports—coconut oil, cordage, cigars and cigarettes, embroideries, and pearl buttons—were likewise dependent on free entry to the States.

The Filipinos, under the provisions of the Tydings act, were now to reap the harvest of this ill-conceived policy. The bill provided for a ten-year transition period within which the Philippines was to adjust its economy. Specifically, the Philippines was obliged to assess a progressively increasing export tax on items shipped to the United States. These taxes, which were to go into the Philippine treasury, were to be increased until 1946 when they would amount to 25 percent of the then existing United States duties. This provision could only lead to economic disaster for the new nation. Not only was there no inducement for the Filipinos to develop new industries or new markets gradually, but the provision failed to increase the export tax until it equalled normal United States duties. The Tydings act, in effect, announced with the finality of a time bomb that in ten years the full United States tariff would be imposed on Philippine products.[58]

Congress created additional Filipino apprehension. In the spring of 1934 the Jones-Costigan bill was proposed. It would have imposed a retroactive quota for the importation of sugar into the United States. If it went into effect, the Filipinos would automatically have a surplus of 400,000 tons of unmarketable sugar. Even more serious was the 1934 proposal to levy a three-cents-per-pound excise tax on coconut oil imported from the Philippines. Murphy strongly opposed these measures and bombarded Washington with messages pointing out the dire consequences that would result; he warned adoption of these bills would threaten bankruptcy in some provinces, close schools, and cause tax delinquency.[59]

President Roosevelt agreed with Murphy's pleas and sent his objections to Capitol Hill. F.D.R. told the legislators the coconut oil bill was particularly serious, since the Tydings act specifically stated that there would be no restriction placed upon Philippine coconut oil coming into the States until after the inauguration of the commonwealth. By using the guise of an excise tax, said the President, Congress was violating the spirit of the independence bill.[60] But his and Murphy's efforts were unavailing, and both bills passed Congress.

Another economic matter was more successfully handled. When the President reduced the weight of the gold dollar, this increased the value of Philippine currency reserves deposited in United States banks. These reserves constituted about 77 percent of the total currency reserves of the Philippine government and had always been considered by the Filipinos as the equivalent of gold reserves. In 1934 the Roosevelt administation pushed through Congress a bill authorizing the Philippines $23,862,750.36 in compensation for the loss in value of its reserves.[61] But in 1936 a bill was introduced to repeal the 1934 act. Murphy radioed the President his objections. F.D.R. in turn asked his secretary to "slip the word to the speaker that it would do no harm if this Bill did not come out of Committee."[62] Accordingly the bill was killed.

In Manila, Murphy urged the Filipinos to seek congressional sympathy for modification of the Tydings economic provisions. The way to do this, he said, was to offset the large unfavorable trade balance with the United States by increasing American imports—thereby meeting a legitimate congressional complaint. Part of the governor-general's motive was also to counter Japanese economic penetration. The influx of Japanese textiles became of such concern by 1934 that Secretary of State Cordell Hull negotiated a gentleman's agreement with Japan to limit its shipment of textiles to the Philippines.[63]

The Philippine economy received its greatest assist from Murphy when he persuaded Washington to find alternatives to the Tydings trade provisions. Many others, including Senator Tydings, helped. But Murphy had the determination to see that something was actually done—using his easy access to the President to push for action. In anticipation of Murphy's 1935 visit an interdepartmental committee was formed within the administration, headed by Francis B. Sayre, to study Philippine-American trade relations.

After discussions with Murphy the committee proposed F.D.R. give the governor-general a letter expressing his intention to call a mutual-trade conference.[64]

A year later the United States and the Philippines arranged for a joint trade conference. Before the conference met, Murphy returned to the States to reenter Michigan politics; nonetheless his influence was felt. In a letter to Secretary Hull he outlined what he thought the scope of the conference should be and, in particular, the position the United States should take. He stated unswervingly his colonial policy that the United States must accept full responsibility for Philippine independence:

> Perhaps too much, in the past our economic attention has been centered on the problems of mainland competition and immediate trade, to the exclusion of the long-range view which seems peculiarly needed in reference to the Philippines.
>
> I have exerted myself to keep alive the Joint Conference idea, not to make haste, but to forestall local attitude to consider it a gesture. As I have stated above, American preparation must be thorough in respect to policy. Consideration should be comprehensive and include general Far Eastern Relations, the Japanese situation, relations with the British and Dutch outposts, Insular revenues and financial stability, the rapid increase of Philippine population, the future extent and character of trade and production in the Islands, their defense and protection and their sound internal political and social development. . . .
>
> Primarily, the responsibility for a successful Conference rests with the United States. The Philippine Commonwealth Government is limited in men capable and willing to take a long-range realistic view of economic matters. It is a natural result of insularity and a generation of political preoccupation. It also lacks men of sufficient training to design a technical plan of the breadth required by present circumstances.

They should be discouraged from entering the Conference only to ask the maximum of trade advantage in each bracket with the idea of bargaining for immediate position. An avoidance of fundamental decisions on their part may be anticipated. I write this not to detract or criticize in any way but only to set in bolder relief the need that the American delegation enter the Conference instructed as to basic considerations and prepared with a well-rounded adequate plan and, also, to anticipate the situation that the United States may be forced to make some decisions for the Philippines themselves.[65]

The conference, which became known as the Joint Preparatory Committee on Philippine Affairs, issued its report in 1938. The committee suggested a series of amendments to the Tydings act. They involved changing the date upon which the full United States tariff would be applied to Philippine products from 1946 to 1961 and, secondly, provided for a gradual reduction of duty-free trade between the two countries during that interval. In considering amendments to the act, Congress rejected the first proposal but accepted the second recommendation which instituted gradually declining duty-free quotas instead of gradually increasing export taxes on four major classes of goods.[66]

After World War II the United States renewed its trade relations with the Philippines on the full basis advocated by the joint preparatory committee. Thus Murphy's campaign to prevent a sudden erection of tariffs became accepted policy.[67]

In addition to the economic problem facing the Philippines, Murphy was concerned about the political future of the new nation. The existence of social unrest, armed uprisings, and obvious political immaturity did not promise an easy transition to full independence. The governor-general was therefore anxious to

115

maintain American influence in the islands during the common-wealth period.

As soon as the Filipinos had approved the Tydings act in May 1934, Murphy wrote the chief of the Bureau of Insular Affairs it was of "utmost importance that the position, status and authority of the High Commissioner be clearly defined, . . . and understood before surrendering control."[68] In particular, Murphy wanted the President to make a clear statement to the high commissioner that the latter could use as written authority.[69] Yet the War Department, which had jurisdiction over the Bureau of Insular Affairs and the Philippines, was not able to decide whether such a statement should be made.

On his 1935 visit to Washington Murphy took the opportunity to explain why explicit instructions should be given to the high commissioner.[70] He received sympathetic consideration, but still no action was taken. However, he was consoled with the knowledge the President was going to appoint him high commissioner of the new commonwealth.[71] At least Murphy knew he would be in a position to continue pressing for the clear outline of authority he felt was necessary.

In August 1935 instructions were finally sent to Murphy. The governor-general found them adequate for administrative routine, but in all other respects most inadequate.[72] Exasperated, he cabled President Roosevelt at Hyde Park and asked for a personal review of the situation.[73] Unfortunately, his action caused displeasure in certain quarters of the War Department. What had once been merely a policy struggle now became a personality conflict as well. Murphy found himself pitted against former Chief of Staff Douglas MacArthur.

MacArthur had become acting secretary of war in September 1935 during a temporary absence of Secretary Dern. The general had a deep interest in the Philippines because of earlier years of military service in the islands. Now that interest was revived with his recent appointment as military adviser to the Philippine Commonwealth on the request of President-elect Quezon. Moreover, President Roosevelt had flattered MacArthur by asking him to become high commissioner succeeding Murphy, when and if the latter resigned.[74] As acting secretary of war, MacArthur countered Murphy's direct plea to the President with a message of his own to the chief executive. In blunt language he challenged the governor-general's thesis that the high commissioner needed to be bolstered by an explicit declaration of authority. Further, MacArthur accused Murphy of wanting to usurp power from both the Philippine Commonwealth and the United States:

> A review of the Governor-General's suggestions . . . indicates that he seeks for the High Commissioner even greater authority with regard to government in the Philippine Islands than he now exercises as Governor-General. . . .
>
> . . . The Governor-General's recommendations if carried out would, in effect, make him a super-President of the Commonwealth, and in addition to increasing his authority over the Philippine nation would place in his hands many of the powers heretofore exercised only by the President of the United States himself. Such a delegation of power not only would be indefensible administratively but no suggestion that such delegation should take place can be found in the Tydings-McDuffie Act. The War Department knows of no appointive official in any government having powers as great as those desired by Governor-General Murphy. In effect, his recommendations would make the High Commissioner locally independent of any agency of government, either the Commonwealth or the United States Government. . . .[75]

No wonder a War Department aide exclaimed, "Hell's apopping!"[76]

The President avoided making a decision which would offend either one of the two proud men. Instead he asked Murphy to wait and talk over the situation with Secretary Dern when the latter came to the Philippines for the inaugural ceremonies. Meanwhile, MacArthur set sail for the islands to assume duties as military adviser to the commonwealth. He found a willing ally in President-elect Quezon who submitted a detailed memorandum to Murphy supporting the omission of detailed instructions for the high commissioner.[77]

But, as Murphy had predicted, friction developed because the United States failed to make clear its authority in the commonwealth. The issue came to a head over the inaugural ceremonies. President-elect Quezon announced that as head of state he should receive the twenty-one gun salute which the United States customarily accorded heads of nations. Murphy felt this symbol of sovereignty should not be accorded a Philippine leader while the islands were still under United States jurisdiction. Such action, he argued, would subordinate the status of the high commissioner, who was the representative of the United States government in the Philippines, and thereby make an effective exercise of American sovereignty impractical. He recommended the twenty-one gun salute be reserved exclusively for the President of the United States and that both the high commissioner and the president of the commonwealth should receive a nineteen gun salute.

General MacArthur sided with Quezon, but he was the only American to do so. The vice-governor, all the members of the governor-general's staff, and the chief military and naval officers, with the exception of MacArthur, agreed with Murphy. Secretary Dern did not choose to make the decision on the gun salute and cabled President Roosevelt. F.D.R. finally was forced to make a firm decision on the issue of American authority. He decided the

United States must not give up its symbol of sovereignty, and Quezon accordingly had to accept the nineteen gun salute.[78]

A few days after the inauguration a French war vessel made an official international call, and respects were paid to the high commissioner and not President Quezon. This incident raised the sovereignty issue again. But Murphy felt President Roosevelt was behind him now and publicly stated that although he was disinterested in honors for their own sake, he believed the position of the United States should be made unequivocal to enable it to serve the Philippines during this critical period.[79]

On December 10, almost a month after the inaugural ceremonies, Murphy decided to write his own instructions since the War Department had not yet sent him what he wanted.[80] His draft of the instructions gave the high commissioner the right to keep himself and the President of the United States fully informed on all activities of the commonwealth government. Furthermore, in case of emergency, the high commissioner was permitted to take any action—consistent with the Tydings act and his position as representative of the sovereign United States—which might be required to protect the legitimate interests of the United States. Murphy sent a copy of his draft to the War Department with the comment that unless he was advised or instructed to the contrary, it was his intention to act as if the instructions were approved. Dern replied no formal action would be taken and until further notice Murphy could adhere to them.[81] Murphy finally won his case, even if by default.

As high commissioner, Murphy was careful not to overplay his hand in the Philippines. He had insisted on United States authority not because he wanted to bludgeon Filipino leaders into total acceptance of American policy, but because he wanted to temper Filipino actions if they went too far astray. He tactfully emphasized this by calling on President Quezon at 8:00 A.M. the day following the commonwealth inauguration. The high commissioner went alone and did not publicize his visit, which was incorrect by protocol. Although some Americans considered his action a betrayal of United States sovereignty, Murphy obviously felt it was necessary if he were to establish amicable relations between the Philippine president and the high commissioner's office. He thereby assuaged, as far as he was concerned, any bad feeling that may have carried over from the gun-salute controversy. However, his successors as high commissioner discovered the sovereignty question was far from settled.[82]

Murphy soon was able to write F.D.R. that "already President Quezon and members of the Cabinet are soliciting the friendly advice and judgment of this office on important matters of governmental policy and legislation, in a manner and to a degree beyond that proposed in the draft of formal instructions that I submitted."[83] Thus Murphy retained what Vice-Governor Hayden termed the "intellectual and moral ascendancy" over the Filipino leaders that he had earned as governor-general. Hayden further observed it probably was easier for the Filipinos to come to Murphy now as high commissioner than when, in a sense, they had had to consult him as governor-general.[84]

Murphy's understanding of the weaknesses of the colonial-trained Philippine government had compelled him to insist on American authority during the commonwealth period. In the face of opposition and delay from Washington he had carried through his idea with determination. On other issues, especially those pertaining to the Philippine economy, he had persuaded administration officials of the rightness of his cause.[85] On the whole, Murphy was successful in obtaining what he wanted from Washington.

Murphy did not have the opportunity to create dramatically new policies in the Philippines as had Governors-General William Howard Taft and Francis B. Harrison. But Murphy did help make possible the realization of the goal of all past policies—a stable and independent Philippine nation. Because of this he found thorough satisfaction in his work and stay in the islands.[86] The Filipinos appreciated Murphy's work and bestowed affection upon him. This contrasted sharply with his experience in Detroit where he often had faced bitter criticism. When it was rumored Murphy was about to leave the islands to reenter Michigan politics, the Philippine newspapers reported the news with apprehension, revealing the affection of the Philippine people for him.[87] Even the Republican national committeeman from the Philippines asked President Roosevelt to keep Murphy in the islands.

The only unhappy aspect of Murphy's stay there was the relatively poor health he endured. Although he was never seriously incapacitated, the tropical climate did cause him sinus trouble and influenza. On his trip to the States in 1935 he was admitted to the Detroit Harper Hospital for treatment and a tonsillectomy. The operation helped, but other ailments continued to bother him. Undoubtedly Murphy's imagination magnified the seriousness of his illnesses. His aide, Edward Kemp, always depreciated any news about Murphy's illnesses. He observed: "The Murphys are never sick, they are always VERY SICK!" And J. Weldon Jones remembered Murphy as a vigorous and robust man.[88]

Socially Manila was a gay city, and Murphy participated freely in its activities. His sister accompanied him as official hostess and both brothers made extended visits as did other relatives and friends. Their upkeep was paid for entirely from public funds, which created problems for the insular auditor. While Murphy had discretionary funds at his disposal, there were limits even to these. Jones finally decided to stop worrying about it, rationalizing

121

that if Murphy's "discretion turned out to be indiscretion, that was for him and his conscience to answer." In the hot season Murphy retired to the summer residence of the chief executive in Baguio, a mountain health resort spread over a large, rolling, pine-covered plateau over a mile above the sea. Murphy's recreation was horseback riding, and he had the U.S. Army build and maintain for his benefit a cross-country course with twenty or thirty jumps.[89]

Thus there were various reasons to cause Murphy regret when the time came for him to leave the islands in the spring of 1936. Roosevelt had asked him to enter the governor's race in Michigan, and the high commissioner felt obliged to acquiesce. In anticipation of leaving, Murphy described his feelings to Hayden in near-sentimental terms: "When my ship sails out of Manila Bay, my heart will be anything but light. These people are so kind and tender and spiritual that you know they want to be led upward in life. My three years here have been as happy as any of my adult years."[90]

Murphy's interest in the Philippines remained lifelong. He reviewed portions of his former vice-governor's manuscript about the islands which was published a number of years later.[91] He continued his friendship with Manuel Quezon; when the Philippine President visited the United States in 1937, he attended the christening of Murphy's niece, and Mrs. Quezon was asked to be the child's godmother. The former high commissioner continued to advise F.D.R. and the administration on Philippine matters.[92] It was even proposed Murphy pay an official visit to the islands on behalf of the President, but this did not materialize.[93] Finally, after World War II, Murphy did return to the Philippines, although on a melancholy mission; at the request of President Harry Truman he accompanied the return of Manuel Quezon's body to the Philippines.

Chapter IV

Michigan Politics:
Victory and Defeat

Frank Murphy returned from the Philippines in 1936 on a poorly concealed political mission. Ostensibly he had returned to confer with administration leaders about Philippine policy. While he did hold lengthy discussions in Washington on Philippine affairs, the real reason for his homecoming was for him to become the reluctant gubernatorial candidate of the Michigan Democratic party. The high commissioner would have been willing to announce the true purpose of his journey before he boarded the ship in Manila if the matter had been settled. But he had not yet committed himself, and, until he had personally investigated the political scene in Michigan and Washington, he remained undecided.

The background to Murphy's final agreement to run in 1936 and to that campaign itself, is a history in miniature of rudimentary and successful New Deal politics. No one foresaw how easily F.D.R. would win the 1936 election. The seemingly difficult political problem facing the New Deal that year was how to repeat the victory of 1932 in a nation that had been, until 1932, predominantly Republican. Obviously the solution was to ensure that the political conversion of 1932 would stick; this in turn necessitated that New Deal preaching permeate state politics and inspire local Democratic victories.

Michigan exemplified the difficult situation facing F.D.R. and his political strategist, James Farley. The year 1932 was the first since 1856 that Michigan had given its electoral vote to a Democratic presidential candidate; it was only the third time since 1854 that the state had elected a Democratic governor. Not unexpectedly, the victory of 1932 was followed by defeat on the state level in 1934. After the Roosevelt landslide the state Democratic party broke discipline—not being accustomed to political power—and split into factions competing for the rewards of victory. In the process Democrats repudiated the incumbent governor, William Comstock, and ran Arthur J. Lacy as the gubernatorial candidate in 1934. Lacy was unable to unite the party before the election, and the Democrats were defeated.

In the midst of this fiasco President Roosevelt wrote impassionedly to the governor-general in the Philippines: "You are much missed in the Michigan campaign!"[1] It was logical for the President to turn to Murphy, for he was one Democratic leader from Michigan who was not allied with any faction. At the same time he was an ardent New Dealer with proven ability as a vote-getter. By bringing Murphy back to head the Michigan party, F.D.R. hoped to achieve party unity and to assure New Deal control of state Democratic politics.

With this in mind the President had asked the governor-general to visit Michigan on his previous return trip from the islands in 1935. He also assigned Murphy another political mission in Michigan at that time.

In 1935 political extremists, among them Father Charles Coughlin of Royal Oak, Michigan, began challenging the New Deal. Coughlin attacked the administration for not enacting inflationary cure-all legislation which he, Coughlin, believed would end the depression. When not castigating the administration, Coughlin turned his wrath on the Godless communists and Jewish businessmen whom he termed usurious money-lenders.[2] At first the priest limited his activities to forming pressure groups, but by 1935 there were indications he might directly enter politics in competition with the Democratic party.

Shortly before Murphy's 1935 visit to the States Coughlin had demonstrated his strength by helping to defeat United States membership in the World Court. In response to his anti-World Court appeal, forty thousand telegrams were sent to the Senate. Yet Coughlin's greatest threat lay in the possibility of his mobilizing hundreds of thousands of dissatisfied citizens through his National Union for Social Justice; soon after the union's creation in 1934, the priest had claimed its membership had reached 5,000,000.[3]

The Roosevelt administration began to watch Coughlin carefully after the national union was formed. The administration made an elaborate study of the broadcasting network through which the priest inflicted his attacks on the New Deal; Postmaster General Farley checked receipts at the Royal Oak post office to measure the response to one of the priest's appeals for funds; and Louis Howe received regular reports on Coughlin from G. Hall Roosevelt in Detroit.[4]

Murphy had been a close friend of Coughlin's although their relationship subsequently cooled following the priest's open attacks on F.D.R. Murphy thus was the ideal emissary for the President to send to Coughlin, and when he came back in the spring of 1935, F.D.R. asked him to dissuade the priest from entering the 1936 campaign. Carrying out the wishes of his chief, the governor-general held several lengthy conversations with Coughlin. As a consequence of these talks Murphy reported to F.D.R. that Coughlin would not align himself with disaffected elements in 1936; he predicted the priest might even support President Roosevelt—especially if the administration gave Coughlin "persistent attention."[5] Murphy's report later proved to have been a mistaken hope.

After his conversations with Coughlin, Murphy went on the air in Detroit to counter Coughlin's appeal in Michigan. He began his broadcast by praising the priest, referring to his "prophet-like zeal for Social Justice." Then the governor-general discreetly shifted his emphasis. He explained how the New Deal wished to effect great social and economic changes and urged patience, asking his listeners not to turn from the President and be dazzled by the panaceas offered by "extremists." Although he did not identify Coughlin as one of the extremists, the occasion of his broadcast made it obvious he had Coughlin in mind.[6]

While quietly trying to restrain Coughlin, Murphy also was attending to the breaches in the state Democratic party. His immediate task was to solve the patronage squabble which had been intensifying factionalism ever since the 1932 victory.[7] The federal administration had refused to give out any Michigan jobs until the state party agreed on its own patronage policy. Murphy brought Democratic leaders together and persuaded them to forget personal differences in the interest of the party. After two months of negotiation the party leaders accepted Murphy's suggestion that the elected party officials dispense patronage; in short order approximately six hundred federal vacancies were filled in Michigan. Former Governor Comstock, who had lost control of the party in the 1934 primary, remained the only major dissenter.[8]

Through his role as mediator Murphy made himself the unofficial head of the Michigan Democratic party. Around him grew the hope that the party would gain a new earnestness and that it would reject as inadequate the old practice of building up a machine for dispensing favors to the faithful. At its worst the old practice had led to the corruption of party leaders, as the indictment of a few of them for tampering with 1934 election returns revealed.

In a final effort to achieve party unity the Democratic National Committee called Michigan Democratic leaders to Washington in February 1936 to plan strategy for the coming national election.[9] President Roosevelt and Farley recognized the Michigan peace was built on a superficial harmony. They felt a unified party could not win in Michigan on that basis alone; this traditionally Republican state would need a Democratic candidate who could attract Republican votes as well.

A preferential poll conducted by Murphy's friends indicated Murphy was this candidate; of four possible Democratic gubernatorial candidates, only Murphy encouraged switches among Republican voters. The poll revealed, in fact, that 25 percent of the Republicans sampled who had voted for Republican Governor Fitzgerald in 1934 would now vote for Murphy. Furthermore, Murphy had great appeal among younger members of the Democratic party.[10]

The other critical aspect of the Michigan political situation was Coughlin's role. Since Murphy's 1935 visit the national administration had witnessed a graphic portrayal of the strength of the extremists who opposed the New Deal. One of Coughlin's ideological allies, Governor Huey Long of Louisiana, was matched in a secret presidential poll against Roosevelt and an imaginary Republican candidate. In the mock ballot the tallies were: Roosevelt, 18,203,359; the Republican, 15,940,874; and Long, 2,750,-164. Clearly, Long had sufficient strength to throw Michigan's electoral vote to a Republican candidate should Long run in 1936; in Michigan, Long was strong enough to reduce F.D.R.'s 1932 plurality of 131,936 votes to 11,245 at the time of the poll in 1936.[11] Before 1935 ended, Long was assassinated, leaving

Coughlin as the strongest rabble-rouser in opposition to the New Deal.

The factors of Democratic minority and Coughlinism necessitated Murphy's 1936 gubernatorial candidacy from President Roosevelt's point of view. The question in the President's mind throughout 1935 was not should Murphy return, but when would he be willing to return. F.D.R. indicated his early decision to call Murphy back in March 1935 when he limited Murphy's appointment as high commissioner to a nominal three months—just long enough to set up a standard of administration.[12]

But Murphy was reluctant to leave the Philippines and become the Democratic gubernatorial candidate. He had been willing to negotiate a peace among the party factions and to calm his ebullient former friend, Coughlin, but it was something else again to leave his comfortable position in the Philippines for the turbulence and uncertainty of state politics. Murphy recognized Michigan party leaders did not consider him a regular Democrat, for his entry into politics as judge and mayor in Detroit had been on a nonpartisan basis. Further, the national administration's efforts to have him run would probably be viewed by old-time state Democrats as a violation of state sovereignty. Particularly bitter was Comstock who had been left out of the patronage settlement that Murphy had arranged in 1935.[13]

Winning the party nomination in itself would be a struggle requiring nasty infighting. Even then, the effort probably would not lead to Murphy's victory in the fall, for he was not expected to win the state election. President Roosevelt spoke frankly of Murphy's making a "sacrifice."[14] Machiavellian reasoning lay behind the New Deal strategy. A close race between Roosevelt and Landon in Michigan was anticipated—with Landon winning; although Murphy would probably lose, the national administration hoped he would bring enough votes into the Democratic column to assure F.D.R.'s victory in the state.

Under these circumstances, understandably the high commissioner was most unenthusiastic. As Joseph Hayden observed in a letter to J. Weldon Jones: "No one likes to take a licking in a political fight, even though he may know that he is making a sacrifice hit for his Chief."[15] On the other hand, Murphy was devoted to the President and would do anything F.D.R. asked him to do. The high commissioner expressed these ambivalent thoughts when the President sounded him out in early 1936 about becoming the gubernatorial candidate. Murphy began his letter of response with an honest assertion: "I will become a candidate for Governor of Michigan or undertake any other mission that might be helpful to your success next fall." He then began to hedge; he reached for his best excuse, telling the President he should remain in the Philippines to preserve "the present satisfactory state of affairs." Eventually, Murphy came to his main point. He described the dismal prospect of becoming the state Democratic standard-bearer:

> Concerning the situation in Michigan, reports that reach me . . . suggest that party success in the State this fall, if not hopeless, is at least very doubtful. While my candidacy would perhaps be popular in Detroit and might aid materially in the re-election of Democratic Congressmen from that district, there appears to be a general belief outside of strict party circles that the State at large will go Republican.
>
> Notwithstanding the creditable achievements of the 1933-4 Democratic administration, the confidence of the public has been seriously, if not irretrievably, impaired by political in-aptitudes of party leaders, frequent disregard of popular sensibilities, open and bitter dissention within the ranks, and finally the pending indictment and trial of prominent party

leaders in Detroit on charges and strong evidence of fraud and manipulation in the recount of the ballots cast in the 1934 State election.[16]

Murphy could not make a firm decision even after his return to the States. As late as June 1936 he urged his supporters to align with other potential candidates if they so desired.[17] In early July he finally committed himself to run.

In retrospect the decision appears inevitable. Murphy was ambitious; his political future was irrevocably tied to F.D.R.'s wishes. If he denied the President this time, could he be sure of a second opportunity to show his loyalty? For, if he did say no, he might well "rot in tropical sun" forever, as one of his Michigan supporters put it.[18] But in agreeing to run, he made the President beholden to him—whether Murphy won or lost. He made the only decision a professional politician could.

Although Murphy didn't decide to become a candidate until July, he nonetheless had prepared the way for his possible candidacy by accepting his party's endorsement given at its state convention in May. (The convention had selected candidates among whom voters were to choose in the September primary.) The high commissioner worked zealously to obtain a "clean and invulnerable" slate of candidates for all state offices, for if he were to run in the fall, he wanted a strong ticket to accompany him.[19]

At Murphy's suggestion the convention took the unusual action of endorsing the Republican senator, James Couzens, who shared the ideology of the New Deal and who was up for reelection in the fall. Like Murphy, he faced a primary contest in September. Unfortunately, Murphy would need Republican votes to win the primary and thus would be competing with Couzens for the same liberal votes. Either Murphy or Couzens, as a result, would probably lose the primary to his more conservative opponent. To prevent this, Murphy had tried to persuade Couzens to switch parties; Couzens understood the logic of the proposal, but procrastinated. The convention endorsement was designed to encourage him to make the party shift.[20]

Murphy strove to achieve party accord at the convention. He would have succeeded in winning at least surface unity had it not been for Comstock, who, representing old-line Democrats, resented the Farley-Roosevelt intrusion and instigated a primary fight for Murphy. Comstock threw his strength behind George A. Welsh who had been elected lieutenant governor in 1925 as a Republican and who now made his bid for the governorship as a Democrat on the theory that he would appeal to Republicans.[21]

Murphy—in fact, if not knowingly—based his primary campaign on the strategy recommended to Farley by Michigan Democratic national committeeman Edmund C. Shields. Shields thoroughly investigated the primary situation in July 1936 and reported Murphy would surely win. He found Democrats did not trust Welsh because he had failed to announce himself a Democrat well in advance of his decision to be a gubernatorial candidate; furthermore, Shields reasoned, if Comstock, as an incumbent in 1934, could not win the primary, he hardly was in a position to have his candidate defeat Murphy in 1936. The wise policy, Shields suggested, was to let the two candidates have their contest—but without vituperation; then, when Murphy won, he would be able to appeal to Welsh's supporters in the final election.[22] Following this strategy, the high commissioner even refused to debate with Welsh. He told his audiences in justification that the Democrats would win only if they presented a united front and stopped the bickering that had cursed the Democratic party in Michigan.

In his speeches Welsh contemptibly accused Murphy of being a

Farley candidate. Murphy refused to be badgered into an angry retort on this issue; he contented himself with equivocal replies:

> It has been suggested that I have been ordered into this campaign and that I have been imposed upon. Nothing is further from the truth, on that you have my word of honor. I have never discussed the subject with James Farley, as has been suggested. Not that I would not have been glad to, for I admire Mr. Farley very much. And I am happy and proud to have the support of President Roosevelt.[23]

Frequently Murphy stated that he had entered the campaign to help the President. The high commissioner correctly assumed most people approved of the New Deal program. He emphasized, therefore, that Republicans and Democrats alike should rally together and vote Democratic to continue the New Deal. "The presidential battle," the *News* (September 9, 1936), quoted him as telling the voters, "is being fought out right here in Michigan. This is one of the six states that will determine the result."

Murphy viewed the primary campaign as dog work. He spent four days a week in Washington discussing Philippine affairs and then returned to Michigan to plead for votes on the remaining three days. He confessed to his confidant Joseph Hayden: "Many things have made me sad these past two or three months. Right now I am just droning away for the President and progressive government in Michigan."[24]

In late August a lift came from Senator Couzens. Although he could not bring himself to betray his independence and run for the Senate as a Democrat, Couzens did see his way to endorsing F.D.R. publicly. His decision doomed his chances for Republican nomination in the primary, although the chances were already slight because of his decision not to campaign against his old guard opponent, Wilber Brucker.[25]

132

As expected, Couzens lost the nomination to Brucker in the mid-September primary. But Murphy won a solid victory over Welsh. Within two years Welsh returned to the Republican party—such was Michigan politics.[26]

In spite of Murphy's comfortable victory two disquieting factors marred the primary results. As usual, the Republicans polled almost a two-to-one plurality over the Democrats. This did not augur well for Democratic victory in Nevember, although in 1932 a similarly heavy Republican primary vote had not brought Republican victory in the election. Equally serious, Coughlin made a strong showing. Murphy's 1935 prediction that the priest would not ally himself with dissident elements had proven incorrect. In June 1936 Coughlin had joined forces with the late Huey Long's followers and those of another extremist, Dr. Francis E. Townsend, to form the Union party—a loose coalition aimed at toppling the so-called communistic New Deal. The new political party hoped to elect Union party congressmen and to gain bargaining power in the electoral college between the two major presidential candidates. As its presidential standard-bearer the party chose an agrarian reformer from North Dakota, William Lemke.[27]

In September Louis B. Ward ran in the Michigan Democratic primary as Coughlin's candidate for Senate. Ward shocked Murphy Democrats by receiving 120,000 votes, leaving his opponent, Prentiss Brown, with a plurality of only 7,466.

There was additional evidence of Union party strength. A few days before the September 15 primary, Murphy sent to Washington the results of the most recent secret poll taken by the Democratic National Committee in Michigan. In a three-way election it showed Landon winning 47.3 percent of the vote, Roosevelt next with 43.9 percent, and Lemke with 8.6 percent. A breakdown of the Lemke vote revealed almost all of it had been won from Roosevelt supporters. If Lemke could be kept off the ballot or otherwise discredited, his votes would go to Roosevelt, giving the President 52 percent of the Michigan electorate.[28] Reports sent to Farley by Michigan politicians substantiated the results of the poll; almost unanimously they expressed concern about the Union party threat. A candidate for representative, who had just won a grueling primary fight with a Coughlinite, complained that Coughlin's "forces were organized [in] the nature of crusade" and, consequently, his victory was "dearly achieved."[29]

While it seemed imperative Union party candidates should be kept off the November ballot, Michigan Democrats were only partially successful in achieving this. The secretary of state ruled the name Union party could not appear on Michigan ballots, but he did permit Lemke to run under both Third party and Farmer-Labor labels. Likewise, ward and house of representatives candidates appeared on the ballot under the Third party heading.

The national administration also attempted to discredit the Union party. This was prompted by a national poll revealing that President Roosevelt had slipped in voting strength from 53.5 to 49.3 percent over the summer, while Lemke had increased from 1.8 to 5 percent in the same period. In a national address F.D.R. accepted Coughlin's challenge to repudiate the support of the Communist party.[30] On the suggestion of Wyoming Senator Joseph C. O'Mahoney, Reverend Maurice S. Sheehy of the Catholic University of America traveled through the West visiting bishops and priests. He assured the White House "some extraordinary things" were being attempted to offset Coughlin's influence. Meanwhile, Monsignor John Ryan gave a radio talk acquitting the President of alleged tendencies toward communism.[31]

During the state campaign, which began in earnest in October, Murphy ignored Coughlin as much as possible. Yet, when Coughlin endorsed the Republican candidate for governor, Frank D. Fitzgerald, Murphy felt obliged to speak out. He spoke gingerly—

first pointing out, as the *News* (October 20, 1936) reported, that in the past he had "had great admiration for Father Coughlin." Murphy then attacked Coughlin indirectly by accusing him of sponsoring the third party because he wanted to see the Republican candidate, Alfred M. Landon, elected President. As for Fitzgerald, Murphy spared no scorn: "There is nothing in this campaign more ridiculous than a man like Fitzgerald, with his smug, complacent, reactionary viewpoints, posing as a friend of social justice."

Murphy faced other obstacles as well. No major newspaper in the state supported him, and only the *News* tried to be neutral. The other newspapers strove to publicize the Republican image of the high commissioner as a demagog, a self-seeker who changed jobs when it was to his advantage, and a waster of public money.[32]

As in his mayoralty campaign Murphy's religion became an issue. His running mate for lieutenant governor was also a Catholic. Propaganda soon spread through the upper parts of the state that the Democratic ticket had theocratic aims. The knowledge that never before had a Catholic been elected governor increased Protestant fears.[33]

Republican employers tried to intimidate workers by placing in pay envelopes wage-reduction notices stating that all salaries would be cut beginning January 1 because of the New Deal. It was not explained that the scheduled reduction was due to social security payroll taxes. To counter this, Democrats distributed handbills explaining social security outside industrial plants and at bus and streetcar transfer points. Murphy also used radio time to denounce the employers and defend the social security bill.[34]

The Democrats remained officially united throughout the campaign. The powerful highway commissioner, Murray Van Wagoner, broadcast his endorsement of the whole state and national ticket, and Comstock chose not to sabotage the campaign even though his candidate, Welsh, had been defeated in the primary. Had Comstock and Welsh continued to oppose Murphy, Democratic strategists believed the two could have brought about Murphy's defeat; these were the indications of the secret September poll.[35]

Although the Democratic State Central Committee lacked enthusiasm and never effectively coordinated efforts, Murphy overcame the handicap of not having an effective political machine.[36] Machineless politics suited him well, for he enjoyed putting on a one-man show. His campaign speeches followed the same colorful and naively eloquent pattern he had perfected as mayor. He attacked Governor Fitzgerald for corrupt practices and for inviting racketeers into the state.[37] As for his own administration, he promised it would be guided by the motto a " 'public office must be a public trust.' "[38]

Whether or not the New Deal should continue in Washington became the main issue of the campaign. To assist the cause the national administration sent Cordell Hull into Michigan. But the all-important event was F.D.R.'s tour in mid-October. The President made brief stops in Grand Rapids, Lansing, Flint, and Pontiac, with a climactic appearance in Detroit where he toured the city and spoke to an outdoor rally in front of City Hall. Murphy accompanied the President and made a few remarks at each stop on the itinerary. Couzens, who was ill, left a hospital bed to lend his prestige to the Democratic President and the gubernatorial candidate. A week later Couzens died.[39]

Murphy put all his energy into the campaign and by the last week was too emotionally and physically exhausted to eat solid food. But his extreme efforts brought results, for to everyone's surprise he edged out his opponent to become the third Democratic governor in the history of the state.[40] For the first time in Michigan history every elective administrative post—except the one to be voted on in the spring—also went to the Democrats. The main reason for the state victory was F.D.R. himself who earned a 300,000 plurality in Michigan as compared to Murphy's 40,000. The Democratic senatorial candidate, Prentiss Brown, received a plurality of 150,000 in his three-way contest with Brucker and Ward. Coughlin, for his part, had little influence in the voting.

The election of 1936 was above all a Roosevelt victory. F.D.R.'s dynamic personality and program gave his party its majority. Without this leader Michigan, in particular, would have remained Republican. But only the most optimistic Democratic politician would have ignored the harsh statistical facts of Michigan Republican strength—which polls and past performances had indicated—and predicted victory solely on the basis of F.D.R.'s personality.

The Coughlin fizzle is explained primarily by his inability to translate discontent into votes. While many voters expressed a preference for Lemke in public opinion polls, they did not want to throw their ballot away on a sure loser come election day. Few Lemke supporters wished to have Landon in the White House rather than Roosevelt. In addition, traditional American distrust of third parties influenced voters to forego their flirtation with Coughlinism.[41]

The fact that the Union party label did not appear on the Michigan ballot inevitably hurt Coughlin's cause. In September Ward's showing was impressive, in part because he was a legitimate contender in the Democratic primary. But in November he and other Union party candidates were ignominiously relegated to the bottom position of twelve ballot columns and were amorphously classed as Third party candidates.[42]

Undoubtedly the September polls had overrated the drawing power of the Union party. F.D.R. had not yet begun his campaign, while, in contrast, Lemke forces had made their greatest impression on the public during the summer months at the time that the Union party had been formed. While the new party had appeared to be a threat, in comparison to the Roosevelt performance of the fall, the Union party's act was merely a curtain-raiser for the star performer.

Since he was now governor-elect of Michigan, Murphy tidied up his Philippine affairs and resigned as high commissioner, effective December 31, 1936. Even before he took office, events occurred that colored his whole administration. In December a few auto workers began a sit-down which soon spread to the key General Motors plants, forcing the corporation to stop production. The workers demanded union recognition—a principle which the manufacturer did not want to concede. Within a few months the sit-down strike became a fever, leaping from industry to industry throughout the nation. Meanwhile, the newly elected governor assumed the task of negotiating the strikes within Michigan and became the center of a raging controversy between traditional employers' property rights and workers' job rights. Because of the prominent role Murphy played in the sit-down, this subject is discussed in the next chapter. However, knowledge of Murphy's participation in the strike negotiations is basic to understanding other aspects of his gubernatorial administration.

As in the past, Murphy prepared himself for this new office by seeking expert advice. Joseph Hayden, who had returned to the University of Michigan in 1935 following the termination of his appointment as Philippine vice-governor, opened doors for Murphy to university and other professional personnel who might be willing to join his administration.[43] For specific guidance, in November 1936 the governor-elect asked experts to prepare a series of studies about such subjects as social security, welfare and relief, prison administration and parole policies, election laws, and workmen's compensation.

In his inaugural address to the legislature on January 7, 1937 Murphy boldly declared his goal of bringing the New Deal to Michigan:

> On the third of November last, by a substantial majority, the people of Michigan gave adherence to the philosophy of government represented by the New Deal of President Franklin Roosevelt and the Democratic Party. To the extent of our means and authority as their chosen representatives, Republicans and Democrats alike, it is our duty as conditions demand it, to translate into law and practice in this state this new social and political philosophy, this broader conception of the responsibility of government for the economic health of the state and the social welfare of all inhabitants.

To carry out his little New Deal—according to *News* articles during early 1937—the governor appointed men of ability and integrity who would be willing to "work in close co-operation with the national administration." These men came from both political parties and were chosen without consulting Democratic leaders. Bragging of his nonpartisan appointment policy, Murphy told reporters, as quoted by the *News* (April 15, 1937): "Until I tell you the name of the man I have selected, there isn't a person in Michigan, excepting me and the man himself, who knows who it will be." Typical of his appointees was Charles T. Fisher, Jr., a Republican chosen as banking commissioner, who, for nearly two years prior to this appointment, had been a member of the central board of the Reconstruction Finance Corporation in Washington. As director of the state welfare department, the governor selected James G. Bryant, who was formerly with the CWA and WPA and the social security board. And to the chairmanship of the Liquor Control Commission Murphy appointed an economics professor from Wayne University, Edward W. McFarland.

The governor's first task was to submit a program to the legislature which began its regular biennial session in January 1937. He submitted proposals in broad areas of both public welfare and governmental reform. When it became apparent that labor legislation also was needed, Murphy requested action in this area.

In the field of public welfare, Murphy asked for amendments to the state Unemployment Compensation Act, passed just a few days before he took office. (A special session of the legislature had been called at the end of December by Governor Fitzgerald in cooperation with the governor-elect to enable Michigan to meet the federal deadline for eligibility under the social security law.) As Murphy requested, the state act was amended to permit benefits to commence on July 1, 1938, six months earlier than originally set. But the legislature also included a provision that dismayed Murphy—in particular, the removal from the Unemployment Compensation Commission of his appointee, William Haber, a University of Michigan professor.

In addition, the governor obtained a liberalized old age assistance act that reduced the eligibility age to sixty-five and increased appropriations for the aged. The legislature also passed, in response to Murphy's request, an occupational disease law bringing thirty-one occupational diseases and conditions within the provisions of the state Workmen's Compensation Act.

The Democratic legislature willingly authorized $4,000,000 in additional appropriations for schools and supported Murphy's interest in mental health by granting $6,000,000 for a two-year program to improve state mental hospitals. For the first time a state Board of Libraries was created to develop a statewide library program.[44]

Murphy began governmental reform by reorganizing state welfare agencies. Under his predecessor a commission had been appointed that recommended centralizing the various state welfare functions; this need had become imperative when, with the depression, greater strains were placed on these agencies. Murphy accepted the study commission's recommendations, and ten bills based upon the commission's report were enacted.

The governor's victory was short-lived, however. Township supervisors and county commissioners of the poor did not relish giving up their control over the dispensation of relief. They strongly objected to the integrated state and county Department of Public Assistance and to the abolition of the state Institute Commission—both brought about by the welfare reform measures. Taking advantage of the referendum provision in the state constitution, the local officials forced a popular vote on these issues and won. The other two major acts of welfare reform legislation—reorganization of the state Hospital Commission as a separate department, and creation of a state Department of Correction with comprehensive powers to deal with adult offenders—and several minor measures either were unopposed or declared automatically valid by the attorney general.[45]

Governor Fitzgerald had also appointed a study commission to make civil service proposals. Using the commission's report as a guide, Murphy pushed through a civil service law despite strong legislative opposition.

The sit-down strikes vividly illuminated the need for labor legislation in 1937, for there was no legislation applicable to that controversy. The Wagner act, openly defied by corporations, was awaiting a Supreme Court decision as to its constitutionality. Michigan's only pertinent law was a statute making strikes illegal. Murphy proposed a comprehensive program of state legislation to fill the void, including a labor relations act and a wages and hours bill.

As finally passed by the legislature, the labor bill provided for a three-man board of industrial relations, empowered to investigate industrial controversies, order elections, and make findings. The board could also suggest mediation and arbitration. Elections for union representation were to be decided by majority rule with spokesmen for the majority given the right to be exclusive bargaining agents. Picketing was legalized but was placed under severe restrictions. Specifically forbidden was picketing of a struck plant by any person who was neither an employee nor a party to the dispute and, further, by officials of allied labor unions.

These drastic limitations on picketing disturbed leaders of the CIO. They pointed out to Murphy that wives of strikers and their allies from other plants or cities would become law violators subject to fines and jail terms. The governor had not asked for these provisions, and, because of labor's objection to them, he vetoed the entire labor act. Although critics accused him of bowing to CIO pressure, the governor preferred to think positively on the matter and stated that this type of bill needed to have the support of both labor and industry in order to succeed.[46]

Murphy's legislative accomplishments were modest—especially considering that two of his measures, civil service and welfare agency reorganization, had bipartisan support. His defeats, in addition to the labor bill, included a minimum wages and maximum hours act and a financial reorganization bill.[47] Yet, his accomplishments served as more than merely caretaker functions; they represented a first step toward a Michigan New Deal. Even the modest amount he did win from the legislature required skill and persistence, for the legislature was conservative, particularly in the upper house. Seventeen votes were required to pass a bill in the senate in which there were sixteen Democrats and sixteen Republicans. A seventeenth Democrat had been elected, but he was serving a prison term for attempting a fraudulent recount in the 1934 election. Murphy had bemoaned this malfeasance in his letter of early 1936 to F.D.R. stating his reasons for not wanting to enter the gubernatorial race.

In all too typical legislative fashion confusion dominated the 1937 session. In the first four months the legislators passed only one important bill; then, when they decided to act, they irresponsibly authorized expenditures totaling nearly $18,000,000 in excess of estimated revenues and left the problem of balancing the budget to the governor. Using his best judgment, he cut expenditures. However, as of January 1938, the budget for that fiscal year remained $5,000,000 out of balance.

Murphy relied heavily on the political power of the various state departments, particularly the highway department, to push his program through the legislature. Yet the governor's own patience and determination were equally responsible; he never relented in his activity for getting his bills passed, and in the last days of the regular session he won both his welfare reorganization program and his labor relations bill. Meanwhile, Murphy's civil service act was left unpassed. Murphy promptly called the legislators back for a special session in August, and a half hour before the adjournment deadline they enacted the civil service bill. Murphy had hoped the legislature would also reconsider his labor bill, but the senate only repassed the bill he had vetoed and then adjourned in a huff. To no avail the house members complained the senate action was illegal, because no concurrent resolution for adjournment had been passed.[48]

Murphy believed in the principle of a strong executive, and, using to the full his constitutional powers, he tried to institutionalize his creed of good government. As he had in Detroit and in the Philippines, he strove for tight financial control. For budget director he chose Harold L. Smith, former director of the University of Michigan's government bureau. The governor authorized Smith to go into state agencies to examine expenditures; Murphy also asked Smith to make long-range studies of state income and expenditure. The governor wanted a balanced budget and, according to the *News* (April 23, 1937), what he termed a "progressive economy movement in government."

Murphy's administration adopted new accounting methods as an adjunct to effective budgetary control. Further, it revised purchasing methods so that the limit on purchases without sealed bids dropped from $3000 to $500. Because of this feature, and others, four times as many firms shared in the state's business. Also, the state tax commission was reorganized and made more efficient; methods of assessing utilities were revised; a study of the tax receipts in mining regions revealed the state provided $1,000,000 a year in these areas to meet deficiencies in revenues, and efforts were made to correct this.[49]

Murphy streamlined and increased the activities of welfare agencies. He reorganized the state parole system and established psychiatric clinics in the prisons. After persuading the legislature to invest in a mental hospital building program, Murphy hired an able director for the hospitals, Dr. Joseph E. Barrett, who had been the Massachusetts assistant commissioner of mental diseases. And, with the help of federal grants in 1938, the governor strengthened local health departments.[50]

In September 1938 the governor called a statewide health conference to discuss medical care from the consumer's viewpoint. The conference discussed group health insurance, group medicine, and area clinics. Murphy envisioned a system whereby the best possible medical care would be given to the indigent and to persons of moderate incomes, but he was unable to do more than force a discussion of this sensitive subject. In this small effort Murphy again indicated his belief that the people, through their government, should provide for the unmet needs of their fellow citizens.

144

Having forced the civil service bill on the legislators, the governor implemented the act with equal ardor. To administer the civil service system he hired William Brownrigg, formerly the executive officer of the California Personnel Board. In spite of the fact that Brownrigg had been a Michigan resident, Michigan politicians considered him an outsider and viewed his appointment with suspicion. Under the new system, beginning in 1938, Brownrigg administered qualifying examinations to all state employees—regardless of political connections—and he dismissed those who failed the examinations.

Political leaders howled. Republicans warned they would not consider the act honestly administered unless 50 percent of the present state employees lost their jobs. Democrats declared no one should be dismissed. Edward J. Fry, the Democratic state chairman, gave an anti-civil service speech in which he blatantly defended patronage.[51] Meeting the challenge of the bipartisan opposition, as quoted by the *News* (May 19, 1938) Murphy stubbornly announced: "The enemies of civil service are starting out to cut my throat. Well, let them cut away. We are going to see this thing through." And he did.

But old practices died hard. In spite of Murphy, state officials asked their employees to contribute a small percentage of their salaries to the Democratic party. Murphy also was compelled to warn Democratic politicians not to coerce contractors and liquor licensees into making contributions to the party. As customary for him, he refused political contributions from professional gamblers; he observed: "You cannot accept contributions from a slot machine gang or a gambling syndicate and have free government."[52]

Murphy had campaigned in 1936 on the promise that he would bring the New Deal into Michigan. In many areas he carried out that promise by effecting programs requiring federal and state cooperation. In addition to the unemployment insurance and old age assistance acts he encouraged rural electrification in Michigan, and, by having the state adopt federal grades for agricultural products, he increased the markets for such products.[53] But the 1937-38 recession led to even greater federal and state joint action.

The economic collapse was totally unexpected. Indeed, federal spending had been reduced in early 1937 for fear that an uncontrollable boom might otherwise be stimulated. Michigan was particularly vulnerable to economic collapse due to its automobile industry—one of the first industries to feel any loss in purchasing power. The recession began in the fall of 1937, and by April Murphy estimated Michigan unemployment at 470,000. He resolved to use all the state's powers and all the aid President Roosevelt would give him to reduce the effects of this new depression. With this in mind, he went to Detroit to tell the unemployed his program. The scene was familiar to the former mayor: ten thousand unemployed or part-time workers were massed before City Hall. The *News* (April 10, 1938) quoted him as assuring his disheartened audience: "The difference between this depression and the last one is that you have a Governor who will fight your battles and do what he can to help you. And you have a President in Washington who will do the same thing. So keep up your hearts."

Murphy's first effort was futile. In line with the national administration he attempted to fix the blame for the recession on business. He made the auto manufacturers' encouragement of installment buying his scapegoat; he discussed regulation of installment buying in Washington with President Roosevelt and the president of General Motors. Nothing came of the discussion, and Murphy contented himself with appointing a study commission to investigate the problem. Later economists realized the recession had been caused by the New Deal's tight-money policies in early

1937. Murphy himself came to accept this interpretation by the end of 1938.[54]

In April 1938 Murphy negotiated a massive federal assistance program in Washington. By this time the state and local communities had about exhausted their relief funds. With Harry L. Hopkins, WPA administrator, the governor arranged to lift Michigan WPA quotas and transfer all employable persons then on relief rolls to federal work-relief projects. This would remove sixty thousand persons from local rolls and save the state and local communities about $1,500,000 a month. Within a remarkably few days the machinery for making this transfer was operating, and Murphy wrote Hopkins: "We are getting action and results—the sort of thing you and I like."[55]

Through conversations with Harold Ickes, Murphy won approval of a plan whereby the federal government would match the $6,000,000 state appropriation for mental hospitals. Murphy also received a promise from the Farm Security Administration to expand its direct relief efforts in Michigan rural areas, for farm income had dropped precipitously beginning in the summer of 1937. In June 1938 this federal aid was supplemented with the distribution by the federal Surplus Relief Corporation of surplus farm commodities to communities that lacked relief money.

Still, this assistance did not do enough. As in the early 1930's, the cities had exhausted their relief funds and had turned to the state for additional help. Murphy, in 1938, found himself abused for not releasing more state funds, even as he had abused the governor in 1932 and 1933 when Murphy was mayor of Detroit. The *News* (June 26, 1938) quoted acting Detroit Mayor Edward J. Jeffries, Jr. as declaring: "I realize that Murphy is telling the truth when he says that the State had already spent in Detroit and elsewhere all of this year's welfare appropriation and most of next year's but he has to find more money." Jeffries suggested that perhaps Murphy had kept welfare expenses down to forestall charges in the fall campaign that he had run the state into debt.

Murphy fumed at the county relief commissions which, he said, had imposed unjustified cuts in local relief expenditures. He felt they had ordered some of their budget cuts for political purposes, not because of financial stringencies. The counties, he implied, had found it all too easy to shift more of their relief burdens to the state or federal governments.

Murphy finally called a second special session of the legislature to appropriate additional relief funds. He timed the session carefully—just a few weeks before the September primary. He asked the legislature for $10,000,000 more in relief funds and, anticipating conservative criticism, prefaced his request with a description of the economies he had instituted as governor. In spite of unexpected relief expenditures, he noted, he had actually spent $12,000,000 less than the legislature had appropriated for all expenditures. In light of this, he concluded, $10,000,000 was not too much more to ask, even though additional taxing revenue was not authorized.

In the same session Murphy asked for and received legislation qualifying Michigan cities for federal housing projects. He also won an extension of land contract and mortgage foreclosure moratoriums.

In addition to his gubernatorial duties Murphy embarked on a host of extracurricular activities that led him all over the country. His ambition and temperament would not let him do otherwise. On out-of-state trips he hobnobbed with important people, received honorary degrees, or made speeches. His frequent excursions prompted the lieutenant governor to try to collect Murphy's salary for the approximately seventy days the governor had been out of the state in 1937. The gesture was not exactly a friendly one but was typical of Michigan faction-ridden politics.[56]

The demands for speechmaking became too great for Murphy to continue writing his own speeches. In the past aides had often written his addresses, but now he hired a young man, Charles Hedetniemi, specifically for that task. Murphy had not hired Hedetniemi because of his own inability. Indeed, Hedetniemi respected the governor's talents as a creative thinker and phrase maker. It was a question of insufficient time on Murphy's part.

The governor devoted many speeches to support of the national administration. In February 1937—before President Roosevelt's court-packing plan was announced—Murphy joined the New Deal chorus in asking for liberalized Supreme Court decisions. Murphy called for an amendment to the Constitution which would endorse the New Deal. It was a tragedy, Murphy told a radio network audience, that agencies such as the Agricultural Adjustment Administration and the National Recovery Administration had been abolished by the court. He declared that because of the Supreme Court's actions: "We are still in no man's land as far as the power of government to protect its citizens against nature and the play of blind economic force is concerned."[57]

A year later—in the midst of the 1938 recession—the Democratic National Committee asked Murphy to give a network address in defense of the President's renewed program of government spending. The governor urged prompt congressional action on the $4,500,000,000 program and warned delay might inadvertently lead to a worsening of the recession. At the same time he held out an olive branch to business—asking Congress to remove "unnecessary and unreasonable handicaps" to free enterprise.[58]

Murphy likewise aided the President politically. Since his landslide victory in 1936, F.D.R.'s popularity had dropped because of the defeat of his 1937 court-packing attempt and the 1937-38 recession. Among the disenchanted were the Progressives, most of whom had been allied with the New Deal, but who, in 1938, began to consider disengaging themselves from the Democrats to form their own party. In May 1938 the La Follette brothers openly proposed a new National Progressive party. Murphy expressed admiration for the brothers but otherwise gave the new party a cool reception.

The following November, after Democrats had suffered serious defeats in the national election, the Progressives made another unification attempt. Mayor Fiorello LaGuardia of New York City asked Murphy and other Progressive sympathizers to discuss with him the future of the movement in America; he implied that he no longer viewed the Democratic party an adequate medium for Progressivism. Murphy accepted the invitation but only for the purpose of healing over the fissure that had come between Progressives and Democrats. At the close of the conference he declared any efforts to give the Progressive movement "adhesion" would not work unless they were under the President's leadership. Moreover, the governor said, Progressives should keep an "open mind" on the question of a third term for F.D.R. The day after the conference Murphy went to Washington and reported on it to the President. Following his conversation with the chief executive, Murphy asserted Progressives must work through the Democratic party, if they wished to achieve their objectives.[59]

This service to the New Deal occasionally incapacitated Murphy; he needed rest and often couldn't get it. By the end of 1937 he had lost eighteen pounds, suffered a collapse, and had to be hospitalized. He had not only been through a tough legislative session but, in addition, had conducted months of grueling sit-down strike negotiations.

Fortunately the governor took time for holidays, frequently spending them in California or Florida. Once F.D.R. rewarded

him with a weekend of fishing on the presidential yacht in Chesa-
peake Bay.[60] Murphy's favorite Michigan vacation spot was Mackinac Island; there he played tennis, swam, or rode. He enthusiastically wrote Hayden: "This island has every other place
in the country beat for health and I'm trying to spend as much
time on it as possible."[61] Often the governor invited his friends to
the island. But rest served only as preparation for more labor. In
the fall of 1938 Murphy faced another election campaign.

In June 1938 Michigan's Democratic senator, Prentiss Brown,
wrote F.D.R. that Murphy had only a slim possibility of a victory
in the fall. Moreover, he said, Murphy had already become discouraged about the outcome.[62] An obstacle to success was the
continuing factional dispute within the state Democratic party.
As in 1936, the party was, at best, lukewarm in support of
Murphy's candidacy.

Murphy had attempted to gain Democratic support by making
an impressive record in legislation and executive action. He dis-
liked achieving unity by dispensing favors to party members. He
told the Young Democrats of Michigan, as reported by the *News*
(October 17, 1937), party members are too often "obsessed by
the notion that patronage and other forms of political domination
are the keys to party strength, they fail to see that in the long
run there is never anything lost in advancing the interest of the
general public. As a matter of fact," he insisted, "the party that
puts public interest first, will flourish."

Unfortunately for Murphy this approach failed to elicit party
support. Moreover, his failure was made worse by a personal
factor. An astute reporter observed in the *News* (July 31, 1938)
that while the party leaders believed Frank Murphy did his duty
as he saw it, they also noted his ambition and felt that this, as
well as duty, must have motivated him to righteously take politics

out of politics. In other words, when Murphy neglected politics, party regulars believed they were being sacrificed for his glory. Resentment led to an almost open revolt against the governor's renomination. The first signs occurred after Murphy had been in office six months. A party leader wrote F.D.R. in June 1937 that Murphy was not doing well politically. He reported many county chairmen asserted they would not support the governor again. Indeed, seventy-two out of eighty-two chairmen secretly opposed him.[63] A year later the party leader's prediction was proven nearly correct. Dissident elements tried to persuade the most powerful Democrat in the state, Highway Commissioner Van Wagoner, to enter the primary against Murphy. They would have succeeded in this had not Van Wagoner decided to wait until after the fall election to challenge Murphy's leadership of the party.[64]

Belatedly the governor attempted to assuage embittered party members. In the summer of 1938 he held a series of meetings with Democratic leaders during which he explained his policies to them. At the first session—held at Traverse City for the northern counties—Murphy encouraged criticism of his administration.[65] The Traverse City meeting, and those which followed in the same pattern, were in themselves highly successful, because they were perfect vehicles for Murphy's effusive charm. However, as a party leader observed, "Wounds are not quickly healed," and the Murphy reelection campaign never won the enthusiasm of party workers.[66]

Because Van Wagoner had decided not to enter the primary, Murphy ran unopposed. As in the past, Republicans received more votes than Democrats in the primary, giving the Republicans confidence that they needed only to hold their own to win.

The Democrats went into the final campaign with still another liability, the 1937-38 recession. The recession had forced the governor to trim government services. Most important was his reduction of old age pensions. Of the $10,000,000 appropriated by the 1937 legislature for this purpose, Murphy cut out $3,000,000 —which meant the federal government deducted an equal amount. Capitalizing on Murphy's predicament, the Republicans promised increased aid to the aged, and Fitzgerald, again the Republican gubernatorial candidate, even came out for the discredited Townsend Old Age Pension Plan.[67]

Murphy also cut back state funds for schools. The legislature had appropriated $4,000,000 more per year for schools than had ever been appropriated previously; Murphy trimmed $1,000,000 off this amount during his second fiscal year. In addition, inequalities in the distribution of school funds had caused discontent, and the governor took the blame for these inequalities.

However, these two issues—reduction of old age and of education appropriations—were only symptoms of deep voter dissatisfaction rooted in the recession. Murphy hoped his Michigan New Deal would not be blamed for loss of personal income but instead would be praised for coming quickly to the aid of those in distress. Making his hope his strategy, he gambled everything on the issue of the New Deal.

As expected, organized labor supported Murphy. The governor had done much for labor, as the mailing of the first Michigan unemployment checks under social security on July 1, 1938 conveniently demonstrated. Although in 1938 labor had nowhere near the political strength of later years, it had organized itself enough to help deliver the big city vote. Frank X. Martel, president of the Detroit and Wayne County Federation of Labor, created a Federation of Labor political action committee, while William Taylor chaired a CIO political committee. In addition, Labor's Non-Partisan League, headed by Homer Martin of the UAW, actively campaigned for the governor. The problem shortly became one of making labor's support more discreet to prevent it from frightening off other potential Murphy supporters.[68]

To add luster to his New Deal image, Murphy urged the President to tour Michigan. President Roosevelt tentatively agreed to dedicate the Port Huron bridge and stop in Detroit for a Labor Day speech, but he was unable to do so. F.D.R. did plead for Murphy in a radio fireside chat.[69] F.D.R. also promised the governor to cut red tape on the Mackinac Straits bridge project, hoping thereby to woo upstate Republicans who would benefit from the bridge.[70] Although Roosevelt did not tour Michigan, Harold Ickes came to endorse Murphy.[71]

Clinging to the coattails of the national administration, Murphy's campaign ground out its daily oratory. But in the middle of October it was delivered an unexpected broadside when Representative Martin Dies and his House Committee on Un-American Activities attacked Murphy's handling of the sit-down strikes. Dies asserted that Murphy had condoned the sit-downs by the workers in violation of private property rights and in defiance of the courts. Dies further implied he saw in the governor's actions the machinations of a Communist conspiracy. He held a series of hearings in which anti-Murphy witnesses reviewed the dramatic events of the sit-downs; the witnesses indicated the unfortunate incidents would never have happened had it not been for Murphy's toleration of Communist activity. No one appeared before the committee in the governor's defense.[72]

Dies had hit the Michigan New Deal at one of its most vulnerable points—its liberal, pro-labor orientation. Murphy's opponent, Frank Fitzgerald—buoyed up by the revelations of the Dies committee—declared that after January 1 he would end the sit-downs and promised the Communists would be kept in bounds if Republicanism were restored.[73] Communism in the New Deal had become a major campaign issue.

To counter the Dies committee's attack, President Roosevelt took the unprecedented action of criticizing the Un-American Activities Committee. Allowing direct quotation of his remarks, F.D.R. told reporters, as quoted by the N.Y. *Times* (October 26, 1938): "On the threshold of a vitally important Gubernatorial election, they [the comittee] permitted a disgruntled Republican judge, a discharged Republican city manager and a couple of officious police officers to make lurid charges against Governor Frank Murphy." The President then praised Murphy's handling of the sit-downs.

Murphy himself offered to come before the committee as a witness and bitterly observed, as quoted by the N.Y. *Times* (October 22, 1938): "It is significant and interesting that while politicians thunder long and loud about violations of the rights of private property, the very men who owned the property that was involved approved of what we did to keep the peace."

To compound Murphy's troubles, the Communist party publicly endorsed him. The opposition seized upon this effectively, especially when Murphy failed to repudiate the endorsement unequivocally.[74] President Roosevelt had flatly rejected Communist support in 1936, but Murphy chose not to follow his example—whether due to political expediency, or conviction, or a combination of both is uncertain. Murphy's statement explaining his postion was:

> I do not consider myself as having anything in common with the Communist Party, or with Communist principles.
> If I have been indorsed {sic} by any Communist group, I am not aware of it, and it has been without my knowledge, solicitation or approval. I have no alliance or understanding with Communists or with any other radical group, with respect either to labor policies or to any other matter affecting the administration of government. . . .

It is my policy, however, to be tolerant of all political groups, to permit men to assemble together peacefully and voice their views and grievances, to exercise public authority with moderation and restraint. And if to some persons I appear at times to be unduly tolerant of radical views, it is because I so thoroughly believe in the principles and the practice of democracy.[75]

In 1940 Earl Browder, the leader of the Communist party, claimed Murphy gladly had accepted Communist support in 1938 and had held many long and intimate conversations with Communist leaders to discuss strategy.[76] It is possible that, considering his civil rights convictions, Murphy did justify Communist support—hoping the few votes might keep him in office. And the governor's long-standing guarantee to protect minority rights might have been sufficient reason for the Communists to give him their support.

In any case, the Communist label was pasted on Murphy. The governor fought back strenuously, charging his opponents with a plot to smear him. The *News* (October 27, 1938) quoted him as saying: "So the reactionary politicians said: 'We will call Frank Murphy a red. There is nothing we can say against the honesty and humanity of his government. We will keep away from the great social and economic issues. We will stir up prejudice and bias. We will call him a communist.'"

The governor's countermeasures took hold. His chances for winning appeared much improved at the end of October, even over what they had been before the Dies committee smear.[77] He had a magical effect on the crowds that came to hear him. Surprisingly, many voters in normally Republican areas greeted the governor, although observers could not tell whether this represented admiration or curiosity.[78] Liberal Republicans also assisted him. Mayor LaGuardia addressed a rally in Detroit; former Michigan Governor Chase Osborn quietly used his influence among independent Republicans. By election day the Murphy camp expressed cautious optimism.[79]

But the optimism was ill-founded. Fitzgerald defeated Murphy in a moderately close race. Immediately the postmortem began. The first impulse, as expressed in the press, was to credit the Dies committee and the sit-down controversy for Murphy's defeat. Dies himself accepted this interpretation, as did President Roosevelt.[80]

However, F.D.R. too quickly credited Murphy's defeat, and the defeats of other liberals, to purely local conditions.[81] The fact that Republicans gained eighty seats in the House and seven in the Senate indicated a national trend away from the New Deal. Considering the anti-Democratic sweep, Murphy did well. He lost by 90,000 votes; in 1936 he had won by less than 50,000 while F.D.R. carried the state with a plurality of 300,000. Murphy, in 1938, had 46 percent of the electorate and Fitzgerald 52 percent. In defeat Murphy received far more votes than any other Democratic candidate had received in an off-year election.[82]

Politicians eager to remove Murphy from Michigan politics seized upon the theory that the sit-down controversy had caused the governor's defeat. Edward Fry, chairman of the Democratic State Central Committee, mailed letters to county party chairmen asserting that Murphy's labor policies had prompted party defeat and implying that the governor should be banished from Michigan politics. Fry had been the chief party critic of Murphy's civil service law, and he may well have been searching for another, more acceptable, issue with which to discredit Murphy.[83]

More convincing were analyses of the election which state party leaders sent to James Farley. They concluded the sit-downs were of less importance than two other factors: the recession—as it had affected farmers and workers—and an inadequate state party effort. In a letter to Farley, Murphy emphasized the recession as having been the "basic cause." Wage-earners and farmers, he said, had simply registered a protest vote against the decline in their purchasing power. Farmers especially had experienced a precipitous drop in income beginning in mid-summer 1937 and reaching a low point in mid-summer 1938. Had farm prices stayed up, Democrats might have continued to receive the farmer vote they had attracted since 1932. Turning to a larger issue, Murphy explained that he felt the election represented voter concern over the New Deal's failure to bring an end to the nine-year-old depression. The voters recognized work-relief as only a temporary answer to unemployment. "To a discovery of a solution," he concluded, "a progressive, liberal government, working in close co-operation with industry and business, must increasingly direct its efforts."[84]

Other state politicians echoed Murphy's interpretation. The farmers, a Grand Rapids correspondent told Farley, had given a protest vote against low farm prices, increased state taxes, and the small share of public works projects which rural districts received.[85] Murphy had lost upper Michigan by ninety thousand votes, which politicians considered a tremendous margin. The farmers "were up in arms, not only against the state but against the national administration as well," declared a county chairman. He added that the same pattern had occurred in the neighboring states of Ohio and Indiana.[86]

WPA workers made up another discontented group. Noting this, during the campaign Republicans had driven sound trucks around WPA projects and announced that Fitzgerald would secure wage increases up to sixty dollars a month. Murphy, in contrast, had been conservative in his promises. Many of these workers voted for Fitzgerald; others, being torn between the candidates, chose not to vote at all.[87]

The second reason for defeat, according to Michigan politicians, was inadequate political organization which went back to the feuding between Murphy and the party leaders—feuding which had almost erupted in a pre-primary rebellion against Murphy. During the campaign a veneer of unity was achieved, but no enthusiasm for Murphy's reelection was evident.[88] The powerful Van Wagoner went on record for the ticket but did little else. And Murphy's old rival, Comstock, ran a Constitutional Democratic ticket in competition with Murphy. Although this ticket never attracted much interest, its existence revealed the depth of the fissures in the state Democratic party.[89]

Murphy blamed the lack of party support on the civil service act for which he had pressed in spite of vocal Democratic hostility.[90] Senator Prentiss Brown agreed, as did several other party leaders. But while the civil service issue became the target of Democratic complaints, it was only symptomatic of a larger problem. Shrewder politicans, who were aware of this larger problem, emphasized the civil service factor less in their analyses of the defeat. One wrote Farley he agreed with Murphy that politics should be kept out of state affairs when it was used for personal gain, but he also believed: "There is such a thing as smart politics . . . in [the] interest of the people."[91]

When Murphy found himself the head of the state party in 1936, he knew of the factional rivalries among the Democrats, yet he neglected to correct the situation. He totally ignored party leaders in matters of appointments and policy.[92] He seemed not to realize that a political party is like an army in that loyalty must go down as well as up through the ranks so that those lowest in rank will be motivated to further the cause of their leader. But the governor concentrated on making a good record for the party in legislation and executive administration. Had he both done this and attended to party reorganization, he might have been reelected. Instead, he broke the morale of the party workers.

The explanation for Murphy's actions lay in his lifelong belief in progressive, nonpolitical government. As mayor he had served his political apprenticeship as the chief executive of a city that prided itself on its nonpartisan character. Had the Democratic party held office on a state level with any regularity prior to the 1930's, Murphy would have undoubtedly held a more practical view of politics. But the Democrats had left organized politics to the Republicans. Significantly, when Governor Comstock was elected in 1932, he made the same error Murphy made four years later. Both tried to be capable governors and both ignored strengthening their party.[93]

Victory for Murphy in 1938 would have demonstrated to the country, and to him, that his decisions as governor—especially those regarding the sit-down strikes—were at least understood by the people as having been well intentioned. Instead, his defeat was regarded in the popular press and in the country at large as a defeat for evil un-Americanism and a victory for good traditional American values.

Yet Murphy's defeat must be kept in perspective. The fact remains that he lost by a small margin in a traditionally Republican state. Six years of New Deal rule in Washington had not been enough to educate the electorate to switch parties and make Michigan a Democratic state—although in a few more years it was to become one.

Despite his defeat, Murphy did not slow his pace. He desired the transition for the new government to be easy and fruitful. He was quoted by the *News* (December 6, 1938) as saying: "It will not hurt us [Democrats], but really help, if we help our successors to get as good a start as is possible."

Murphy had always been interested in the science of government, and he used this interim period to pull together his experiences as governor for the new administration. His major effort was to prepare his farewell address in which he planned to give a realistic picture of the state's condition. To assist him, he asked six private agencies to make analyses that could be incorporated into his speech.

The final document encompassed many topics, including civil service, finance, office space, health, the National Guard, agriculture, housing, and highways.[94] Of all the topics, Murphy considered governmental reorganization to be the most significant. His approach was scholarly; he tried to distill abstract principles as to what good government should be.

Murphy had begun his study of governmental reorganization in the summer of 1938. At that time he appointed his friend Hayden, to chair a study commission for this purpose. In its December preliminary report the commission pointed out the weakness of the state government's executive branch—which consisted of an administrative board of seven elected officials including the governor—and it recommended consideration of a cabinet-type government modeled after the federal government, which would give the chief executive much greater powers.[95]

In his farewell message the governor referred the report to the new administration with the hope action would be taken. If Murphy had been reelected, undoubtedly he would have pushed for fundamental reform of Michigan government; he confided as much to Hayden.[96]

The new legislature's reception to Murphy's farewell address sharply contrasted with the dedication Murphy had put into the message. Only two minutes had been devoted to reading the document when, according to the *News* (January 6, 1939), a Republican legislator moved that "the report be considered read and printed in the House and Senate Journals." The motion carried. Not since 1931 had a gubernatorial message received so curt a reception. Further repudiation of Murphy's administration came when the 1939 legislature crippled the civil service system. Governor Fitzgerald had defended civil service in his inaugural address, but, following his sudden death, the legislature passed amendments which exempted outright three thousand employees and which deprived the Civil Service Commission of jurisdiction over legislative employees and the unclassified services under which were enumerated eighteen specific classes of employees.[97]

Murphy's own party also rebuffed him. At the state Democratic convention in February 1939, Murphy's candidate for state chairman lost to one who was supported by Van Wagoner. As a further indication of the party's return to normalcy, the convention named to the state Democratic committee the former state senator who was serving a prison sentence for a recount vote fraud.

Chapter V

"Sit Down! Sit Down!"

When they tie the can to a union man,
    Sit down! Sit down!
When they give him the sack, they'll take him back,
    Sit down! Sit down!
When the speed-up comes, just twiddle your thumbs,
    Sit down! Sit down!
When the boss won't talk, don't take a walk,
    Sit down! Sit down!

        Sit down, just take a seat,
        Sit down, and rest your feet,
        Sit down, you've got 'em beat.[1]

The year 1937—Murphy's first as governor—was a time of triumph for organized labor. The national economy had achieved a modest recovery—just enough to make labor want more of the economy's fruits. Labor found itself favored by the Democratic administration, which coincidentally had been given an impressive vote of confidence in the 1936 election. This same administration had passed the Wagner act which outlawed unfair labor practices and assured collective bargaining. In industry after industry, during 1937, the unions called workers out on strike and won concessions from employers. Altogether 1,860,000 men and women took part in 4,740 strikes, making 1937 the most industrially chaotic year of the depression.[2] Under the agressive leadership of John L. Lewis and his newly formed CIO, the large assembly-line industries—steel, auto, glass, and rubber—capitulated to organized labor's demands. Previously, large corporations had successfully kept the AF of L from challenging management's right to determine working conditions.

The sit-down strike to which unionists resorted in 1937 had no definite origin, although there were precedents for it. In 1892 steelworkers had seized the Homestead mills, and in the women's garment industry in 1910 employees had stopped operations by staying in the shop. In 1936 rubber workers used this technique to win recognition of their union. Yet theirs was a partial victory, for management retained its right to negotiate with the company union as well. But sit-downs were not an American phenomenon, for Europe experienced them as well, with the sit-downs in France during 1936 being the most spectacular.[3]

American labor leaders hesitated to endorse this tactic. In nearly every instance of its use the workers spontaneously employed it, presenting union leaders with the dilemma of whether to approve of, or repudiate, the action. In private, union leaders agreed it was illegal. However, when the General Motors auto workers in Flint, Michigan sat down on December 30, 1936, John L. Lewis boldly endorsed the technique, his reason being more that he thought the action would defeat GM than that he approved of it.[4]

In Michigan during 1936 the CIO had concentrated on organizing workers in the automobile industry, particularly General Motors. By November the CIO had enrolled enough men to make a bid for power. The workers were responsive, for they had many long-standing grievances they wished removed. Among the grievances were the prolonged layoffs that made a mockery of the five-dollar day established by Henry Ford, the conveyor system that compelled the body to keep pace regardless of how tired one became, and the speeding up of the assembly lines by foremen. A Buick employee related how many a night he came home from work exhausted and how his wife had to wash his face to keep him awake long enough to eat. The exhausting assembly lines forced many men, when they reached forty, to quit the factories. When employees sought protection in unions, the corporations considered their action treasonous and financed espionage activities to ferret out defectors. The guilty were fired. From January through July 1936 General Motors alone spent $994,855 on private detective services.[5]

Without waiting for union leadership, workers struck two Flint General Motors plants in early December 1936. On December 21, 1936 John L. Lewis and auto union leaders wired William Knudsen, executive vice-president of GM, asking for a collective bargaining conference to discuss recognition of the United Auto Workers, affiliate of the CIO. Knudsen rejected the proposal, saying individual plant managers would deal with all employee grievances.[6]

On the morning of December 30 the workers in GM's Fisher Body plant no. 2 in Flint seized possession of the factory and began a sit-down to protest management's transfer of union inspectors to other jobs. That night men in Fisher plant no. 1 were alarmed to see dies being loaded onto boxcars bound for non-union cities. With the help of railroaders the auto workers kept the dies in the plant. Then, to prevent the assembly line from starting again, they, too, took possession of the factory with a sit-down.[7]

Since Fisher no. 1 cut dies for about half of the body parts in GM cars, it became the focal point of the struggle between the UAW and the corporation. With the production of this plant cut off, most other General Motors factories eventually stopped operation. Before the sit-down was over, 140,000 of the 150,000 production workers were idle, and automobile production dropped from a mid-December peak of 53,000 units to 1500 units per week.[8]

The workers had chosen an effective weapon. In occupying the plants they nullified all the usual strikebreaking practices. The owners could not continue production by hiring scabs, for the strikers possessed the means of production. Also, the strikers no longer faced the hazards of bad weather and police or scab battles. General Motors was placed on the defensive. It hesitated to evict the strikers forcibly for fear of damaging its property and machinery.[9]

On January 2, 1937 GM secured an injunction in Flint from Judge Edward Black ordering the strikers out of the plants. The workers retaliated by defying the sheriff who served the eviction order, but the UAW knew this defiance could not continue for long without provoking public disapproval. The union's lawyer, Lee Pressman, then discovered that Judge Black owned 3365 shares of General Motors stock valued at $219,000. Since under Michigan law no judge could preside over a case in which he was an interested party, Black's injunction was invalid. Having no alternative, General Motors filed a new injunction in another court.[10]

On January 4 Lewis submitted eight demands to the corporation, including recognition of the UAW as the sole bargaining agent for all GM auto workers. Angered by an increasing number of plant seizures by strikers, General Motors refused to answer the letter.[11] Neither of the opponents was in a mood for compromise. The immediate objective of both became winning—or retaining—control of the Flint plants. The corporation needed to break the strike to resume production; the union needed to continue the sit-down to assure that manufacturing could not be resumed.

When the strike went into the second week of January with no sign of settlement, Governor Murphy started mediation efforts. With his intervention the first phase of a prolonged series of conferences began. During the second phase mediation efforts shifted to Washington where Secretary of Labor Frances Perkins attempted negotiation. Upon her failure, Murphy again became the central figure, and during the third and final phase he brought about a settlement. Even when he alone was the principal negotiator, the governor worked closely with Washington; federal mediators came from Washington to assist him, and he maintained almost daily contact with Secretary Perkins and President Roosevelt. Thus Murphy acted with the approval of the national administration even though he was not its direct agent.[12]

Murphy's first task was to bring the two opponents together. The union wanted to begin talks, but the corporation hesitated to meet with UAW leaders for fear of giving tacit recognition to the union. General Motors refused to negotiate until the sit-down strikers had vacated the factories. The union admitted vulnerability on this issue because of its illegal seizure of property; union leaders promised to call the strikers out of the Fisher plants if GM would give written guarantees that it would not remove the dies. This the company refused to do.

At this point General Motors received support from another quarter. George E. Boyden, a past paymaster of the Buick Motor Company, created the Flint Alliance, an employee organization that claimed to represent thousands of loyal GM workers. The alliance announced that if there were any collective bargaining, it must be consulted. Although the alliance was not sponsored by General Motors, its sympathies were with the corporation for which it became a faithful ally.[13]

On January 11 the strikers' growing tension erupted into violence, the immediate cause of which was the company's shutting off of heat in Fisher plant no. 2. A few hours later Flint police blockaded the plant entrance to stop shipment of food to the strikers. This twofold action jeopardized the success of the sit-down, for, without heat and food, the strikers would quickly be forced to give in. In response Victor Reuther, a UAW organizer, drove a sound car to the plant entrance and asked the police to allow food delivery. Failing to gain permission, his appeals became more belligerent. Aroused by the loudspeaker, the strikers took matters into their own hands. Shortly before 7:00 P.M. pickets rushed the plant door, pushed police aside, and moved coffee and bread into the factory.

Two hours later the police returned with their strength increased to fifty and armed with clubs; they charged the pickets at the doors, driving some inside the building. One policeman discharged a tear gas gun through a broken factory window. Other officers fired buckshot at pickets and through the factory windows at strikers. The striking workmen fought back with sticks, metal pipes, nuts and bolts, and soft-drink bottles. For three hours the fighting went on. Before it ended, the strikers had captured four police cars. At midnight the police regrouped for a renewed attack on the plant, but the men inside were ready. At the signal from the sound car the strikers emerged with a spouting fire hose. Unable to withstand the powerful, icy stream, the police retreated one hundred yards across a bridge that approached the plant gate. Although fourteen auto workers had to be removed for medical treatment of gunshot wounds, it was nonetheless a union victory and was named the Battle of Running Bulls.[14]

At midnight Murphy heard of the outbreak of violence. He immediately drove to Flint for an inspection. He found the situation serious and called out the National Guard on riot duty. He instructed the guard to be neutral, its only mission being to prevent violence. To assure the day's incidents would not be repeated, Murphy insisted General Motors make no further efforts to shut off the heat or stop the supply of food. In addition he denied a request of the county prosecutor to serve John Doe warrants on three hundred persons connected with the battle. These decisions aided the UAW because they thwarted the plans of the corporation.

Murphy also had favored the union earlier when he had ruled that strikers' families should be given relief on the basis of need, like anyone else. Yet there was a limit to Murphy's patience with labor. He warned the union he would not stand for hordes of outside agitators and strong-arm men coming into Michigan to defend the Flint strikers. He condemned the practice whereby outsiders filtered into the factories. Frequently when a striker went out on a pass—ostensibly to change clothes and see his family— a substitute slipped back on his pass. This procedure risked violence and, as Murphy pointed out, was morally repugnant.[15]

Four days after the Fisher plant battle Murphy succeeded in winning a truce between General Motors and the UAW. The governor had taken the position that, as the public's representative, he had a right to see that settlement was reached. Therefore he insisted the disputants confer to resolve their differences. After offering a series of alternatives that would not require direct talks—such as filing a statement in the presence of the union and then leaving—the corporation reluctantly consented to meet with UAW president Homer Martin in the governor's office at the capitol. At the close of a fifteen-hour session Martin and the company representative, William Knudsen, had agreed to a truce; formal negotiations for a strike settlement were to begin on Monday, January 18. By that time the union was to have the plants evacuated. The union also removed its earlier demand for recognition as sole bargaining agent as a prerequisite to negotiation. In return, the corporation promised not to withdraw dies, machinery, materials, or other equipment during negotiations and consented to discuss the entire union list of eight demands, including the all-important one of recognition of the UAW as sole bargainer.

But on Sunday, January 17, the truce was shattered. A reporter discovered Knudsen had also agreed to negotiate with the pro-management Flint Alliance. Martin was appalled, for, in effect, General Motors had ruled out the key issue—sole bargaining rights for the UAW. He ordered the workers to remain in the plants. Some had already begun to leave, but, on hearing the news, they raced back to their positions. The company had planned to delay announcement of its meeting with the alliance until Sunday evening by which time the factories would have been vacated by the strikers.

General Motors took the view that it had not violated the terms of the truce. Technically this was true, for there was no mention of the status of the Flint Alliance in the truce.[16] However, as the UAW observed, the agreement with the alliance was obviously designed to make it unnecessary for the company to consider the sole-recognition issue. Murphy had attempted to forestall this development by discouraging efforts of the alliance and of other groups of workers to arrange collective bargaining conferences. But he had been unable to persuade the alliance to remain silent.

With the collapse of negotiations the scene of activity moved to Washington. Secretary of Labor Perkins immediately took charge. Her strategy was to persuade the top men on both sides to accept personal responsibility for a settlement; she invited the president of General Motors, Alfred P. Sloan, Jr., and John L. Lewis to Washington.

Lewis had little respect for Miss Perkins; he believed she was not accustomed to the rough-and-tumble of the power struggle between the UAW and GM. While he obligingly conferred with Perkins, he gave greater attention to increasing his bargaining strength. He had the CIO call off strikes in the aluminum and plateglass industries in order to insure an uninterrupted flow of materials to General Motors' competitors. He also tried to maneuver President Roosevelt into publicly supporting the UAW. With the United Mine Workers' $500,000 political campaign contribution in mind, Lewis announced to a news conference:

> The administration asked labor for help . . . and labor gave its help. The same economic royalists now have their fangs in labor. The workers of this country expect the administration to help the workers in every legal way and to support the workers in the General Motors plants.

F.D.R. chided: " 'Of course I think in the interests of peace that there come moments when statements, conversations, and headlines are not in order.' "[17] In the meantime Sloan had read Lewis' statement in Washington and boarded a train for New York City. Lewis had not only failed to win F.D.R.'s support but had initiated the collapse of Perkins' mediation efforts.

In spite of numerous appeals by Secretary Perkins and a public statement by President Roosevelt, Sloan refused to return to Washington to negotiate with Lewis.[18] Unless F.D.R. was prepared to risk the prestige of his office by trying to force a settlement when General Motors and the union were not even conferring, he had no alternative but to give Murphy a second try at mediation.

The time lost in Washington only built up tension in Flint.

Increasingly the Flint Alliance and other pro-General Motors organizations pressed Murphy to drive the strikers out of the plants. When it became clear Murphy would not risk violence, the alliance denounced him in a public meeting. Soon there was talk of vigilante action. One plan envisioned persuading Murphy to move the National Guard troops away from the Flint strike area, opening the way for a citizen invasion of the plants. Another scheme called for raiding the two Fisher plants, thereby forcing the governor to order troops to clear the plants as a public safety measure. Murphy was disturbed by these plots and feared the situation might get out of hand. To forestall further talk of vigilante action he appealed to General Motors for help; the N.Y. *Times* (January 30, 1937) quoted him as saying: "General Motors officials have stated to me privately they do not want the strikers evicted by force. I believe the time has come for them to make such a statement publicly if they mean it."

The UAW as well tried the governor's patience. Many strike leaders wanted a dramatic new action to maintain rank-and-file enthusiasm. In part this desire reflected the activist philosophy of some Communists in the UAW. But this ideological view did not dominate the union, for there were few Communists. Even the leading Communist on the scene could claim giving no more than "loyal backing and support to the strike."[19]

Strike leaders decided the month-long sit-down needed new aggression. Of the several plants that made up the Chevrolet works, the motor assembly division, plant no. 4, was the most critical for maintaining Chevrolet production. Its capture became the next goal of the union. UAW leaders leaked the news that Chevrolet plant no. 9 was their target. When, on February 1, the workers in no. 9 acted suspiciously, plant police converged on the factory with tear gas and clubs. Meanwhile, plant no. 4 quickly fell without company opposition.[20] Informed of this new development, Murphy ordered twelve hundred additional National Guardsmen to Flint.

The daring capture of an additional General Motors factory revealed how seriously the workers took the sit-down strike. They viewed the conflict as a war, albeit an industrial one, in which discipline and obedience were the crucial elements. If through boredom or outside pressure their will faltered, the cause of the union would be lost. Strike leaders in part achieved discipline by holding court each morning; the most serious offenses were smuggling in liquor and circulating rumors.[21] They also maintained discipline with the sound car; heard for more than a city block, its martial music and encouraging voice braced the strikers.

Having a highly successful weapon in the sit-down, labor leaders lost their original shyness toward it. They now said labor need not be disturbed because the sit-down involved seizing property illegally; they pointed out most weapons employed by labor had been declared illegal at first.[22] Moreover, as Homer Martin said:

> What more sacred property right is there in the world than the right of a man in his job. This property right involves the right to support his family, feed his children and keep starvation away from the door. This property right is the very foundation stone of American homes.[23]

While it was sophistry to infer from this that a sit-down was legal, the naiveté of the statement won sympathy for labor.

On February 2, the day after the strikers seized Chevrolet no. 4, the principle of management's property rights was upheld when the courts awarded General Motors a new injunction for the expulsion of the strikers; Judge Gadola ordered evacuation of Fisher plants nos. 1 and 2 within twenty-four hours. He also enjoined union picketing, under the provisions of Michigan law.

Workers in Fisher no. 1 sent Murphy a telegram of defiance less than twenty-four hours later:

> We have carried on a stay-in strike over a month in order to make General Motors Corporation obey the law [Wagner act] and engage in collective bargaining. . . . We fully expect that if a violent effort is made to oust us many of us will be killed, and we take this means of making it known to our wives, to our children, to the people of the state of Michigan and the country that if this result follows from the attempt to eject us, you are the one who must be held responsible for our deaths.[24]

This was more than strategy. The issue had become too grave for the men to give up calmly. If more evidence of their determination was needed, it was visible on the roads into Flint. The twenty-four-hour deadline was to end at 3:00 P.M., and all morning long, workmen from neighboring cities streamed into Flint. Rubber workers came from Akron; Walter Reuther led five hundred auto workers from the west side of Detroit. The men congregated at Fisher no. 1, for Fisher no. 2 had been cut off by National Guard troops. As three o'clock drew near, strikers inside Fisher no. 1 increased from four hundred to two thousand; a line of almost five thousand workers, two abreast, circled on the lawn in front of the plant. They held in their hands clubs, heavy sticks, pipes, and crowbars. Murphy chose not to risk bloodshed, and 3:00 P.M. passed with the strikers secure in the plant and the troops as yet uncommitted.[25]

With the injunction ordered and defied, Murphy had to produce a quick settlement. The threat of violence was already severe and would increase each day that the union ignored the court order. The governor asked F.D.R. personally to request

General Motors' participation in talks with the union. Responding to presidential authority, GM agreed to come to the bargaining table in spite of its prior refusal to negotiate while strikers still occupied its plants.[26] This procedure permitted the corporation to claim that "the request of the President of the United States left no alternative."[27] However, the sit-down had virtually stopped all production by General Motors, and its competitors were dividing up its market. At the beginning of the strike GM had sought to prevent this by asking other auto manufacturers to form a united front and shut down the entire industry. But the others had refused; the temptation of profit at GM's expense was too great.[28] Murphy's reluctance to enforce the injunction had now given added force to the union's tactic. Sloan commented: "Under such circumstances, the corporation stood powerless. Manifestly, it became a matter beyond its power to control."[29]

Lewis, meanwhile, had arrived in Detroit. The site for negotiation, which began February 4, was the Detroit courtroom of Frank Murphy's brother, Judge George Murphy. For the most part the participants did not meet together; Lewis and his aides sat in Judge Murphy's office while Knudsen, with his corporation assistants, remained in the jury room. Frank Murphy went back and forth between the two groups carrying proposals.

The immediate problem was the court injunction that had been defied on Wednesday, February 3. On Thursday General Motors prepared a writ of attachment compelling the sheriff and the governor to force the workers out of the plants. Murphy persuaded the company to postpone asking for the writ for twenty-four hours; he believed progress would be made in the negotiations if he could prevent further exacerbating action. But on Friday morning John Smith, chief counsel for GM, told Murphy the corporation had decided to go ahead with the writ of attachment. Murphy again asked for a deferment, this time only until

175

tion of workers who really wanted UAW representation. This Lewis categorically rejected. By Monday night, February 8, the cautious optimism of Friday had evaporated; neither side was willing to yield on the basic issue of sole bargaining privileges for the UAW.

The failure to reach an agreement resulted in greater uneasiness in Flint. On Thursday, February 4, a new group of armed strangers had come to Flint.[35] Thereafter Murphy took personal command of the Flint situation and requested hourly reports. When Murphy refused to enforce the writ of attachment, the sheriff and Flint police decided to enforce it themselves and prepared to move on Fisher no. 1 with a brigade of men from the American Legion, the Sheriffs' Association, and GM police. Murphy retaliated by ordering National Guard troops to strategic points in the vicinity of plant no. 1. Pro-GM forces refused to be outdone. The Flint city government enrolled one thousand special reservists in its police force and placed them under the command of the mayor, who was also a Buick distributor. The city was serving notice on Murphy that if he didn't restore law and order, Flint would. Seldom in an industrial struggle was sheer power revealed as it was in Flint. Each side had its hastily armed followers. Only the National Guard remained neutral.

Murphy decided to wait no longer for the two powers to find their way to industrial peace. On Monday night, February 8, he telephoned his decision to the White House:

> We have one chance left out of this. I have not made any statement thus far about my position as Chief Executive. I feel I cannot delay that longer than tonight, and the Chief Executive of the State must be in the position of upholding the authority [of the state]. . . .[36]

Murphy had resolved to arbitrate the dispute. He chose as his model a Toledo agreement which the CIO had recently signed with a glass company. In that settlement the union had agreed to bargain collectively on the basis of its members only, and, in return, the company had given a protective guarantee to the union. Murphy won acceptance of this formula from General Motors. As its guarantee to the union, GM agreed to give Murphy a letter stating it would not bargain collectively with any other organization for three months, unless Murphy sanctioned it.[37] The time limit, however, was negotiable, for GM was concerned in this experiment only by the phraseology that might deal with exclusive bargaining rights during the period.[38]

With General Motors' acceptance, the problem was to win Lewis' approval. The substance of what the CIO leader desired was in Murphy's proposed settlement—but not recognition of sole collective bargaining rights—and Lewis remained unyielding. When, by Tuesday evening, Lewis still had not accepted the formula, Murphy quietly visited the CIO leader in his hotel suite. There he served Lewis with a letter stating Murphy's obligations as governor to uphold the law and threatening to evict the strikers by force unless an immediate settlement were attained.[39] For strategic reasons Murphy did not inform General Motors representatives of this action.[40]

By the end of Wednesday Lewis had yielded, and on Thursday morning the representatives signed Murphy's imposed agreement. As the participants filed into George Murphy's courtroom, the spectators burst into applause—such was the relief at the termination of the forty-four-day strike. Only Lewis was absent from the ceremony. He had excused himself with a cold, and Murphy carried the agreement to him for his signature.

After voting to accept the agreement, the strikers marched out of Fisher no. 1 singing "Solidarity Forever." Heading the procession was the color bearer with a large American flag. Behind him followed the strikers, each carrying a smaller flag. Still to come

were the wives and other women who had marched in the
Women's Emergency Brigade. These women, who had provided
able assistance throughout the strike, wore brilliant red or green
berets and arm bands. When the victorious evacuation march was
completed, the entire group went to Fisher no. 2 and Chevrolet
no. 4 to repeat the performance.

The evacuation was part of the general agreement between the
UAW and General Motors. The corporation dropped its injunction, and all factories reopened without discrimination against
the unionists. In accordance with Murphy's formula, GM recognized the union as bargaining agent for its members only in the
seventeen plants that had been struck. The crucial part of the
agreement was covered in a letter which Knudsen wrote Murphy.
It began with a statment that General Motors would not enter
into any agreement that would have the effect of denying to any
group of employees the right of collective bargaining. Knudsen's
letter then gave the assurances Lewis had insisted on, declaring
that GM would not inspire collective bargaining ambitions in
other groups for the purpose of weakening the UAW. As evidence of its good faith, the company promised not to bargain
with any other employee group for a period of six months.

Murphy's settlement was an adroit solution to an uncompromis-
able issue: the union surrendered the principle but achieved the
substance of its demand; General Motors won the principle but
lost the purport of what it wanted. Both sides believed they had
won. Lewis had correctly judged the direction history was moving
and swung the vast majority of auto workers into the UAW
during the six-month bargaining period the agreement granted
him—thereby obtaining a permanent victory. Had he been unable to do this, the corporation's position would have been
vindicated.

General Motors regarded it wrong for the UAW—only one of

179

many worker organizations—to have *sole* collective bargaining rights. In a statement to stockholders on the strike Alfred P. Sloan, Jr., the president of GM, declared: "The Corporation cannot do anything to deny the rights of collective bargaining to [all] those entitled to same." But, recognizing the need for consistency, Sloan agreed "that in collective bargaining the bargainers should be truly representative of a body of General Motors workers." GM was willing to have an arbiter decide if a group were truly representative. This, said Sloan, was the purpose of Knudsen's letter to Murphy: it only designated him as the arbiter; it did not strengthen the union's position.[41] By coincidence AF of L President William Green agreed with Sloan, calling the agreement between Lewis and Knudsen a defeat for the principle of the closed shop.

The nation responded to the settlement with jubilation. Murphy could not be praised enough. Sloan and Knudsen hailed his handling of the negotiations. Other automobile manufacturers, including Walter P. Chrysler of the Chrysler Corporation and A. Edward Barit of Hudson Motors, echoed the statements of the GM executives. Even the Detroit *Free Press,* a consistent Murphy critic, endorsed his actions.[42] President Roosevelt headed the chorus of New Dealers and labor leaders who extolled the peace Murphy had achieved. Perhaps Secretary Perkins, as reported by the N.Y. *Times* (February 12, 1937), was the most generous in praising Murphy's "patience, intelligence and fortitude" and in venturing that the negotiations under his direction were "an educational experience for the whole country."

Murphy made the most of his newly won glory. Following the settlement he delivered three radio broadcasts. And the evening after the agreement he disobeyed his physician's order to remain in bed and took a train to New York to attend a dinner of the Irish-American Historical Society. When he was asked on his arrival if he thought his political star was rising, the N.Y. *Times* (February 14, 1937) reported he grinned and replied: "I have no political star."

Following the General Motors settlement Murphy escaped to Florida for a rest. Before he had completed his vacation, a rash of sit-downs broke out in Detroit. No business in this open-shop city was immune; the businesses affected included aluminum, iron smelting, drug, grocery, shoe, hat, cigar packing, soft drink, and other automobile companies. Even thirty members of a National Guard company staged a sit-down strike in demand of unpaid wages from the Flint strike assignment. Reluctantly the governor returned to Michigan to mediate settlements.

Many Detroit strikes were solved within a few days. But, in hopes of achieving a permanent end to sit-downs, Murphy sponsored a Law and Order Committee to rally public support for obedience to law and rational solutions to labor grievances. Committee members included representatives of labor, capital, government, and the general public. Murphy warned that continued flouting of public authorities by sit-down strikers would impair public confidence in the government and open the door to vigilante action and mob rule. The committee passed two resolutions: one, urging Michigan mayors to mediate and, if that failed, to arbitrate strikes in their cities; the other, advocating passage of a state labor relations law along the lines Murphy proposed. However, the committee's effectiveness was stunted by Homer Martin's refusal to join it.

Taking their cue from the Law and Order Committee, Detroit police broke up several small sit-downs. Murphy himself accompanied the police to a department store where a strike was in progress. Among the strikers he discovered an ex-convict whom he had sentenced when Murphy had been a judge. In an obvious

effort to discredit irresponsible sit-downs, the governor termed
the seizure of the store by labor organizers banditry.

Homer Martin protested against the police raids and threatened
to call a general strike in all organized Detroit automobile plants
unless the police stopped forcible evictions. Murphy's firmness
compelled Martin to limit his action to calling a protest meeting.

While Murphy was mediating these sit-downs, a new sit-down
of serious proportions erupted at the Chrysler plants. The corporation immediately requested an injunction ordering the union to
evacuate the eight Chrysler plants affected. On March 15 the
court awarded the injunction, and Murphy declared the court
should be obeyed.

The strikers defied the injunction, and on March 19 the court
ordered them arrested. The sheriff conferred with Murphy about
carrying out the court order but did not formally request intervention by the governor. Murphy's official position was that he
could take no action until the sheriff exhibited inability to handle
the situation and requested intervention. Subsequently the sheriff
made no effort to evict the sit-down strikers. Murphy avoided
exacerbating the situation by having to forcibly evict the strikers,
and, in contrast to his position in the General Motors strike, he
also avoided having to bear the onus of rejecting a sheriff's request
for military assistance.

Murphy took over the Chrysler strike negotiations on March
18. By March 24 he won from John L. Lewis and Walter Chrysler
an agreement for a truce during which negotiations were to take
place. Under the terms of the truce the UAW evacuated the
plants, and the company promised not to resume production
while talks were in progress.

This agreement had not been easily won. Murphy had to
threaten the forcible eviction of strikers before Lewis and Chrysler
would even agree to meet. While the two opponents talked with

Murphy at the capitol, the National Guard colonel, who had commanded the troops in Flint, and the State Police commissioner waited outside the governor's office for the outcome. Preliminary to the talks the colonel had made several obvious inspection trips to occupied plants. It was evident Murphy intended to order troops and police into the strike area if the conference failed.

With brief interruptions, Murphy kept Chrysler and Lewis together until they reached a final settlement on April 6. The settlement was similar to the GM agreement. The UAW gave up its demand for sole bargaining rights and achieved recognition for its members only. However, the corporation guaranteed preferential bargaining treatment for the union. Immediately after the Chrysler settlement, the Reo Motor Car Company and Hudson Motors settled their strikes on the same terms.

From Murphy's point of view the Chrysler strike revealed a more realistic attitude on the part of both labor and management. Neither wished to repeat the bitter maneuvers of the GM strike. Although for a few days the court eviction order had been ignored, the workers did evacuate the plants before formal negotiations began, and no violence necessitated the mobilization of the National Guard.

While the end of the Chrysler sit-down terminated the most prolific month of sit-down strikes, throughout 1937 Murphy was called on to mediate sporadic sit-downs and conventional strikes. General Motors was beset with wildcat strikes at various times. Other Michigan industries affected by strikes included trucking, lumber, brass, and electric power. In the power strike Murphy intervened on two occasions to order the strikers back to work. In exasperation at one point, as quoted by the N.Y. *Times* (May 20, 1937), he publicly denounced the power workers: "The conduct of labor in this case is as despotic as capital's ever has been."

In June a strike at the Republic Steel plant in Monroe, Michigan compelled Murphy to order out the National Guard for the first time since the Flint crisis. On May 28 a minority of workers had gone on strike as part of a general walkout against Republic Steel, perhaps the most anti-union corporation of the little steel group. The strike was not to be settled in Monroe, and Murphy limited his efforts to maintaining peace until a corporation-wide settlement could be achieved. This was not to come about, and before the year was out the union had to admit failure.[43]

Monroe was a strongly anti-union town. When the company announced plans to reopen its plant despite picketing, Mayor Daniel A. Knaggs offered his assistance. He swore in 383 untrained deputies and equipped them with tear gas grenades, guns, police clubs, and baseball bats purchased by Republic Steel. Hoping to prevent violence, Murphy pressed peace negotiations from June 8 until the plant opened, but he failed. On June 10 armed deputies and police, with loyal employees lined up in cars behind them, marched to the plant while deputized American Legion members patrolled the business district. Nearing the plant, the police force found the road blocked by pickets. As the armed group maneuvered for position, two tear gas shells were unexplainably fired. Shortly thereafter the police deputies moved in and quickly dispersed the pickets. No one was seriously hurt.[44]

Murphy hastened to prevent a retaliatory raid by the CIO. But the CIO organizers insisted on some measure of revenge and called for a tri-state rally at Monroe to protest the forcible breaking of the picket line. The Monroe City Commission sought to prevent the rally and asked Murphy to declare martial law. He refused, reminding the commission of its obligations under the first amendment to maintain free speech; however, he did promise to police the rally. He persuaded the local deputies and vigilantes to lay down their arms and ordered a National Guard battalion and one hundred State Police to the city. Murphy himself made an appearance in Monroe on the day of the labor rally. Afterwards, he negotiated with Mayor Knaggs a definition of peaceful picketing which allowed the union to picket the Republic plant in a peaceful demonstration, providing pickets did not prevent employees from entering or leaving the plant.

A few days before the Monroe rally the most dramatic event in the aftermath of the GM sit-down took place. As an outgrowth of the arrest of pickets at the Capital City Wrecking Company in Lansing, on June 7 the CIO staged a labor holiday in the state capital. Union members stopped work throughout the city, paralyzing its activity. Not content to picket, workers mobbed the streets and halted traffic. Other brigades of workmen invaded the City Hall, and one group battled with college students in East Lansing. Murphy was en route from Detroit to Lansing when the holiday began. On his arrival the waiting unionists greeted him with cheers.

But Murphy deplored their action and called their leaders into his office for an explanation. One of them said they were trying to educate the public. To this Murphy replied: "The public will educate you," and followed with a short but stinging lecture on the unionists' duties and obligations to the public. In compliance with his demand, the unionists promptly dispersed the City Hall blockade.[45] The governor then arranged bail for the pickets whose imprisonment had caused the agitation; this brought an end to the holiday.

The euphoria of the first days following the GM settlement ended after the sit-downs spread—closing numerous industries, retail stores, and other business throughout the nation. That March 192,642 people resorted to sit-downs, making this the month with the greatest number of strikes in the entire New Deal era.

185

Using the sit-down technique as its spearhead, the CIO rapidly increased its membership. Founded in 1935, it had 1,460,000 members by December 1936; by September 1937 it had more than doubled this number to an impressive 3,718,000.[46] As a consequence of the sit-downs and the rise of the CIO, American labor became a power that business was compelled to recognize.

Many Americans had second thoughts about those fateful days when Murphy had postponed enforcement of the court injunction; they wondered: "Was civil war averted or social disintegration begun?"[47] The answer to this and the key to understanding Murphy's actions lie in the astute contemporary observation of Arthur Krock, a N.Y. *Times* columnist who at times was highly critical of the sit-downs. He observed that Murphy was "a conservative in the broad sense of the term."[48] Krock meant that, whatever Murphy did, he did not because he wanted to change American values, but to preserve them. After the February 11 settlement the N.Y. *Times* (February 14, 1937) quoted Murphy as describing his accomplishment in this way: "There was no fatality, no violation of civil liberties and no suspension of democratic institutions." That labor gained significantly in its status meant less to Murphy than that the gain was won peacefully. He viewed the amicable settlement as a moment of greatness for American democracy—as an occasion when a belated and needed change in the social and economic status quo was accomplished while human rights remained inviolate.

Murphy could have used the powers of his office to break the GM strike. But his sensitivity to needs around him prompted a different course. He believed in the dignity of the individual and that factory conditions negated this. "A human being," Murphy observed, according to the N.Y. *Times* (March 22, 1937), "does not want to be an infinite sort of nothing in the face of mass production." To protect himself the worker had turned to a new type of labor organization, the CIO, which, unlike the craft-oriented AF of L, included all the workers of a given corporation and therefore presented a united front before management. Murphy rejected the interpretation that the new unions endorsed the Marxian concept of the class struggle: "No basis for classes exists in our land, and our people are not disposed to give that factor more than scant notice."[49] Instead, he held the conflict between employers and employees to be an acute manifestation of labor's long struggle to protect itself by receiving a larger share of its own product and to escape the fear of insecurity by consolidating itself in its job.[50]

For Murphy it would not have been only a tragedy but a moral lapse as well, had American democracy failed to adjust to the economic and social changes of the thirties. "It may well be true," the N.Y. *Times* (March 22, 1937) quoted him as saying, "that the leader in government, as well as in labor and industry, who does not recognize this need of harmonizing his views with the realities of the day and with the changing needs of our people, is spiritually a lost man, simply because he is . . . of a bygone day."

Traditionally, governors had had few qualms about calling out the National Guard to break strikes. In the years 1933-37 there were eighty-three instances throughout the United States in which the militia was called on to intervene in strikes or demonstrations. With few exceptions the guard had acted to aid employers against employees.[51] Murphy could have followed these precedents. He would have been justified: it was clearly illegal for strikers to seize the property of General Motors. But he had observed that force used in recent strikes had not been used by the authorities to obviate the situations—to permit social and economic change—but had been used only to suppress agitation.[52]

In the GM strike Murphy was convinced that the workers had

187

real grievances and only because they had been deprived of a peaceful recourse had they resorted to seizing their employer's property. Moreover, the use of force would have led to open warfare and bloodshed. When the Flint police tried to evict the strikers early in the GM strike, their action resulted in the wounding of fourteen men. Similarly, at a steel strike in Massillon, Ohio in the spring of 1937 police and deputies attacked a group of strikers, killing two of them and wounding others.[53] And in South Chicago on Memorial Day 1937 police killed ten strikers and wounded many more in a labor battle. Murphy's belief that civil war was imminent in Flint was not an exaggeration.

Thus he had decided not to meet the seizure of property with force. It had been impressed on him, he commented, "that government, in its essence, is a fragile and tenuous thing which is easily damaged. In its ideal form, it is never haughty and arrogant, for when it assumes those characteristics, it becomes a hateful thing, without real value and without a worthwhile cause."[54] Years after the General Motors sit-down Murphy confided to a friend how alone he had felt during the strike in trying to implement his philosophy that democracy operates only when men are willing to use reason and justice, not force, to arrive at decisions:

> I was impoverished of spirit. It seemed that all those who knew me had lost serenity of spirit. Not for a single moment did I harbor the thought of encouraging any lawlessness. Quite to the contrary, I carefully prepared an order . . . which demanded obedience to the courts' decisions. That order [the letter given to Lewis] . . . helped break the resistance and brought the General Motors strike to an end.
> . . . I had ambitions to weather the complicated question by what I conceived to be the American way, and the Christian way. . . . The rule of reason guided me. I wanted it held aloft. It was reason at the conference table I sought

Friday afternoon. Smith agreed, but, beyond his control, an associate went to Flint and asked for the writ. At 11:00 A.M. it reached Murphy. At the same time he received a wire from the sheriff requesting military assistance to enforce the court order. Murphy told the sheriff he believed a negotiated peace was imminent and suggested he postpone action until after the weekend.[30]

Talks continued Friday on the basis of a concession by Lewis, who reduced his demand for exclusive UAW bargaining rights for all sixty-nine GM plants to just those plants struck by the union. Although the number of struck plants by February had increased to seventeen, the three plants in Flint remained the pivotal ones throughout the GM-UAW struggle. Discussion turned to the possibility of limiting the period of exclusive bargaining rights. F.D.R. conferred with Lewis by phone and tried to persuade him to agree to a three-month period. Lewis refused to consider any less than six months. Since the UAW still represented only a minority of the workers, Lewis believed six months would solidify the union's position.[31]

However, from GM's point of view it was useless to discuss any period of exclusive bargaining, since the corporation had consistently rejected the principle of exclusive bargaining.[32] Making matters worse, the AF of L renewed its row with the CIO. William Green, AF of L president, telegraphed Murphy that "any agreement . . . which would give the United Automobile Workers Union sole labor representative authority in the automobile industry would be not only unjust and unwarranted, but the results would be a direct attack against the American Federation of Labor itself."[33] This stand by the AF of L strengthened the hand of the corporation. General Motors believed the recent court injunctions further bolstered its position.[34] The corporation taunted the UAW by suggesting a secret ballot to determine the propor-

and insisted upon. Always in similar situations—although there never had been one of such magnitude—men had reached for the gun. The idea of turning brother against brother, of releasing revolution in our homeland and making monuments of hate of our factories did not appeal to me. I don't blame those who disagreed with me. I understood their viewpoint but they did not understand mine, which was one of reason and Christianity and Americanism.[55]

Murphy did not foreswear the use of force altogether, for, as indicated above, he used the threat of it to break the strike. Rather, his point was that, when force is resorted to in a democracy, by default democracy has failed: "Better and more lasting results are often achieved by the application of moral pressure and emphasis on moral and spiritual values than by resort to physical force."[56]

When Murphy failed to announce the role force had played in the final settlement, he violated one of the canons of elected officials: to make public all their actions so that there will be no doubt as to where they stand on vital issues. But Murphy's reason for keeping it secret—to preserve his neutrality as a mediator— was convincing. Since he was called on many times after the General Motors strike to settle labor disputes, his caution was well advised. Although he did not make known his threat to Lewis until two years later, it was common knowledge that a zero hour had been fixed for labor, by which time either a settlement was to have been reached or the governor would have ordered the National Guard to evict the strikers.[57]

Similarly, when Murphy did not promptly enforce the court order in Flint in spite of the sit-down's obvious illegality, he risked giving the impression he condoned the sit-down. (In July 1937 the courts formally ruled the sit-downs illegal.)[58] He had often expressed sympathy for union grievances, thereby implying approval of the sit-down technique. But Murphy's position as governor made it impossible for him to rule on the legality of the sit-down; he properly left this issue to the courts. He limited himself to mediating the dispute which, under the circumstances, required a postponement in enforcing the court order.

Murphy could not ignore the question of law enforcement. When the court presented him with its writ of attachment, he faced a dilemma. The N.Y. *Times* (January 14, 1939) quoted him as saying: "I believe in vigorous law enforcement. However, when there is widespread disobedience to law, it is not enough to enforce the law; it is also necessary to discover and eliminate the cause of that widespread disobedience."

After the GM sit-down Murphy discussed this philosophical problem and defended his view that social change, guided by human reason, is a higher value than literal enforcement of law:

> The sit-down is not legal. But problems involving human equations so vast and complex as these which we are facing cannot be determined by exact justice. It has been in my mind from the first and I don't know anybody who can determine problems such as we have here by strict legalism. The author of life might do it or some one with divine powers, but no figure I know or have heard of with executive, legislative or judicial powers can work these problems out on lines of exact justice.
>
> It is the duty of all of us to preserve the integrity of the courts and to be obedient to authority. . . . But laws must be just and ample so that the great human movements don't start bursting through legal structures which do not meet their needs.[59]

The lack of recognized legal machinery for settling strikes further complicated Murphy's dilemma. Michigan's only labor statute outlawed all strikes, and GM and other corporations had defied the Wagner act by refusing to bargain collectively with unions. Only after the Supreme Court in April 1937 found the Wagner act constitutional did business abide by its provisions. Thus, Murphy had to devise ways and means of handling the sit-downs as he went along; in lieu of statutory authority, he, himself, had declared that the public must be supreme in the industrial conflict.

Some moderate men in the automotive industry accepted this viewpoint. A few, including the Fisher brothers and Walter Chrysler, were Murphy's personal friends. Not only did they respond to Murphy's cautionary words, but they were prepared to accept a change in the worker's position. They did not want strikers driven from the Flint plants at the price of bloodshed. The Ford company, they remembered, had yet to regain public respect after the deaths during the 1932 hunger march on Dearborn plants.

Two General Motors executives had a compelling reason for approving a moderate course. While touring the automobile shows in Europe in 1936, Lawrence P. Fisher and William Knudsen had had a long and sobering conversation with a French automobile manufacturer. His description of the sit-down strikes that had swept the French automobile industry earlier that year appalled them. Feeling had run high, and strikers had reviled and mistreated management. The French manufacturer himself had been locked in his office for several days. He predicted the sit-downs would soon come to the American automobile industry. In a matter of months they did.

With the help of this moderating spirit from within the corporation, plus pressure from Washington, Murphy succeeded in persuading General Motors to negotiate with the union despite the fact that he had not carried out the court evacuation order. This was the essence of the governor's strategy—to insist on continuing the negotiations.[60] Murphy regarded the negotiations as a trial of endurance in which the opponents would eventually be forced to compromise from sheer exhaustion if for no other reason. The governor knew he would surpass the representatives of labor and management in this endurance trial which the strike negotiations provided, for his training in self-discipline carried on since his youth had prepared him for it.[61]

Largely by personal will, Murphy obtained the settlement of February 11. He was certain his policy had not encouraged social disintegration but had prevented civil war and thereby improved the labor picture for the whole nation.

Many did not approve of Murphy's way of settling the sit-downs. They believed he had condoned lawlessness, and they pointed to events such as the Lansing holiday to prove their point. The Dies committee, which had struck at Murphy's handling of the Flint crisis, attacked his role in the holiday with equal vigor. In a summary of its findings the committee declared:

> Well-known Communists instigated and engineered the sit-down strike and the so-called Lansing holiday, when a mob of 15,000 people barricaded the State capitol and 2,000 of them, many of whom were armed with clubs, were ordered to march on the university and to bring part of it back with them. The evidence shows that the State police sat helplessly by for lack of instructions from the Governor in the face of open rebellion, while the Governor looked down upon the scene from a window in the Capitol. . . . If open and undisguised rebellion is to be countenanced in the name of political expediency, then constitutional democracy will perish in America.[62]

Other distinguished citizens, among them Norman Vincent Peale, joined those shocked Americans who attributed the Lansing holiday to the postponement of the court injunction at Flint. Peale deplored the fact that Murphy was not like other "he-men" governors who refused to capitulate to mob rule.[63]

The Lansing holiday was one of the worst incidents of the entire sit-down movement. It was deplorable, yet understandable, that labor believed it had to resort to such tactics; in 1937 industrial labor was not well-disciplined and had never held responsibility before. The auto workers, for example, were for the most part young, high-spirited men either from immigrant families or from the South.

Murphy's basic defense for his action in the General Motors strike was founded on an iffy argument—that if he had acted as his critics had wished, he believed the consequences would have been loss of life, destruction of democratic values, and the ruination of industrial progress. If Murphy's defense suffered from resting on an unproved assumption, the argument of his opponents rested on an equally unproved one—that as a result of Murphy's capitulation to labor at Flint, the sit-downs were proven effective and therefore became popular. When the Flint crisis is placed in chronological perspective, this assumption loses validity. The sit-downs of the 1930's actually began in 1936 in the rubber industry and by the end of 1937 had served their purpose. After the April 1937 Supreme Court decision upholding the Wagner act, strike activity steadily declined until the end of the year. The GM sit-down received widespread attention because of the size of the corporation, the bitterness engendered in the struggle, and the issue of recognition for the UAW as sole bargaining agent.

Murphy's way of handling the sit-downs had sacrified man hours of work and respect for the principle of rule by law; his critics' way would have upheld the law while sacrificing both lives and the principle of providing for social and economic change. As quoted by the N.Y. *Times* (April 19, 1937), Murphy observed: "It is important that our laws and political institutions keep steady pace with changes in the political and social economy of the country in order that government shall not lack power and means to deal with new conditions."

Ardent New Dealers defended Murphy's handling of the sit-downs; other distrusted his judgment. Like the New Deal itself, Murphy became controversial. When he was defeated for re-election in 1938, many interpreted this as a repudiation of his policies.

Murphy failed to communicate the convictions that determined his actions at Flint, and this misunderstanding by the public became a sore which afflicted him the rest of his life. He could never adequately explain to people conditioned to polarized argument that there were gradations involved in law enforcement when one tried to achieve justice. He wanted not everyone's approval but more understanding of the immense problem he had faced.

In the midst of the sit-down controversy his attention was called to a critic who termed his sit-down policy a "corruption of American ideals." Murphy took time to write his critic patiently:

> It isn't pleasant to know that a well-meaning citizen, like yourself, holds me in such low esteem because of an earnest effort I have made to advance industrial peace and to have the Government represent to the people something that is friendly and clean rather than something that is hateful and oppressive.
>
> I greatly fear that your opinion of me is likely to grow worse because with each day I am more determined than ever to do the kindly and right thing for big and little alike. Sowing the seeds of kindness in the vineyard of 1937 is not altogether an easy errand.[64]

After his unsuccessful bid for reelection as governor in November 1938, Frank Murphy's future plans were uncertain. Although he was a lawyer, he did not declare any intention to retire to private practice in the tradition of most defeated political candidates. Neither did he accept a position offered by an automobile company.[2] He undoubtedly secretly enjoyed the offer, in view of the recent sit-down crisis, but he had no desire to squander his energies in the business world. He divulged only his immediate intention of taking a vacation in the Philippines following his successor's inauguration.

Murphy avoided making any commitments, for he knew President Roosevelt was obligated to find him a place in the administration. Since his return from the Philippines, Murphy had served his chief well—both in state politics and in mediating the sit-down strikes. Not surprisingly—because Murphy's chances of reelection were poor—F.D.R. had begun to talk about finding a position for Murphy even before the Michigan voters went to the polls.[3]

The President's search ended when Attorney General Homer Cummings announced his retirement. The one difficulty was that F.D.R. had previously led Robert Jackson, the solicitor general, to believe he would succeed Cummings. To mollify Jackson the President informed all concerned that Murphy's appointment would be temporary. Before long, F.D.R. explained, he would transfer Murphy to the secretaryship of the War Department and thus leave the attorney general post open for Jackson. But this contemplated cabinet shuffle could not take place until Harry H. Woodring, then secretary of war, would agree to serve as minister to Canada and the assistant secretary of war had had a short spell as acting secretary.[4] This risky scheme, in which ambitious men would be pawns, could not but portend trouble.

Yet, for the moment, F.D.R.'s plan appeared feasible. Murphy cancelled his Philippine vacation and on January 2, 1939 took the oath of office as attorney general. The Bible used for the occasion was that given him by his mother when he graduated from grammar school. Many pages were loosened from constant use. In a news conference following the ceremony Murphy called attention to his favorite Biblical text, Isaiah 11:4: "But with righteousness shall he judge the poor, and reprove with equity for the meek of the earth."

The appointment was an interim one, pending Senate confirmation. The press foresaw difficulties in winning confirmation because Murphy symbolized the New Deal's alleged disregard for property rights. A recent report of the House Committee on Un-American Activities had attacked Murphy for his tolerance of the sit-downs. To publicize the Dies committee report, a member of the House carried into a chamber a suitcase and an orange crate, from which he produced clubs and other weapons that he said had been used by the strikers.

But this theatrical gesture did not typify the Senate proceedings. Much to the surprise of the press, the Senate judiciary subcommittee quickly approved Murphy's nomination without requesting a public hearing. Led by Vice-President James Garner, who had been impressed with Murphy's efforts in the Philippines, Senate conservatives quietly supported him.[5] Once again Murphy's attraction for conservatives was revealed. Murphy invariably convinced critical observers that, despite his New Deal political philosophy, he was dedicated and honest.

When the judiciary subcommittee announced its approval, Murphy created a stir by asking for a public hearing. "I want to be heard because I believe it is in the public interest that there shall be confidence in the Department of Justice . . .," the N.Y. *Times* (January 13, 1939) quoted him as saying. The hearing revealed Murphy's secret conference with Lewis during the closing days of the General Motors strike, when Murphy had threatened Lewis with forceful eviction of the strikers unless a settlement were reached. Letters of commendation from prominent men were read at the hearing, including one from Harry H. Bennett, the anti-union Ford executive. Murphy had requested the public hearing to offset criticism that he expected to arise during debate on the floor of the Senate. In this the hearing was successful. Only Senator Bridges of New Hampshire fought Murphy's confirmation with any energy. In the final vote on January 17, 1939 Murphy was confirmed with a mere seven votes in opposition. The N.Y. *Times,* which editorially had voiced reluctant acquiescence before, switched to enthusiastic approval for the new attorney general: "No one ever doubted his humanitarianism, and no one need doubt now his respect for law."[6]

The circumstances surrounding Murphy's appointment left little room for innovation in the Justice Department. In part this was because his appointment was temporary. Had Murphy's predecessor been incompetent, the situation would have been different; but Attorney General Cummings had served well, and his guidelines became Murphy's program. In a midyear report to the President, Murphy cited the instructions F.D.R. had given him on taking office. What was revealing was their failure to be exceptional:

On January 1, 1939, upon appointing me to the office of Attorney General of the United States, you directed me to endeavor in every possible way to continue the efforts of my predecessor, Homer S. Cummings, to strengthen the Department of Justice. You directed me to improve the federal judicial system and provide vigorous and honest law enforcement; to eliminate congestion in the court dockets; to guard against privilege and favoritism; to modernize and improve personnel practices wherever possible within the Department; and to effect such additional administrative measures as might be necessary and advisable. . . .[7]

But by temperament Murphy was a reformer. He brought to the attorney generalship great personal energy, a sense of duty, and a flair for publicity. Moreover, he headed the Justice Department at a time when national and international affairs were rapidly approaching crisis. On the domestic scene the political parties were unifying their ranks and jockeying for position in anticipation of the 1940 presidential election. In Europe and the Far East the first battles of World War II had been fought. These factors—the attorney general's temperament, domestic politics, and the World War—were to magnify and sometimes distort what Murphy was to undertake in 1939.

In reorganizing the Justice Department Murphy retained three key officials: Robert Jackson, solicitor general; Thurman W. Arnold, head of the antitrust division; and J. Edgar Hoover, FBI chief. However, he liberally appointed his own candidates to other posts.[8] Two personal friends and confidential advisers of long standing, Edward Kemp and Joseph Mulcahy, became special assistants to the attorney general.

Murphy brought William Brownrigg, his Michigan civil service director, to head a personnel program. With this appointment Murphy implemented within the Justice Department a presidential order of the previous year to broaden civil service within the federal government. Brownrigg's immediate task was to set up a program of personnel training and management.[9] By the end of the year Brownrigg had outlined his program, and Murphy issued a departmental order creating a division of personnel supervision and management with Brownrigg in charge.

Murphy also appointed several committees to study various legal problems; most important was the committee dealing with administrative law. Attorney General Cummings had called President Roosevelt's attention to the need for improving the procedures of administrative agencies in order to protect individual rights. Murphy pursued this matter. It was 1941 before the committee made its report; five years later the report became the foundation of the administrative procedure act.[10]

While the development of a personnel program and the appointment of study committees served future needs of the Justice Department and of the nation, events in 1939 demanded immediate action. In March Stephen Early, secretary to F.D.R., wrote Murphy urging him to accept a speaking invitation. This otherwise insignificant message ended with the revealing postscript: "You [will] speak from New York City where Mr. [Thomas E.] Dewey has been very active of late. This fact, too, has its advantages."[11] Dewey, then a young New York City district attorney, had won national attention by conducting a well-publicized campaign against crime. He hoped thereby to catapult himself into the 1940 Republican nomination for the presidency. The administration had no wish to let Dewey and the Republican party monopolize virtue; it commissioned the attorney general to direct a broad program for improved administration of justice and crime control.

F.D.R. had a special interest in parole programs, and in early January he asked Murphy to prepare a national parole conference to be held at the White House. "In view of the great to-do" over Tom Dewey, administration friends urged that F.D.R. himself address the conference.[12] The President readily agreed. The conference, which included prison and parole officials, judges, district attorneys, law enforcement officials, and interested private citizens, met at the White House on April 17 and 18. During the brief session the delegates attempted to reach agreement on standards and administrative procedures and on means to stimulate more cooperation between federal and state governments. However, the main purpose of the conference, as Murphy said in his keynote address, was "to sell the ideal of parole to the general public."[13]

Immediately following the parole conference the attorney general called a meeting of U.S. attorneys to promote closer coordination between the Washington staff and the attorneys in the field and to improve the efficiency of the latter.[14] Murphy had already directed U.S. attorneys to submit a thorough, explanatory report on all cases more than two years old. As a result of this twofold prodding the attorney general eliminated much deadwood from the dockets and hastened the final disposition of numerous cases.[15]

One of Murphy's favorite administrative techniques was to make dramatic inspection trips to the offices of the U.S. attorneys throughout the country. His first inspection trip to New York in January led to the resignation of Judge Martin T. Manton of the U.S. Court of Appeals. Murphy disclosed his own inquiry into Manton's affairs the day before Dewey made public his' charges against the judge. Not content with Manton's resignation, Murphy insisted on prosecution. Manton was indicted and found guilty of receiving funds from litigants whose cases he heard.[16] A few months later Murphy ordered the investigation of another federal judge's questionable activities, and he too resigned.

These exposures required a policy statement from Murphy as

to what he intended to do to correct the situation. In a major address to an Associated Press luncheon he pinpointed the weakness of the federal courts in their inefficiency and in their tendency to become embroiled in politics and patronage. The problem of efficiency, he reported, would be solved if Congress would pass an administration-sponsored bill providing for an administrative office for the U.S. courts. In August Congress complied.

Murphy believed the problems of politics and patronage in the federal courts were due largely to the way courts handled receiverships and bankruptcy proceedings. Under the existing fee system referees and receivers and their lawyers received a portion of the final settlement. Murphy suggested a salary basis to eliminate abuses encouraged by the fee system. He appointed a committee to investigate receivership and bankruptcy proceedings; eventually the committee's recommendations led to improvements in the administration of insolvent estates.[17]

Murphy helped to restore integrity to the courts by recommending able men to fill court vacancies. Beginning with his proposal of naming William O. Douglas to the Supreme Court, he consistently suggested men who were recognized for their legal ability; these judicial recommendations were also invariably politically sound. As a part of the administration's peace offering to conservative Democrats Murphy quietly sought recommendations from these congressmen. For example, to fill a judgeship vacancy he chose the dean of the University of Virginia Law School, Armistead M. Dobie, who was a lifetime friend of Senator Harry F. Byrd.

When Murphy turned from administration of justice and crime control to the narrow field of law enforcement, he acted with equal vigor. To improve efficiency in prosecuting commercial frauds, he created a new section in the criminal division devoted exclusively to this type of crime. The section's job was to supervise all prosecutions arising under the securities act of 1933 (as amended), the securities exchange act of 1934, the mail fraud statute, and the public utility holding act of 1935.[18]

Antitrust prosecution was emphasized. The decision to undertake an antitrust drive had been made a year earlier at which time the antitrust division had been doubled in size. Although the Justice Department had a tradition of antitrust prosecution going back to the Sherman act of 1890, the recession of 1937-38 provided the impetus for the current drive. The recession appeared to New Deal economists evidence of the closing of the American economic frontier; they no longer believed a sudden business turn would restore prosperity. However, they reasoned, if competition could be guaranteed through antitrust prosecutions, it might be possible to reduce prices, thereby increasing the standard of living of Americans.[19] This was not trust-busting in the tradition of Theodore Roosevelt, for the economists did not want to make little industries from big ones—they only wanted to abolish restraints in trade that were stifling competition.[20] The architect for this new antitrust policy was the division head, Thurman Arnold. Undoubtedly he had a hand in writing Murphy's statement summing up the intent of the administration:

> The antitrust laws were intended to achieve a constructive, not a destructive purpose. Their purpose is not to harass businessmen but to give businessmen the right to compete in a free field without favor and to give the consumers the benefit of orderly and healthy competition.[21]

During Murphy's tenure as attorney general the antitrust division undertook investigations in many industries; among them were motion pictures, oil, aluminum, news printing, milk, liquor, tobacco, signboard advertising, fish canning, and fertilizer.[22] The largest antitrust investigation in 1939 was of the building industry. Maintaining a free market was particularly difficult in this business; despite government subsidies and credit, and although building had doubled and there was no scarcity of goods or materials, prices had risen 25 percent since 1936. Building material producers conspired to keep prices up, and distributors established fixed markups or refused to supply firms other than their own. Because the conspiracy was nationwide, the antitrust division for the first time carried out a nationwide investigation. However, actual grand jury proceedings were limited to eleven cities; in these cities every restraint of trade that affected the building of a house was investigated. As a result of investigation alone—even before prosecution began—prices often dropped. In one large city lumber prices declined 18 percent and sand and gravel prices declined 22 percent.[23]

When the Justice Department began investigating labor unions for violating antitrust statutes, labor tried to halt the antitrust program. Murphy was castigated at an AF of L convention, and William Green came to the attorney general with a plea to go slow. Thurman Arnold insisted that shutdowns resulting from jurisdictional labor disputes were violations of antitrust laws. The issue finally centered on whether the government should indict "Big Bill" Hutcheson, president of the carpenters' union. Green contacted Murphy again, reminding him that the Clayton act specifically exempted labor and farm organizations from prosecution under the antitrust statutes. But Murphy refused to be pressured and let Arnold press the indictment of Hutcheson.[24] Ultimately the Supreme Court dismissed the indictment on the grounds that Congress had exempted trade unions from antitrust prosecution.

By 1940 the Justice Department had won a series of key cases empowering it to enforce antitrust laws.[25] Generally business cooperated with the department, once the department showed resolution, and it became common practice for the antitrust division to give consent decrees to industries permitting cooperation among them and granting them exemption from antitrust prosecution providing they adhered to the spirit of the antitrust laws.[26] With the coming of World War II the antitrust drive ended.

Even more popular than the antitrust drive was the Justice Department's investigation of organized crime—particularly that phase in which crime and politics were united. The first important prosecution resulted in the conviction of Tom Pendergast, Democratic boss of Kansas City, Missouri. Murphy himself flew to Kansas City the day the U.S. attorney presented the case to the grand jury.[27] More indictments followed in other cities and states; the most outstanding was that of the Long machine in Louisiana. By 1940 the Justice Department had successfully prosecuted thirteen Long supporters on mail fraud charges.[28]

Although the number of indictments was small, the Justice Department's drive against political-crime conspiracy appeared impressive due to Murphy's skill in achieving publicity. He constantly traveled throughout the country on departmental errands, and, wherever he went, he described to reporters the department's struggle against lawlessness. "We have mapped out plans for this national campaign," the N.Y. *Times* (May 30, 1939) quoted him as saying. "The purge is on. We know where we have to fight." In the summer of 1939 he revealed that forty-five agents were carrying out investigations in twenty-six cities and that grand juries would be called in eight or nine cities. Although this proved to be incorrect, at the time it made good newspaper copy. In a similarly enthusiastic moment Murphy told Ickes: "Harry Hopkins once said: 'We will tax and tax and spend and spend.' I will indict and indict and jail and jail."[29]

The campaign against crime even assumed a batting-average appearance when in July Murphy submitted a report to President

Roosevelt stating that the percentage of convictions or pleas of guilty during the past six months was 97.1. He commented that "while the percentage of convictions has always been high, it is doubtful that this figure has ever been surpassed."[30] A member of F.D.R.'s staff advised the President to plant a question at his next press conference permitting him to cite Murphy's 97.1 percent record. "This record," the aide pointed out, "contrasts beautifully with Mr. Dewey's recent figures in the seventies."[31] F.D.R. didn't follow the advice, but the incident reflects the competitive spirit that accompanied Murphy's term as attorney general.

As chief law enforcement officer, the attorney general had the major responsibility of maintaining the nation's internal security. By 1939 the nation's security clearly was in danger. In the years since 1935 Italy had invaded Ethiopia, civil war had broken out in Spain, Japan had invaded China, and Hitler had militarized the Rhineland and forced a union with Austria. Then in September 1938 Hitler had forced the Munich settlement on France and England. Most Americans would have preferred to ignore the import of these facts, but the administration had no choice but to anticipate possible United States involvement. In early 1938 the Federal Bureau of Investigation secretly began training its agents in techniques for uncovering espionage, sabotage, and subversive activities. Whereas in the five years prior to the fiscal year of 1938 there averaged only 35 espionage investigations a year, in 1938 there were 250 such cases, and in 1939 there were 1651. Only two espionage cases had been tried in court in the years since World War I; in 1939 there were four within the year.[32]

But, if the American people wished not to be aroused and the administration was content to prepare without panic for likely danger, Congress insisted on both preparation and panic. In the spring of 1938 the House created the Committee on Un-American

Activities under the chairmanship of Martin Dies. Dies made his own definition of what constituted un-American activity: any action he personally believed opposed the American system. His definition included the activities of Nazis and Communists who were in truth violating criminal laws, but it also included the activities of many liberal New Dealers, among them Frank Murphy. Harold Ickes, too, was suspect because he belonged to the American Civil Liberties Union.[33] Ickes understandably was sensitive about the committee and decided Dies was "smearing the Administration . . . with apparently deliberate intent."[34] This became the interpretation of the whole Roosevelt administration. Meanwhile, the committee rapidly achieved popularity with the electorate. In December 1938, 74 percent of voters who were polled favored a continuation of Dies committee investigations, and throughout 1939 the committee's popularity remained high.[35] Clearly Dies was effectively arousing the people but not necessarily to the same dangers the administration saw.

Against this background Murphy took charge of the nation's internal security program. In order to provide efficient and adequate protection he requested that all investigations involving espionage, counterespionage, and sabotage be centralized in the Federal Bureau of Investigation, the Office of Naval Intelligence, and the military intelligence division of the War Department— thereby eliminating the participation of the State Department, the Treasury, and the Post Office. President Roosevelt ordered Murphy's request be carried out. Murphy also desired that all intelligence data be pooled. Accordingly, F.D.R. urged all state and local law enforcement agencies to give their information concerning subversive activities to the FBI. In addition, the FBI was to supervise the protection of defense plants.[36]

When on September 1, 1939 Hitler invaded Poland, President Roosevelt issued a Proclamation of National Emergency to Enforce Neutrality under which he enlarged the military forces and authorized an additional 150 FBI agents. The Justice Department concurrently undertook studies of presidential war powers and a wartime economy. In December Murphy urged general finger-printing, especially in war plants. F.D.R. initiated the fingerprint-ing campaign by announcing that he himself had been finger-printed.[37]

As these various security measures were undertaken, Murphy made every effort to keep the public informed. He publicized his trips about the country with J. Edgar Hoover to check on sabotage and subversion. He also issued frequent press statements. "There will be no repetition of the situation in 1917 when a democracy was unprepared to meet the espionage problem," the N.Y. *Times* (September 1, 1939) quoted him as saying. He tried to explain why a free country must subject itself to security restrictions:

> There are well-meaning individuals who fear that by taking action to protect democracy against that kind of activity [espionage and subversion] we will in fact make inroads upon democracy.
>
> I recognize the sincerity of that position, but I do not believe it is based on a realistic view of the nature of democracy.
>
> I do not believe that loyalty to democratic ideals precludes a democratic nation from bracing itself against realities in a world where, for the moment at least, might is the test of survival.[38]

At times Murphy appeared to be in competition with Martin Dies. But, for every call to defend America, Murphy also made a plea for caution. As the N.Y. *Times* (October 1, 1939) reported, he told the National Police Academy: "We will not act on the basis of hysteria. We are just as anxious to protect the rights of our own citizens as to see that those who attack the United States do not go unwhipped of Justice." He had in mind the violations of civil liberties in the name of patriotism that had occurred during and after World War I.

One way to protect civil liberties, he believed, was to limit anti-espionage and anti-subversive work to the FBI and take it from the hands of amateurs and local law enforcement agencies who lacked training and discretion. The test of this policy came after President Roosevelt's emergency proclamation. The President's order inspired the formation of a number of citizens' committees appointed by sheriffs and local officials whose idea of cooperating with the Justice Department was to spy on their fellow citizens. Murphy repudiated these committees and refused to recognize them; having no support, they dissolved.[39]

But closing down the citizens' committees ended only one anxiety in the huge problem of maintaining civil liberties. Murphy realized violations could occur in infinite ways. He revealed his concern by the frequency and eloquence with which he spoke on civil rights. His basic theme was that a democracy must protect simultaneously the individual rights of the citizen and the country from its enemies. "Let us prove for all time," he said, "that ours is a two-fold strength—the physical strength of self-defense and the moral strength of unflinching devotion to our ideals."[40] He proposed observing Oliver Wendell Holmes's dictum of a "free trade in ideas." "Simply stated," Murphy said, "that concept means that a democracy gives a hearing to every idea." But to defend itself a democracy can and should use the "criminal laws that protect us against violence and the incitement to violence."[41] Murphy was convinced existing laws were sufficient and proposed no new ones for fear any new legislation would be too restrictive.

By exposing American citizens to the "free trade in ideas" doctrine, Murphy hoped to rally public opinion to the defense of free speech and other civil liberties. Only when citizens became aware of the threat to their liberties did Murphy believe they would defend them. Until then the government should intervene on behalf of the citizens:

> Public opinion crystallizes slowly, and in times like this when there is so much that is confusing and misleading, the process is abnormally slow. And until public opinion *does* reach the point where it will not tolerate violation of civil liberties, there can and will be such violation—*unless government takes a hand and refuses to permit it.*
>
> In a sense, the part that government can play is purely negative. But it would be a serious mistake to conclude that it is therefore of little significance. Let government play its part vigorously, and with a clear responsibility, and it is bound to be a powerful bulwark of civil liberty, not only as an agency that imposes penalties but as an influence on public thinking.[42]

In assigning to government this additional responsibility, Murphy acted consistently with his view that government should intervene to protect the individual. Always before he had advocated intervention in the economy; now he extended the obligations of government into the sensitive area of ideas. Yet, as he said, it was negative governmental intervention he advocated; therefore he avoided endangering freedom under the guise of protecting it.

To implement this policy Murphy created a civil liberties unit in the criminal division of the Justice Department. Its task was to protect the liberties of citizens in instances of law violations in race relations, labor practices, and the exercise of religious beliefs, as well as in national security matters. Intolerance aroused by fear of depression as well as by fear of war had prompted Murphy to establish the civil liberties unit.[43] Murphy may also have had the Dies committee in mind when he established the unit. F.D.R. had wanted the Senate to appoint a committee to review the actions of the Dies committee.[44] This had not been done. Although the civil liberties unit could hardly undertake this review, it could call the attention of the nation to the value of civil liberties, which at that very moment the House committee chose to undermine.

Murphy encouraged considerable fanfare about the civil liberties unit, but what the unit could actually do was quite circumscribed. There were few civil rights statutes; most of those passed during Reconstruction had since been declared unconstitutional by the Supreme Court. The chief remaining laws were Sections 51 and 52 of title 18 of the U.S. Code, and these required criminal, rather than civil, proceedings. Criminal proceedings were cumbersome and unsatisfactory. Nearly always the complaint was not popular in the community, and the penalties prescribed for violators of Section 51 were so harsh that juries hesitated to see them imposed. As a result Murphy did not undertake new prosecutions under civil rights laws although he did continue a few cases initiated by his predecessor.[45] However, the Justice Department did recommend prosecutions under the Hatch act, which was passed in 1939 and was designed to prevent harmful political activities and to restrict campaign efforts of rank-and-file federal employees.[46]

Although the civil liberties unit could not prosecute effectively, it did quietly influence state and local governments to find solutions to civil rights violations. Also, the mere existence of the unit served an important function. Before its creation the Justice Department had received few complaints of violations of civil liberties; after its establishment the large amount of mail on this subject indicated a growing civil rights consciousness. In the fiscal year 1940, eight thousand complaints came to the department;

most cited violations of civil liberties in which there was no federal jurisdiction. Nonetheless, the Justice Department suggested possible remedies to the plaintiffs.[47] Despit severe limitations, the civil liberties unit provided leadership and some action at a time when citizens needed to have their faith in liberties renewed. The unit thereby won the commendation of the American Civil Liberties Union.[48] The civil liberties unit set a precedent for government initiative in the protection of individual rights. Such had not been evident since Reconstruction.

In the realm of national security and civil liberties Murphy's efforts were complicated by the investigations of Dies and his Committee on Un-American Activities. Dies's attacks on the administration's alleged leftist tendencies had too much popular support to be ignored, especially with an election approaching. In an effort to counteract Dies's influence President Roosevelt spoke out against the committee's methods and purposes. He also asked congressmen to moderate the effect of the committee. After Congress voted to continue the Dies committee for 1939, the President told committee members John J. Dempsey and Jerry Voorhis that he was counting on them "to preserve civil liberties on the Dies Committee." They replied in the affirmative.[49] Likewise, F.D.R. acted to maintain the La Follette Civil Liberties Committee in the Senate. Considerable pressure—much of it originating with Dies—mounted for discontinuing the La Follette committee.[50] To counter this, F.D.R. wrote Senators Robert La Follette, Jr. and Lewis B. Schwellenbach of his "off the record" concern.[51] Later, when the Civil Liberties Committee was fighting for more funds, F.D.R. wrote Senator James Byrnes:

> I hope much you will go through with the Schwellenbach-Thomas-La Follette request for more money for the Civil Liberties Committee. From the point of view of the preserva-

tion of civil liberties, I recommend it strongly—and from
the point of view of good politics, I recommend it equally
strongly.

Can I make a stronger statement to you?[52]

President Roosevelt had decided to pursue the Dies committee's
findings to determine their validity. A few days after he appointed Murphy attorney general, the President told him to have
the FBI investigate the organizations Dies was attacking. Shortly
thereafter F.D.R. announced his decision at a news conference
and said that investigations of "alleged violation of criminal
statutes" by Nazis, Communists, and other organizations were
underway.[53] This initiated a series of prosecutions that eventually
reflected unfavorably on Murphy.

No more was heard about the investigations until the fall of
1939. In September the Committee on Un-American Activities
won an admission from Earl Browder, secretary of the Communist party, that he had traveled in Europe with a fraudulent
passport. Representative J. Parnell Thomas seized on this and
issued a statement on behalf of the Republican National Committee, charging—as quoted by the N.Y. *Times* (October 23,
1939)—that while the attorney general was "enthusiastically and
tirelessly swooping by airplane all over the country in pursuit of
lesser violators of the law," he was "strangely indifferent and list-
less in the case of Browder." The Justice Department countered
that it had already prepared Browder's case.

Dies, a Texas Democrat, chided Thomas for the partisanship of
his attack on Murphy; then Dies himself accused the administration of laxity and demanded that the Justice and State Departments move immediately to prosecute Communists and Nazi Bund
organizations for failing to register as foreign agents, as required
by law. If the two departments did not act, he threatened to place
the cases before a district attorney for prompt action. Murphy

quickly responded with an offer to assign a special staff of Justice Department attorneys to work on the issues raised by the committee.[54]

Somewhat pacified on the Communist and Bund investigations, Dies turned his attention to the American League for Peace and Democracy. Believing the league was communistic and wishing to expose its followers, Dies gave newspapers its membership list for Washington, D.C. He thereby blackened the reputation of innocent people. At the same time he roused the ire of President Roosevelt; at a news conference F.D.R. referred to the matter as a vile procedure.[55]

Dies next formally asked that Murphy prosecute the league for alleged violation of the statute requiring registration of foreign agents. Murphy refused, though he said he would have the evidence examined, and wrote the committee a dispassionate letter explaining his decision. He reminded the committee the Justice Department had to prove every factor of the alleged offense beyond a reasonable doubt for prosecution to be successful. This, he believed, was not possible in this case. He then spoke of his duty to uphold the rights of free citizens:

> In the performance of its duty to enforce compliance with the laws and prosecute any violation thereof, it is the obligation and responsibility of the department to safeguard and protect the rights of citizens as well. At the cost of whatever inconvenience and annoyance to individual citizens and government officials, the fundamental rights and privileges of free assembly, free opinion, and free speech as guaranteed by Federal and State Constitutions must be respected and observed.[56]

Dies had pressured the attorney general for action, but Murphy was resolved not to prosecute an organization because of its professed ideas. Some in the administration were apprehensive that Murphy would not be able to avoid this, for any prosecution of subversives risked blurring the distinction between subversive acts which threatened the nation, and subversive ideas which the Constitution protects because they are not in themselves dangerous.

Murphy soon announced his strategy. At a cabinet meeting in December he revealed that he was ready to call a federal grand jury in Washington to hear a number of espionage and subversion cases prepared by the Justice Department. Ickes feared the grand jury investigation would start a Red-hunt. Murphy's intent, however, was not to start, but to stop, the Red-hunt of the Committee on Un-American Activities—this was aside from his official concern as attorney general to prosecute known law violators. He hoped that a grand jury sitting in Washington and taking evidence would steal the headlines from the Dies committee. Accordingly, when Congress met in January, there would be no necessity for continuing the Dies committee, which by then would have exhausted its appropriation and could be allowed to expire by limitation of law.[57]

Murphy went ahead—with Ickes reluctantly concurring—and called the federal grand jury into session. The jury indicted two businesses and several persons of alleged Communist connections for failure to register as agents of foreign powers. Meanwhile, Browder and two other Communists were convicted for passport frauds. The attorney general tried to avoid giving a Red-hunt image to the Justice Department prosecutions; simultaneously with the Communist prosecutions, he warned Americans of the anti-Semitic virus and indicated that purveyors of religious hate would be prosecuted by the government even as Communists were.[58] In Brooklyn a few weeks later the FBI apprehended seventeen members of the anti-Semitic Christian Front.

In the midst of the Justice Department's roundup of subversives, President Roosevelt named Murphy to the Supreme Court. Justice Pierce Butler, a Roman Catholic, had died in November 1939, leaving a vacancy. Since the attorney general was an ardent New Dealer and a Catholic, the President's announcement of Murphy's appointment on January 4, 1940 evoked no surprise. At the same time F.D.R. moved up Solicitor General Jackson to the attorney general's post.

With the announcement of the new appointments the previously suppressed rivalry between Murphy and Jackson broke into the open. At the time of Murphy's appointment as attorney general in 1939 Jackson had felt slighted that he had not been chosen to succeed Cummings. The situation was made worse by F.D.R.'s scheme to ease Woodring out of the cabinet, thereby making room for Murphy as secretary of war and for Jackson as attorney general. The newspapers had soon learned of the plan, reducing the chances for its success to zero. Woodring adamantly refused to give up the War Department, and the President felt he couldn't force Woodring because of the latter's anticipated control over the Kansas delegation to the Democratic convention in 1940.[59]

By the fall of 1939 both Murphy's and Jackson's morale was low. Murphy believed he had completed his revitalization job in the Justice Department, and he was impatient to move to the War Department. He eventually expressed the opinion that someone ought to tell F.D.R. what a mess the situation was.[60] By the time the death of Justice Butler provided F.D.R. with an honorable solution in Murphy's appointment to the high court, the followers of both Murphy and Jackson were overly ready to promote the ambitions and defend the pride of their benefactors. The fact that both men were frequently discussed as possible presidential and/or vice-presidential candidates in 1940 intensified the rivalry.[61]

215

Shortly before the new appointments were announced, Jackson had discussed his impending job with F.D.R. and expressed dissatisfaction with Murphy's performance in several matters. He singled out Murphy's drive on subversives for special criticism. Jackson cited a December 28 press conference in which the attorney general had declared that the department would prosecute subversives through income tax, passport, and foreign agent laws. Jackson told F.D.R. the government would be greatly handicapped in court should its prosecutions for income tax or statutory offenses be suspected of being efforts to punish opinions and attitudes; this would be a direct violation of free speech. He asserted that he would not continue this policy. F.D.R. dismissed Jackson's concern with a laugh, and Jackson felt a little "contemptible and cowardly" for having complained to the President.[62]

Murphy sensed what Jackson would do if he inherited any of Murphy's cases. Consequently, after being named to the Supreme Court, he called a news conference and said he planned to remain a month or so to complete his work in the Justice Department. Jackson rightly interpreted this to mean Murphy feared that he, Jackson, would drop cases that Murphy believed should be prosecuted.[63]

Later, a newspaper story, (perhaps leaked by Murphy), stated that Murphy was being kicked upstairs because he was unwilling to make deals with big political organizations that would assure F.D.R. a third term.[64] Murphy had indictments pending against Democrats Mayor Edward Kelly of Chicago and Hudson County boss Frank Hague and was, in fact, only waiting for a presidential go-ahead, which never came. Because "they" (the President's office) would not let him prosecute these corrupt politicians, Murphy felt he was being eased out.[65] The furor this raised in the administration necessitated a denial by Murphy. In a press conference he then denied that proceedings against Kelly or

Hague were being suppressed and claimed that the department wasn't prosecuting because there was no evidence of violation of federal laws. But the denial itself indicated the first account might be true and reflected on Jackson by intimating that Jackson's appointment was a part of the plot to suppress the indictments. This angered Jackson's supporters even more.

To stop the rumors and mounting antagonism President Roosevelt quickly had Murphy and Jackson sworn into their new offices. Tempers did not die; instead, what Arthur Krock, in a N.Y. *Times* article (March 26, 1940), called a "smear" in the best tradition of intra-administration rivalry was directed against Murphy. The attacks against him were often without specifications. He was accused of being a poor administrator, of seeing Reds in honest radicals, of lacking ability, and even of being a homosexual. The fomenters of the smear, Krock reported, were Jackson's supporters and also J. Edgar Hoover's critics who counted on the animosity between Murphy and Jackson to effect Hoover's removal from office.

The specific action arousing the anti-Hooverites was the arrest, ordered by Murphy, of sixteen Loyalists in Detroit for recruiting Americans to fight in the Spanish Civil War. The arrests occurred after Jackson became attorney general, but he was unaware of Murphy's order. The Dies committee had cited such recruitment as a law violation against which the Justice Department should press indictments. Undoubtedly it was for this reason that Murphy had ordered the arrests. Since there was considerable public sympathy for the Loyalist cause, Murphy's attackers felt they could successfully smear his decision in this case. For his part, Jackson disapproved of prosecuting the Loyalists because so many nationalities were recruiting Americans for foreign armies that it would have led to endless prosecutions. Accordingly, he dismissed the indictment.[66]

A further question of violation of civil liberties in the Loyalist case caused Murphy even more embarrassment. The FBI zealously had carried out its duties. Its agents had raided the homes of suspects at an early morning hour, held the accused incommunicado for nine hours, and denied them prompt access to counsel.[67] The American Civil Liberties Union felt the FBI had used "indefensible methods of arrest and detention."[68] Public opinion was aroused, and Jackson held an investigation. However, in this part of the affair, Jackson publicly backed the FBI and its chief.[69] Opponents of J. Edgar Hoover discovered they had been mistaken in hoping Jackson might fire the head of the FBI.

Although Jackson did undo Murphy's decision in the Loyalist case, as attorney general he made few other changes in departmental policy. For the most part he retained Murphy's personnel, and he proceeded with the indictment against Christian Front members.[70]

In writing about the smear that accompanied his appointment to the Supreme Court, Murphy said his attempt to defend Hoover had precipitated the slander:

> There will always be "smears" during election years. . . .
> Appointed a Supreme Court Justice I had the best press of
> any man in the land. For the first time a record vote was not
> asked on confirmation in the Senate. Two weeks later I was
> something of a cross between a mountebank and a bum.
> What had happened in the fourteen days interlude? There
> was no official act complained of. I was the same man. But
> here was my sin or error: —knowing they were going to
> decapitate Hoover . . . I undertook on my last act of office
> to defend him. That was an apostasy of some sort. It ruined
> the plans of a little group of terrorists. They are not an
> entirely bad lot: they have a mistaken notion of their tough-
> ness. The discharge of Hoover would have been bad for the

country and a serious injury to the President and I undertook to prevent it.[71]

Murphy also mentioned "other reasons" for the slander in his letter but did not identify them. This is unfortunate, for the conflicting ambitions of Murphy and Jackson—two able and energetic men—must have played a part in this affair.

Murphy had left the attorney generalship in the midst of unsettled debate, and inevitably the impression was that he had betrayed the cause of civil liberties—the very cause he had tried valiantly to advance. Unquestionably he had succumbed to Dies committee pressure in instituting the drive against subversives, and he had failed to oppose the heavy-handed methods employed by FBI agents in carrying out the drive. But the most serious criticism leveled against him—that his indictments were designed to punish not overt deeds, but ideas—cannot be substantiated. In its investigation of Murphy's anti-subversive prosecutions the American Civil Liberties Union found no proof for this assertion. However, it did find that several arrests ordered by Murphy had been accompanied by violations of civil liberties.[72]

Murphy's hope had been to convince the public that subversion and espionage could be coped with adequately under existing laws. Murphy feared that Dies committee hysteria might lead to legislation that would infringe upon individual freedoms. He believed it better to demonstrate that prosecution could be conducted under existing laws—even if his showpiece cases did not always involve dangerous enemies—and to forestall excessive restrictions on civil liberties. The civil liberties record of Americans was far better in World War II than in the first World War, with the tragic exception of the Japanese containment camps. To claim this better record was due to Murphy's actions

219

alone would be a mistake. But undoubtedly his effort to convince Americans that they could have both security and freedom had influence. Where Murphy failed was in not crowning this policy with complete success.

While Murphy desired the honor of being an associate justice, he did not look forward to the political isolation this entailed. Ickes observed that Murphy looked and acted unhappy at the swearing-in ceremony.[73] Murphy's consolation was that F.D.R. had promised to return him to the cabinet, probably as secretary of war.

On February 5, 1940 the new justice took his seat. Within a matter of weeks the Nazi army overran Denmark, Norway, Holland, and Belgium. By June, Hitler's forces were deep into France. For Murphy to observe this and not be able to wrestle with the gigantic problems of statecraft was almost cruel. In the past he had thrived on controversy and crisis; now, at the peak of his powers, he was chained to a reflective and scholarly life. Certainly the time had already come for President Roosevelt to call him back into the cabinet, but Murphy received no word. When the summer court recess came, Murphy could no longer contain his impatience and wrote F.D.R.: "It has been my hope that you would go forward with your original plans for me." He put no pressure on his chief, assuring the President that he had no obligation to perform: "You must be free in judgment. You have always done me more than justice. You owe me naught. I am your debtor."[74]

For political reasons President Roosevelt selected, on June 20, 1940, the Republican Henry L. Stimson as his new secretary of war. In the winter of 1940-41 another possibility opened for Murphy. The President asked him about going to the Philippines or Mexico on a diplomatic mission, but nothing came of these suggestions.[75] Then, in summer of 1942, Murphy made one last effort to free himself from the court. Perhaps to prepare himself for appointment as secretary of war, or perhaps simply to catch the President's attention, he joined the army reserves during the court recess and attended the Infantry Officers Training School at Fort Benning, Georgia. He wrote to F.D.R. describing his summer plans and assuring him of his availability: "I did want you to know my plans, to leave my best wishes for your personal safety and welfare and to tell you that if you need me at any time, I can get back to Washington in three or four hours."[76] However, Murphy had long since been cut off from President Roosevelt by men of greater influence, and the President did not seek the justice's services. Frank Murphy's political career had ended.

Notes

Citations of correspondence, unless otherwise noted, refer to letters and are indicated, for example, as: Frank Murphy to Joseph R. Hayden, (followed by the date and source).

Abbreviations:

BIA	Bureau of Insular Affairs, War Department, National Archives, Record Group 350, Washington, D.C. (Where the Record Group number changes, this is noted.)
DJCC	*City of Detroit, Journal of the Common Council*
DN	*Detroit News*
DSN	*Detroit Saturday Night*
DT	*Detroit Times*
EKP	Edward G. Kemp Papers, Michigan Historical Collections of the University of Michigan, Ann Arbor.
FDRL	Franklin D. Roosevelt Library, Hyde Park, N.Y. Citations referring to material in the Roosevelt Library are abbreviated as: OF Official Files PPF President's Personal Files PSF President's Secretary Files
FMP	Frank Murphy Papers, Michigan Historical Collections of the University of Michigan, Ann Arbor.

JRH   Joseph R. Hayden Papers, Michigan Historical Collections of the University of Michigan, Ann Arbor.

MOR   Mayor's Office Records, Burton Historical Collection, Detroit Public Library.

NYT   *New York Times*

Notes to Introduction

1. Frank Murphy, "The Moral Law in Government," *The Commonweal*, XVIII (May 19, 1933), 64. Reprinted by permission of *The Commonweal*.

2. Arthur B. Moehlman to Murphy, July 21, 1948, Arthur B. Moehlman Papers, Michigan Historical Collections of the University of Michigan.

3. Harold L. Ickes, *The Secret Diary of Harold L. Ickes* (3 vols.; New York: Simon and Schuster, Inc., 1953), III, 228.

4. Norman H. Hill to author, March 21, 1964.

5. Charles A. Fecher, *The Philosophy of Jacques Maritain* (Westminster, Md.: Newman Press, 1953), pp. 204-8.

6. Frank Murphy, "The Return of Religion," commencement address, St. Joseph's College, Philadelphia, June 13, 1939, FMP.

7. Ickes, III, 110.

8. Frank Murphy, "The Right Use of Democracy," address at the Second National Catholic Social Action Conference, Cleveland, June 14, 1939, FMP.

9. Murphy to Grace Tulley, secretary to Franklin D. Roosevelt, (cited hereafter as F.D.R.), February 11, 1942, FDRL, PPF 1662.

10. Murphy to Chase S. Osborn, February 22, 1936, Chase S. Osborn Papers, Michigan Historical Collections of the University of Michigan. Cited hereafter as Osborn Papers.

11. Frank Murphy, *Selected Addresses of Frank Murphy, Governor of Michigan—January 1, 1937 to September 30, 1938* (Lansing, 1938), p. 67.

Notes to Chapter I

1. Ickes, II, 181, 372.
2. J. Weldon Jones to author, January 25, 1963.
3. "Address to the Society of the Friendly Sons of St. Patrick in New York City," March 17, 1933, MOR 1933.
4. "A Message from the Mayor to Students of Northern Night School," February 25, 1932, Speeches, FMP.
5. Murphy's speeches and correspondence are full of this expression. For example: untitled radio speech, August 8, 1932, p. 9, MOR 1932.
6. Jones to author, January 25, 1963.
7. "Address to Society of Friendly Sons . . . ," March 17, 1933, MOR 1933.
8. Governor Woodbridge N. Ferris to Murphy, November 1, 1920, Murphy's birthplace, Harbor Beach, Mich.
9. Murphy to *DT,* April 4, 1923.
10. Clarence Darrow, *The Story of My Life* (New York: Charles Scribner's Sons, 1932), p. 306.
11. Irving Stone, *Clarence Darrow for the Defense: a Biography* (Garden City, N. Y.: Doubleday and Co., Inc., 1943), p. 483.
12. *DSN,* December 6, 1930.
13. *DSN,* May 23, 1931.
14. Undated report of Mayor's Unemployment Committee, MOR 1932.
15. Elliott Roosevelt (ed.), *F.D.R., His Personal Letters 1928-1945* (4 vols.; New York: Duell, Sloan and Pearce, 1950), III, 144.
16. *DSN,* November 8, 1930.
17. *DJCC,* March 10, 1931 (Detroit: Inland Press, 1932), II, 466.
18. *DJCC,* January 12, 1932, p. 2.
19. Assistant secretary to J. R. Nix, July 12, 1932, and Joseph F. Majeske to John T. Taylor, January 6, 1932, MOR 1932.

20. *DT,* December 28, 1930; Dr. Frank D. Adams to Senator James Couzens, October 13, 1932, and Murphy to Father Hickey, November 2, 1932, MOR 1932.

21. Roy E. Duquette to John F. Ballenger, May 3, 1932, and assistant secretary to Nix, July 12, 1932, MOR 1932.

22. Murphy to Willard W. Stone, February 23, 1933, MOR 1933; Adams to Couzens, October 13, 1932, MOR 1932; mimeographed itinerary of thrift garden tour, June 29, 1932, pp. 1-4, MOR 1932; Oral History Interview of Josephine Gomon, University of Michigan and Wayne State University Institute of Labor and Industrial Relations, 1959, p. 11, Michigan Historical Collections of the University of Michigan. Cited hereafter as Oral History Interview.

23. Irene Murphy to Frank Murphy, April 23, 1931, Speeches, FMP.

24. Hill to Murphy, February 8, 1932; assistant secretary to Nix, July 12, 1932; assistant secretary to managing editor, *Detroit Mirror,* March 22, 1932; and Henry A. Johnson, secretary, Detroit Thrift Gardens, to committee member, June 22, 1932, MOR 1932.

25. Secretary to Harry Bennett, February 18, 1932, and assistant secretary to Mrs. Boyd, October 6, 1932, MOR 1932.

26. *DN,* June 13 and June 14, 1931; preliminary report on investigation of the Department of Public Welfare, Touche, Niven and Co., public accountants, July 10, 1931, MOR 1931.

27. *DN,* January 11, 1933; Joseph R. Hayden to John A. Hackett, May 17, 1933, Correspondence, (Box XVIII), JRH.

28. *DSN,* May 28, 1932.

29. *DN,* October 1 and November 7, 1930; Mauritz A. Hallgren, "Detroit's Liberal Mayor," *The Nation,* CXXXII (May 3, 1931), 527; William A. Haber to Adams, November 2, 1932, and assistant secretary to Mr. Hollinshead, June 27, 1932, MOR 1932.

30. *DN,* September 26, 1930.

31. Hallgren, *The Nation,* CXXXII, 527; undated report of Mayor's Unemployment Committee, MOR 1932.

32. Murphy to Mrs. Alfred G. Wilson, October 2, 1931, MOR 1931.

33. Harry Barnard, *Independent Man: The Life of Senator James Couzens* (New York: Charles Scribner's Sons, 1958), p. 203.

34. Adams to Couzens, October 13, 1932, MOR 1932.

35. Edward G. Kemp, "Frank Murphy as a Government Administrator," (MS prepared for use at memorial proceedings held by the bar of the U.S. Supreme Court, March 6, 1951, in honor of Frank Murphy), sec. I, p. 1, EKP.

36. *DJCC,* January 13, 1931, I, 1.

37. Hallgren, *The Nation,* CXXXII, 527; *DSN,* December 28, 1930 and February 21, 1931.

38. Kemp MS, sec. I, p. 1, EKP.

39. *DN,* January 11, 1931; Hayden to Hackett, May 17, 1935, JRH; *DJCC,* January 12, 1932, p. 8; *DT,* November 15, 1930.

40. Oral History Interview of Josephine Gomon, p. 16.

41. *DSN,* January 3, 1931.

42. J. B. Matthews to Murphy, March 2, 1932, and Murphy to Matthews, March 8, 1932, MOR 1932.

43. Vivian Pierce to Murphy, March 31, 1932, and Murphy to Pierce, April 1, 1932, MOR 1932.

44. Untitled, undated radio speech, MOR 1933.

45. Murphy to Mr. Taylor, May 25, 1932, MOR 1932.

46. Roy Wilkins to Murphy, June 24, 1932, MOR 1932.

47. Ballenger to Murphy, January 13, 1932, MOR 1932.

48. Murphy to J. Frank Kilroy, M.D., April 21, 1932, MOR 1932.

49. R. L. Bradby to Murphy, April 6, 1932, MOR 1932.

50. Murphy to Adams, October 25, 1932, MOR 1932.

51. *DT,* October 24, 1930 and July 6, 1931; J. Wilson to Murphy, December 5, 1931, MOR 1931.
52. *DT,* April 19, 1931.
53. Murphy to William H. Chaney, August 28, 1931, MOR 1931.

Notes to Chapter II

1. "Final Campaign Address," November 2, 1931, pp. 8, 9, Speeches, *FMP.*
2. Murphy to Frank X. Martel, November 11, 1931, MOR 1931; *DSN,* May 30, 1931.
3. Collection of printed handbills; Hill to radio station WJBK, October 4, 1931 and to J. C. Talley, September 23, 1931, Frank Murphy Papers, Burton Historical Collection, Detroit Public Library. Cited hereafter as Murphy, Burton Coll.
4. Assistant Secretary to Mrs. Etta S. Wilson, September 15, 1931; memo, September 19, 1931; V. M. Lugonja to Murphy, October 23, 1931, Murphy, Burton Coll.
5. Lee A. Fordon to John T. Taylor, October 13, 1931, Murphy, Burton Coll.
6. Hayden to James R. Fugate, April 8, 1933, JRH.
7. *DT,* October 6, 1931; *DN,* September 30 and October 20, 1931.
8. *DT,* October 27, 1931.
9. *DT,* October 30, 1931.
10. Memo: "Tax Delinquency Last Four Years," November 28, 1932, MOR 1932.
11. *NYT,* December 31, 1931, and January 6, 1932; Secretary to editor, Voice of the People column, *Detroit Free Press,* January 26, 1932, and untitled, undated statement, MOR 1932.
12. Henry F. Vaughan to Murphy, February 5, 1932, MOR 1932.
13. Radio talk by C. C. McGill, February 14, 1932, MOR 1932.
14. *NYT,* February 5 and February 7, 1932.

15. *DN,* December 13, 1931.

16. Undated memorandum for department heads' meeting; Murphy to Billy Drummond, March 23, 1932; secretary to editor, Voice of the People column, *Detroit Free Press,* January 26, 1932; Executive Order Number 29, from mayor to all department heads, February 16, 1932, MOR 1932.

17. G. Hall Roosevelt to Murphy, September 1, 1932, MOR 1932.

18. Telegrams: Paul C. Smith to Murphy, March 28, 1932, and Murphy to E. F. Dustan, March 28, 1932, MOR 1932.

19. G. Hall Roosevelt to Common Council, April 13, 1932, MOR 1932.

20. Guy A. Durgan to Murphy, August 8, 1932; Kathryne Donnelly to Josephine Gomon, March 19, 1932; assistant secretary to Mabel Kienecke, June 21, 1932, MOR 1932.

21. Assistant secretary to Mrs. Annie L. Byant, May 2, 1932, MOR 1932.

22. Statement by Charles Novak in *The Proceedings and Transactions of a Conference of the Mayors and other Municipal Executives of the Cities of the State of Michigan, Held at the Invitation and in the Office of Honorable Frank Murphy, Mayor of the City of Detroit,* May 18, 1932, p. 36, MOR 1932. Cited hereafter as *Proceedings, Mich. Mayors' Conference.*

23. The Mayor's Office Records are filled with job requests. Quoted is Joseph D'Angelo to Murphy, July 11, 1932, MOR 1932.

24. Good Friday Proclamation, MOR 1932.

25. John Atkinson to Murphy, November 28, 1932; William G. Woolfolk to Common Council, July 1, 1932; Clarence E. Wilcox to Murphy, November 29, 1932, MOR 1932.

26. Murphy to Brucker, March 12, 1932, MOR 1932.

27. Untitled, undated press release on statement by Ralph Stone, MOR 1932.

28. *Ibid.*

29. Phelps Newberry to Murphy, September 24, 1932, and Murphy to Newberry, September 28, 1932, MOR 1932.

30. Murphy to H. Wirt Newkirk, May 14, 1932, and Murphy to Darwin J. Meserole, June 2, 1932, MOR 1932. Hearst's proposal involved 1) the federal government lending $5,000,000,000 to the unemployed, who would then spend it and thereby revive the economy, and 2) reducing the work day to six hours to spread employment among more workers.

31. *Proceedings, Mich. Mayor's Conference,* p. 4.

32. *Ibid.,* p. 48.

33. *Ibid.,* p. 48.

34. Correspondence with the men involved, MOR 1932.

35. *Proceedings, Conference of Mayors of the United States Held at Detroit,* June 1, 1932, pp. 108, 111, 116, 118, MOR 1932.

36. Copy of resolutions adopted by mayor's conference June 1, 1932, MOR 1932.

37. *Proceedings, Conference of Mayors . . . ,* pp. 133, 134, MOR 1932.

38. Frank Freidel, *America in the Twentieth Century* (New York: Alfred A. Knopf, 1960), p. 289.

39. Stone to Common Council, May 20, 1932, MOR 1932.

40. G. Hall Roosevelt to Murphy, September 1, 1932, MOR 1932.

41. Radio talk by McGill, July 13, 1932, MOR 1932; *NYT,* September 4, 1932.

42. Murphy to George E. Miller, June 30, 1932, MOR 1932.

43. Radio talk by McGill, July 13, 1932, MOR 1932.

44. *NYT,* July 21, 1932.

45. Unidentified newspaper article by James Sweinhart, MOR 1932.

46. *Ibid.*; Hill to Sherman Brown, October 13, 1932, MOR 1932.

47. Article by Sweinhart, MOR 1932.

48. Handout, MOR 1932.

49. *Ibid.*
50. Hill to Brown, October 13, 1932, MOR 1932.
51. Committee on City Finances to voters of Detroit, July 29, 1932, MOR 1932.
52. Stone to Murphy, July 20, 1932, MOR 1932.
53. Handouts, MOR 1932.
54. Untitled radio address, August 8, 1932, MOR 1932.
55. Undated handout by the Communist party, District 7, Detroit, MOR 1932.
56. Statement by Roger Baldwin, March 12, 1932; James K. Watkins to Murphy, March 9, and March 16, 1932, MOR 1932.
57. *Ibid.*
58. *Ibid.*; Murphy to Baldwin, March 18, 1932, MOR 1932.
59. Untitled, undated probable press release, MOR 1932.
60. Handbill, "Protest Against the Bloody Ford Massacre at the Arena Gardens," March 11, 1932, MOR 1932.
61. Baldwin to Murphy, March 30, and May 3, 1932; Watkins to Murphy, April 13, 1932, MOR 1932.
62. Murphy to Baldwin, April 5, 1932, MOR 1932.
63. Baldwin to Murphy, March 30, 1932, and Murphy to Dr. E. T. Olson, May 11, 1932, MOR 1932.
64. Bessie Bavly and Ethal Polinsky to Murphy, April 10, 1932, MOR 1932.
65. Murphy to Baldwin, June 24, 1932, and Baldwin to Murphy, June 27, 1932, MOR 1932.
66. Jack R. C. Cann to Murphy, June 11, 1932, MOR 1932.
67. G. O. Ohlsson to Murphy, March 18, 1932, MOR 1932.
68. Murphy to Baldwin, June 24, 1932, MOR 1932.
69. Baldwin to Murphy, June 27, 1932, MOR 1932.
70. Telegram: Murphy to Ludwell Denny, July 29, 1932, MOR 1932.
71. Durgan to Murphy, June 27, 1932, MOR 1932.

72. Report of Auditors of Wayne County, February 29, 1932, pp. 2-3; Report on Investigation of Detroit Welfare Department by the Citizens Committee, July 26, 1932, [unnumbered], MOR 1932.

73. Assistant secretary to Mrs. Marie Friedrich, September 21, 1932, MOR 1932.

74. Comment by Ballenger on the Report of Auditors, March 1, 1932, MOR 1932.

75. The following discussion is entirely from the Report on Investigation of Detroit Welfare Department by the Citizen's Committee, July 26, 1932, MOR 1932.

76. G. Hall Roosevelt to George Bailey, October 18, 1932, MOR 1932.

77. *DN,* September 22, 1932.

78. Assistant secretary to Nix, July 12, 1932; Report . . . by Citizen's Committee, July 26, 1932, MOR 1932.

79. Murphy to Brucker, December 7, 1932, and Brucker to Murphy, December 14, 1932, MOR 1932.

80. Ruth D. Roth, "Nightmare in February" (Master's thesis, Wayne State University, Detroit, 1956), pp. 61-62; untitled, undated probable press release, MOR 1933.

81. G. V. Branch to Murphy, March 10, 1933, MOR 1933.

82. Murphy to Homer Cummings, April 19, 1933, MOR 1933; "A Mayor's Interpretation of the Encyclical of Leo XIII Forty Years After," November 20, 1932, MOR 1932.

83. Untitled, undated radio address, MOR 1933.

84. Murphy to Cummings, April 19, 1933, MOR 1933.

85. Roth, pp. 61-62.

86. Joseph Brown, article in *Detroit Leader,* February 18, 1933, Joe Brown Collection, Labor History Archives, Wayne State University. Cited hereafter as Joe Brown Coll.

87. Joseph Brown, article in St. Louis County *Independent,* Hinning, Minnesota, March 17, 1933, Joe Brown Coll.

88. Samuel Romer, article in *Leader,* March 4, 1933, Joe Brown Coll.

89. William M. Walder to Murphy, March 30, 1933, MOR 1933.

90. Mrs. Dorothy H. Parker to Murphy, March 28, 1933, and Murphy to Parker, March 31, 1933, MOR 1933.

91. "Address to Society of Friendly Sons. . . . ," March 17, 1933, MOR 1933.

92. *DT,* March 5, 1931.

93. *DN,* July 4, 1931 and January 7, 1932; *NYT,* February 18, 1933.

94. Murphy to M. V. MacKinnon, May 3, 1932, MOR 1932; *Daily Mining Journal,* October 22, 1932.

95. Murphy to O. C. Davis, June 17, 1932, MOR 1932.

96. Murphy to F.D.R., October 21, 1931, MOR 1931.

97. Roosevelt, III, 259.

98. *DT,* June 24, 1932.

99. *DT,* September 23, 1932.

100. Murphy to Louis Howe, October 28, 1932, Democratic National Committee Correspondence 1928-33, Michigan Before Election, (Box 289), FDRL.

101. Barnard, p. 208.

102. George Murphy to Howe, October 19, 1932, Democratic National Committee Correspondence 1928-33, Michigan Before Election, (Box 289), FDRL.

103. Telegram: Murphy to F.D.R., November 9, 1932, Private Correspondence, 1928-32, (Box 124, Group 12—Murphy), FDRL.

Notes to Chapter III

1. G. Hall Roosevelt to F.D.R., April 7, 1933, FDRL, PPF 285.

2. Raymond Moley, *After Seven Years* (New York: Harper & Bros., 1939), p. 124.

3. Forbes to F.D.R., April 10, 1933, FDRL, OF 400.

4. Hayden to John A. Hackett, May 17, 1933, JRH.

5. James R. Fugate to Hayden, April 22, 1933, JRH.

6. Duke (not identified) to Hayden, October 9, 1933, JRH.

7. For the following background material, I have depended on Joseph Ralston Hayden, *The Philippines, a Study in National Development* (New York: Macmillan Co., 1942), and Robert Aura Smith, *Philippine Freedom, 1946-1958* (New York: Columbia University Press, 1958).

8. Reverend Frank Mosher, Episcopal bishop of the Philippine Islands, to Hayden, November 4, 1933, JRH.

9. Hayden to William H. Hobbs, January 29, 1935, JRH.

10. Hayden to Jones, July 21, 1936, JRH.

11. Hill to Martel and Green, November 10, 1933, FMP.

12. Frederic S. Marquardt, *Before Bataan and After; A Personalized History of Our Philippine Experiment* (New York: Bobbs-Merrill Co., 1943), p. 169.

13. Manuel Luis Quezon, *The Good Fight* (New York: D. Appleton-Century Co., 1946), pp. 149-50.

14. Smith, p. 33.

15. *Ibid.,* p. 75.

16. Mosher to Hayden, November 4, 1933, JRH.

17. Duke to Hayden, September 29, 1933, JRH.

18. Hayden to Jesse S. Reeves, February 9, 1934, JRH.

19. Murphy to F.D.R., November 28, 1934, Personnel File, Frank Murphy, BIA. Cited hereafter as Personnel File, BIA.

20. Hayden to Herbert Lyons, January 16, 1934, JRH.

21. Veto message of Governor-General Murphy, December 1, 1934, on Senate Bill No. 4, Veto Messages of Frank Murphy, (Box XIX), JRH.

22. Murphy to Howe, May 14, 1934, FDRL, OF 400.

23. With the exception of one citation, the material for the next seven paragraphs was drawn from Hayden, *The Philippines . . . ,* chap. xxvi. As vice-governor, Hayden directed Murphy's welfare program.

24. *NYT,* August 4, 1935; Jones to author, January 25, 1963.

25. Smith, p. 65.

26. *Manila Daily Bulletin,* January 31, 1934; Marquardt, p. 174.

27. Marquardt, p. 178.

28. *Manila Daily Bulletin,* January 31, 1934.

29. *Manila Tribune,* August 8, 1935; Smith, p. 27.

30. Smith, pp. 25-26.

31. *Ibid.,* p. 26.

32. Hayden, pp. 12-13; George A. Malcolm, *The Commonwealth of the Philippines* (New York: D. Appleton-Century Co., 1936), p. 44.

33. Hayden, p. 13.

34. Hayden to Harry J. Hayden, October 30, 1934, JRH.

35. Hayden to Fugate, May 12, 1933, JRH.

36. Everett D. Hester, American trade commissioner, to Hayden, July 1, 1933, JRH.

37. Hayden to Reeves, February 9, 1934, JRH.

38. *Manila Tribune,* February 22, 1934.

39. *Ibid.*

40. *NYT,* October 29, 1933.

41. *NYT,* February 22, 1934; *Manila Daily Bulletin,* March 5, 1934.

42. *Manila Tribune,* February 22, 1934.

43. Hayden to Harry J. Hayden, October 30, 1934, JRH.

44. Murphy to Hayden, March 16, 1936, JRH.

45. Murphy to Hayden, December 5, 1935, JRH.

46. Draft of letter by Secretary of War George H. Dern for F.D.R.'s signature to Senator Quezon, January 30, 1934, FDRL, OF 400.

47. Copy of text of Murphy's address to the Philippine legislature, April 30, 1934, FDRL, OF 400.

48. Smith, p. 80.

49. Smith, pp. 86-88; Hayden, p. 44.

50. Marquardt, p. 177.

51. Murphy to Hayden, March 16, 1936, JRH.

52. For the discussion of the *Sakdal* uprising I have depended on Hayden, *The Philippines* . . . , chap xv. Hayden was acting governor-general during the uprising.

53. Hayden to Reeves, June 14, 1934, JRH.

54. For the discussion of the presidential election and its aftermath, leading up to the commonwealth inauguration, I have depended largely on Hayden, *The Philippines* . . . , chap. xvii.

55. Murphy to Howe, July 18, 1933, and F.D.R. to Murphy, August 25, 1933, FDRL, OF 400.

56. Murphy to F.D.R., November 28, 1934, and memorandum: F.D.R. to Secretary of War, December 28, 1934, Personnel File, BIA.

57. Press Conference 187, March 1, 1935, Press Conferences of the President, V, 141, FDRL.

58. Hayden, pp. 789-93.

59. Radiogram: Murphy to War Department, March 13, 1934, as quoted in letter from Dern to F.D.R., March 14, 1934, FDRL, OF 400.

60. F.D.R. to Senator Pat Harrison, March 24, 1934, FDRL, OF 400.

61. Memorandum: Creed F. Cox, chief of Bureau of Insular Affairs, to secretary of war as attached to a letter from Dern to F.D.R., March 23, 1934, FDRL, OF 400.

62. Radiogram: Murphy to secretary of war for F.D.R., June 1, 1936, and memorandum: F.D.R. for MAC, June 4, 1936, FDRL, OF 400.

63. Smith, p. 227.

64. Cordell Hull to F.D.R., April 6, 1935, FDRL, OF 400.

65. Murphy to Hull, May 23, 1936, FDRL, OF 400.

66. Hayden, p. 793.

67. Smith, pp. 127-28, 189-90.

68. Cablegram: Murphy to chief of Bureau of Insular Affairs, May 21, 1934, FDRL, OF 400.

69. Murphy to F.D.R., November 28, 1934, Personnel File, BIA.

70. Acting Secretary of War Woodring to F.D.R., March 22, 1935, FDRL, OF 400.

71. Memorandum, March 18, 1935, Visit of Governor-General Murphy 1935, Conversations as Revealed in Memoranda, Record Group 126, BIA. Cited hereafter as Visit 1935, BIA.

72. Cablegram: Murphy to secretary of war, September 23, 1935, Instructions to High Commissioner, BIA. Cited hereafter as Instructions, BIA.

73. Memorandum: Cox for secretary of war, November 4, 1935, Instructions, BIA.

74. Roosevelt, III, 507.

75. MacArthur to F.D.R., September 26, 1935, U.S. High Commissioner to the Philippine Islands, BIA. Cited hereafter as High Commissioner, BIA.

76. McDonald, War Department aide, to Cox, September 23, 1935, Instructions, BIA.

77. Memorandum: Quezon to governor-general, November 2, 1935, High Commissioner, BIA.

78. Radiogram: Dern to F.D.R., November 9, 1935, and F.D.R. to secretary of war, November 9, 1935, FDRL, OF 400.

79. *NYT,* December 1, 1935.

80. Murphy to Hayden, December 11, 1935, JRH.

81. Memorandum for chief, Bureau of Insular Affairs, December 24,

1935, Instructions, BIA; secretary of war to Murphy, January 21, 1936, High Commissioner, BIA.

82. Jones to author, January 25, 1963.

83. Murphy to F.D.R., December 16, 1935, FDRL, OF 400.

84. Hayden to Murphy, March 12, 1936, JRH.

85. *Ibid.*

86. Murphy to Osborn, February 4, 1936, Osborn Papers.

87. *La Vanguardia,* December 21, 1933. (Translation of editorial from Clippings, Personnel File, BIA.)

88. *DN,* January 20, 1936; radiogram: Marguerite Teahan to George Murphy, August 19, 1935, Personnel File, BIA; Jones to author, January 25, 1963.

89. Hayden to Gustavus Pope, August 2, 1935, JRH; Jones to author, January 25, 1963.

90. Murphy to Hayden, March 16, 1936, JRH.

91. Murphy to Hayden, May 9, 1940, JRH.

92. Hayden to Murphy, May 17, 1939, JRH; Murphy to chief, Bureau of Insular Affairs, January 10, 1939, Personnel File, BIA; Ickes, III, 12.

93. Ickes, III, 590; Murphy to F.D.R., April 10, 1942, FDRL, PSF (Box 36).

Notes to Chapter IV

1. Roosevelt, III, 427.

2. Louis B. Ward, *Father Charles E. Coughlin: an Authorized Biography* (Detroit: Tower Publications, Inc., 1933), p. 70; Charles E. Coughlin, *Eight Lectures on Labor, Capital, and Justice* (Royal Oak, Mich.: Radio League of the Little Flower, 1932), p. 66.

3. Richard D. Lunt, "Agitators: Long, Townsend, and Coughlin Versus the New Deal—1932 through 1936" (Master's thesis, University of New Mexico, 1959), pp. 99, 106-7.

4. *Ibid.,* p. 116.

5. Murphy to Margaret LeHand, secretary to F.D.R., May 1
FDRL, OF 400.

6. *DT,* May 12, 1935. This clipping was attached to Murph
to LeHand, cited above.

7. Patrick H. O'Brien to F.D.R., January 26, 1935, FDRL, (

8. *DT,* March 30 and April 3, 1935.

9. Memorandum, Washington, February 21, 1936, FDRL, Ol

10. Hayden to Jones, May 25, 1936, JRH.

11. James Farley to F.D.R., September 26, 1935, with
memoranda on polls taken by Emil Hurja, FDRL, PS
29); detailed breakdown of Hurja poll, FDRL, PPF 869

12. Memorandum, March 18, 1935, Visit 1935, BIA; James
Jim Farley's Story: The Roosevelt Years (New York: N
Hill Book Co., 1948), p. 52.

13. Hayden to Jones, July 21, 1936, JRH.

14. Osborn to LeHand, November 30, 1936, Osborn Papers

15. Hayden to Jones, July 21, 1936.

16. Murphy to F.D.R., March 3, 1936, FDRL, PPF 1662.

17. *DN,* June 23, 1936.

18. Radiogram: Adelaide Williams to Murphy, February 1(
Personnel File, BIA.

19. Murphy to Hayden, October 2, 1936, JRH.

20. Barnard, p. 307; *NYT,* May 22 and August 10, 1936.

21. *DN,* September 16, 1936.

22. Shields to Farley, July 21, 1936, FDRL, OF 300.

23. *DN,* July 31, 1936.

24. Murphy to Hayden, September 1, 1936, JRH.

25. Barnard, p. 314.

26. Martin R. Bradley to Farley, December 23, 1938, FDRL, OF 300.

27. Lunt, pp. 118-28.

28. Murphy to Marvin H. McIntyre, with results of poll attached, September 11, 1936, FDRL, OF 300.

29. Draper Allen to Farley, October 8, 1936, FDRL, OF 300.

30. Lunt, p. 140.

31. Sheehy to LeHand, October 5, 1936, FDRL, PPF 3960.

32. Frank Picard to Farley, September 17, 1936, FDRL, OF 300; Hayden to Jones, July 21, 1936, JRH.

33. Carl M. Weideman to Farley, October 5, 1936, FDRL, OF 300.

34. *DN,* October 24, 1936; Mrs. Howell Van Auken to Farley, October 26, 1936, FDRL, OF 300.

35. Van Auken to Farley, October 26, 1936, and Murphy to McIntyre, September 11, 1936, FDRL, OF 300.

36. George A. Schroeder to Farley, October 22, 1936, FDRL, OF 300.

37. *DN,* October 7, and October 13, 1936.

38. *DN,* November 4, 1936.

39. Barnard, pp. 320-23.

40. Hayden to Jones, November 6, 1936, JRH.

41. Lunt, p. 136.

42. John C. Cahalan to Farley, October 28, 1936, FDRL, OF 300.

43. Murphy to Hayden, November 20, 1936, JRH.

44. *Journal of the House of Representatives of the State of Michigan,* 1939, (Lansing: Franklin DeKleine Co., 1939), I, 49.

45. State of Michigan, *Report of the State Welfare Department of the State of Michigan* (Lansing, 1938), p. 13; Charles E. Misner to Farley, January 6, 1939, FDRL, OF 300.

46. *NYT,* July 30, 1937.

47. Arthur E. Buck, *The Reorganization of State Governments in*

the United States (New York: Columbia University Press, 1938), p. 134; *DN*, August 1, 1937.

48. *NYT*, July 31, and August 1, 1937.

49. Sec. III, p. 3, EKP; *Journal . . . House of Representatives . . .*, 1939, I, 43, 45.

50. *DT*, January 7, 1940; *DN*, November 11, 1937; *Journal . . . House of Representatives . . .*, 1939, I, 47.

51. *DN*, June 6, 1938.

52. Sec. III, p. 4, EKP.

53. *Journal . . . House of Representatives . . .*, 1939, I, 56; *DN*, October 18, 1938.

54. *NYT*, January 21, 1938; *DN*, January 14, 1938; Murphy to Farley, December 7, 1938, FDRL, OF 300.

55. Murphy to Hopkins, April 20, 1938, FDRL, Group 24.

56. *DN*, January 2, 1938.

57. Murphy, *Selected Addresses of Frank Murphy . . .*, p. 3.

58. *Ibid.*, pp. 89-92.

59. *NYT*, November 13 and 14, 1938.

60. *DT*, August 29, 1937; *NYT*, April 2, 1938; Ickes, II, 181.

61. Murphy to Hayden, July 29, 1938, JRH.

62. Brown to F.D.R., June 6, 1938, FDRL, OF 300.

63. Judge Malcolm Hatfield to F.D.R., June 4, 1937, FDRL, OF 300.

64. *DN*, July 31, 1938; Prentiss Brown to F.D.R., June 6, 1938, FDRL, OF 300.

65. *DN*, July 24, 1938.

66. George Marble to Farley, December 16, 1938, FDRL, OF 300.

67. H. O. Clines to Farley, December 12, 1938, FDRL, OF 300; *DN*, October 18, 1938.

68. Picard to Farley, October 31, 1938, FDRL, OF 300; *NYT*, October 21, 1938.

69. McIntyre to Murphy, June 30, 1938, FDRL, OF 200-DDD; *NYT,* September 3, and November 5, 1938.

70. F.D.R. to Murphy, October 18, 1938, FDRL, OF 725.

71. Ickes, II, 482.

72. August Raymond Ogden, *The Dies Committee; a Study of the Special House Committee for the Investigation of Un-American Activities 1938-1943* (Washington: Catholic University of America Press, 1943), pp. 77-78.

73. *NYT,* October 21, 1938.

74. John C. Lehr to Farley, October 31, 1938, FDRL, OF 300.

75. *DN,* November 3, 1938.

76. *NYT,* January 23, 1940.

77. Rudolph G. Tenerowicz to Farley, October 25, 1938, FDRL, OF 300.

78. John D. Dingell, Sr. to Farley, October 26, 1937, FDRL, OF 300.

79. Osborn to Murphy, October 29, 1938, Osborn Papers; *NYT,* October 31, 1938; Shields to Farley, October 28, 1938, FDRL, OF 300.

80. Ogden, p. 152; Farley, p. 149.

81. Farley, p. 149.

82. *NYT,* January 18, 1939; Hatfield to Laurence Wood Robert, Jr., secretary, Democratic National Committee, November 26, 1938, FDRL, OF 300; *DN,* December 25, 1938.

83. *DN,* December 25, 1938.

84. Murphy to Farley, December 7, 1938, FDRL, OF 300.

85. Francis McDonald to Farley, December 21, 1938, FDRL, OF 300.

86. Harry H. Mead to Farley, December 24, 1938, FDRL, OF 300.

87. Gerald J. Cleary to Farley, November 19, 1938, and McDonald to Farley, December 21, 1938, FDRL, OF 300.

88. Marble to Farley, December 16, 1938, FDRL, OF 300.

89. Shields to Farley, October 28, 1938, FDRL, OF 300.

90. Murphy to Farley, December 7, 1938, FDRL, OF 300.

91. Clines to Farley, December 12, 1938, FDRL, OF 300.

92. William J. Delaney to Farley, December 15, 1938, FDRL, OF 300.

93. Hatfield to Robert, Jr., November 26, 1938, FDRL, OF 300.

94. *Journal . . . House of Representatives . . .,* 1939, I, 40-60.

95. State of Michigan, Commission of Reform and Modernization of Government, *A Report of a Preliminary Survey* (Lansing, 1938), p. 12.

96. Murphy to Hayden, June 21, 1938, JRH.

97. George N. Fuller, *Michigan, A Centennial History of the State and Its People* (5 vols.; Chicago: Lewis Publishing Co., 1939), I, 461.

Notes to Chapter V

1. Edward Levinson, *Labor on the March* (New York: University Books, Inc., 1956), p. 179; Joel Seidman, *"Sit-Down"* (New York: League for Industrial Democracy, 1937), p. 9. Reprinted by permission of University Books, Inc. and League for Industrial Democracy.

2. Saul Alinsky, *John L. Lewis: an Unauthorized Biography* (New York: G. P. Putnam's Sons, 1949), pp. 94-95.

3. *Ibid.* p. 90; Seidman, pp. 13, 18; Levinson, p. 146.

4. Alinsky, p. 112.

5. Levinson, p. 150; Oral History Interview of Arthur Case, p. 16.

6. Alfred P. Sloan, Jr., *The Story of the General Motors Strike* (New York: General Motors Corp., 1937), p. 5.

7. Seidman, p. 21.

8. *Ibid.*; Levinson, p. 153; Oral History Interview of Wyndham Mortimer, p. 27.

9. Alinsky, p. 90.

10. *Ibid.*, pp. 116-17.

11. Sloan, p. 6.

12. Press Conference 335, January 8, 1937, Press Conferences of the President, IX, 41, FDRL.

13. Alinsky, p. 119.

14. Levinson, pp. 155-57.

15. Frances Perkins, *The Roosevelt I Knew* (New York: Viking Press, 1946), p. 322.

16. Sloan, p. 7.

17. Alinsky, pp. 124-25.

18. Press Conference 339, January 26, 1937, Press Conferences of the President, IX, 107, FDRL; *NYT*, January 31, 1937.

19. William Weinstone, *The Great Sit-Down Strike* (New York: Workers Library Publishers, Inc., 1937), p. 36.

20. Levinson, pp. 161-63.

21. Seidman, p. 33.

22. *Ibid.*, p. 37.

23. *Ibid.*, p. 39. Reprinted by permission of League for Industrial Democracy.

24. Levinson, pp. 164-65. Reprinted by permission of University Books, Inc.

25. *Ibid.*, p. 164-66.

26. Perkins, p. 323.

27. Sloan, p. 8.

28. Alinsky, p. 136; Union News Service (CIO), Washington, D. C., January 25, 1937, Joe Brown Coll.

29. Sloan, p. 8.

30. U.S. Congress, Senate Sub-Committee of the Committee on the

Judiciary, *Hearing, Nomination of Frank Murphy to Be Attorney General of the United States,* 76th Cong., 1st sess., 1939, p. 9. Cited hereafter as Senate, *Hearing, Nomination . . . Murphy . . .,* 1939.

31. Alinsky, pp. 134, 138.

32. Unsigned memorandum for F.D.R., following telephone conversation with Murphy, February 8, 1937, FDRL, OF 407-B.

33. Telegram: Green, J. W. Williams, and John P. Frey to Murphy, February 6, 1937, FDRL, OF 407-B.

34. Unsigned memorandum . . ., February 8, 1937, FDRL, OF 407-B.

35. Memorandum by Stephen Early, February 4, 1937, FDRL, OF 407-B.

36. Unsigned memorandum . . ., February 8, 1937, FDRL, OF 407-B.

37. *Ibid.*

38. Memorandum: Daniel C. Roper to McIntyre, February 10, 1937, FDRL, OF 407-B.

39. Senate, *Hearing, Nomination . . . Murphy . . .,* 1939, p. 11.

40. Sec. III, p. 8, EKP.

41. Sloan, p. 11.

42. *Detroit Free Press,* October 30, 1938.

43. Levinson, p. 272.

44. U.S. Senate, Committee on Education and Labor, *Report, Violations of Free Speech and Rights of Labor,* 76th Cong., 1st sess., 1939, pp. 150-54.

45. Sec. III, p. 11, EKP.

46. Levinson, pp. 169, 236.

47. Arthur Krock, article in *NYT,* March 21, 1937.

48. *NYT,* February 12, 1937.

49. Murphy, *Selected Addresses . . .,* p. 12.

50. *NYT,* June 10, 1937.

51. Walter Wilson and Albert Deutsch, *Call Out the Militia! A Survey of the Use of Troops in Strikes* (New York: American Civil Liberties Union, 1938), pp. 9, 10.

52. *NYT,* January 14, 1937.

53. Wilson and Deutsch, p. 14.

54. Frank Murphy, "Industrial Peace," *The Christian Front,* II (November, 1937), 158.

55. Murphy to Osborn, June 13, 1944, Osborn Papers.

56. Murphy, "Industrial Peace," *The Christian Front,* II, 157.

57. *NYT,* February 10, 1937 and January 6, 1939; Krock in *NYT,* March 21, 1937.

58. Levinson, p. 184.

59. *NYT,* March 26, 1937.

60. F.D.R. to Osborn, October 25, 1938, FDRL, PPF 2680.

61. Irene Murphy to author, March 10, 1961.

62. U.S. Congress, House, Special Committee to Investigate Un-American Activities and Propaganda, *Hearings,* 75th Cong., 3rd sess., 1938, Vol. 3, 2019-20.

63. *NYT,* June 14, 1937.

64. Murphy to F. J. Thieme, Jr., June 14, 1937, JRH.

Notes to Chapter VI

1. Joseph Alsop and Robert Kintner, "Frank the Just," *NYT,* May 28, 1939.

2. *DT,* January 7, 1940.

3. Farley, p. 126.

4. Ickes, II, 536.

5. *NYT,* December 30, 1938, January 2, and January 11, 1939.

6. *NYT,* January 2 and January 18, 1939.

7. Murphy to F.D.R., July 7, 1939, FDRL, OF 2111.

8. Eugene C. Gerhart, *America's Advocate, Robert H. Jackson* (Indianapolis: Bobbs-Merrill Co., 1958), p. 170.

9. *Annual Report of the Attorney General of the United States for the Fiscal Year Ended June 30, 1939* (Washington: U.S. Government Printing Office, 1939), p. 10. Cited hereafter as *Annual Report . . . Attorney General, 1939.*

10. Murphy to F.D.R., July 7, 1939, FDRL, OF 2111; Leonard D. White, *Introduction to the Study of Public Administration* (New York: Macmillan Co., 1955), pp. 519, 520.

11. Early to Murphy, March 4, 1939, FDRL, OF 10.

12. Ernest K. Lindley to Early, March 14, 1939, FDRL, OF 3563.

13. "Keynote Address, National Parole Conference," April 17, 1939, FMP.

14. Frank Murphy, "Closing Remarks at the Attorney General's Conference of United States Attorneys," April 21, 1939, FMP.

15. Murphy to F.D.R., July 7, 1939, FDRL, OF 2111; *Annual Report . . . Attorney General, 1939,* p. 3.

16. Gerhart, p. 172.

17. Frank Murphy, "The Federal Courts," address to Associated Press, April 24, 1939, FMP; U.S. Supreme Court, *Resolutions,* March 6, 1951.

18. *Annual Report . . . Attorney General, 1939,* p. 59.

19. Thurman W. Arnold, *The Bottlenecks of Business* (New York: Reynal and Hitchcock, 1940), pp. 275-87.

20. *Annual Report . . . Attorney General, 1939,* p. 44.

21. *Ibid.,* p. 36.

22. *Ibid.,* p. 158.

23. Arnold, pp. 44, 196-97.

24. Thurman W. Arnold, "Mr. Justice Murphy," *Harvard Law Review,* LXIII (December, 1949), 292.

25. Arnold, *The Bottlenecks* . . ., pp. 189-90.

26. *Annual Report . . . Attorney General, 1939,* p. 41.

27. Gerhart, p. 170.

28. *Annual Report of the Attorney General of the United States for the Fiscal Year Ended June 30, 1940* (Washington: U.S. Government Printing Office, 1940), p. 85. Cited hereafter as *Annual Report . . . Attorney General, 1940.*

29. Ickes, II, 685.

30. Murphy to F.D.R., July 7, 1939, FDRL, OF 2111.

31. Unsigned memorandum, July 18, 1939, FDRL, OF 2111.

32. *Annual Report . . . Attorney General, 1939,* pp. 61, 153.

33. Ogden, pp. 98-99.

34. Ickes, II, 573.

35. Ogden, p. 101.

36. Murphy to F.D.R., June 17, 1939, and Murphy to F.D.R., September 6, 1939, FDRL, OF 10-B; *Annual Report . . . Attorney General, 1940,* p. 13.

37. Gerhart, p. 182; Ickes, III, 77.

38. *NYT,* September 26, 1939.

39. *In the Shadow of War; the Story of Civil Liberty 1939-1940* (New York: American Civil Liberties Union, 1940), p. 16.

40. Frank Murphy, *In Defense of Democracy* (3rd ed.; Washington, D.C.: American Council on Public Affairs, 1940), p. 7.

41. "Civil Liberties and the Cities," address before the Joint Meeting of the United States Conference of Mayors and the National Institute of Municipal Law Officers, New York City, May 15, 1939, FMP.

42. *Ibid.*

43. Frank Murphy, "The Meaning of Civil Liberty," commencement address at John Marshall College, Jersey City, N.J., June 21, 1939, FMP.

44. Ickes, II, 549.

45. Henry A. Schweinhaut, "The Civil Liberties Section of the Department of Justice," *The Bill of Rights Review,* I, No. 3 (Spring, 1941), 216; *In the Shadow of War . . .,* p. 18.

46. *Annual Report . . . Attorney General, 1940,* p. 78.

47. Schweinhaut, *The Bill of Rights Review,* I, No. 3, 206, 216.

48. *In the Shadow of War . . . ,* p. 18.

49. Memorandum for S.T.E. from LeHand, February 18, 1939, and note signed S.E., February 20, 1939, FDRL, OF 320.

50. Ogden, p. 152.

51. F.D.R. to Robert M. La Follette, Jr., March 8, 1939, FDRL, OF 1581.

52. Memorandum: F.D.R. to Byrnes, July 26, 1939, FDRL, OF 1581.

53. Ickes, II, 549; Press Conference 515, January 5, 1939, Press Conferences of the President, XIII, 41, FDRL.

54. Ogden, p. 155.

55. *Ibid.,* p. 161.

56. *NYT,* November 4, 1939.

57. Ickes, III, 76.

58. *NYT,* January 8, 1940.

59. Gerhart, p. 168; Ickes, II, 592.

60. Ickes, III, 12, 51.

61. *NYT,* December 16, 1939, and January 19, 1940; Farley, p. 253.

62. Gerhart, pp. 185-87.

63. *Ibid.,* p. 189.

64. *Ibid.*

65. Ickes, III, 93.

66. Ickes, III, 132.

67. Charles A. Beard to *NYT,* in *NYT,* April 3, 1940.

68. *In the Shadow of War . . . ,* p. 17.

69. *Ibid.*
70. Gerhart, p. 194.
71. Murphy to Hayden, April 9, 1940, JRH.
72. *In the Shadow of War . . . ,* p. 17.
73. Ickes, III, 111.
74. Murphy to F.D.R., June 10, 1940, FDRL, Group 24.
75. Hayden to Murphy, February 6, 1941, JRH.
76. Murphy to F.D.R., June 1, 1942, FDRL, PSF (Box 36).

Bibliography

A. Manuscript Collections

When this manuscript was written, the private papers of Frank Murphy were not available for research. They have since become available at the Michigan Historical Collections of the University of Michigan.

Burton Historical Collection of the Detroit Public Library.
There is a small collection here of Frank Murphy's papers and a large collection of executive papers, entitled Mayor's Office Records, for the period when Murphy was mayor of Detroit.

Frank Murphy Birthplace, Harbor Beach, Michigan.
Very little manuscript material is located here.

Franklin D. Roosevelt Library, Hyde Park, N. Y.
Abundant, applicable material is in this library—consisting primarily of correspondence between Murphy and F.D.R. or other members of the Roosevelt administration.

Labor History Archives, Wayne State University, Detroit, Mich.
The Joe Brown Collection was especially useful. In the future, as the collection of labor history grows, there will undoubtedly be an abundance of material relating to the sit-downs.

Michigan Historical Collections of the University of Michigan, Ann Arbor, Mich.
The most valuable collection for a study of Murphy is the Joseph

R. Hayden Papers. It deals mostly with the Philippines but includes correspondence between Hayden and Murphy extending through 1941. The next most valuable collection is the Chase S. Osborn Papers. Osborn, a former governor of Michigan, left voluminous correspondence with state and national figures. The Frank Murphy Papers, which, at the time of preparing this manuscript, was a small collection, has since become a very large and important collection. The Edward G. Kemp Papers and the Arthur B. Moehlman Papers include one or two manuscripts pertaining to Murphy.

National Archives, Washington, D.C.

The Bureau of Insular Affairs division of the War Department contains a collection of manuscript material dealing with Murphy's period in the Philippines.

B. Public Documents

Annual Report of the Attorney General of the United States for the Fiscal Year Ended June 30, 1939. Washington: U. S. Government Printing Office, 1939.

Annual Report of the Attorney General of the United States for the Fiscal Year Ended June 30, 1940. Washington: U. S. Government Printing Office, 1940.

City of Detroit Journal of the Common Council, 1930-1933. Detroit: Inland Press, 1930-1933.

Department of Justice. *Federal Criminal Jurisdiction over Violation of Civil Liberties*. Circular no. 3356, Supplement no. 1, May 21, 1940.

State of Michigan, Commission on Reform and Modernization of Government. *A Report of a Preliminary Survey*. Lansing, December 20, 1938.

State of Michigan. *First Annual Report of the Michigan State Civil Service Department*. Lansing, December 31, 1938.

State of Michigan. *Journal of the House of Representatives of the*

State of Michigan, 1937-1939. Lansing: Franklin DeKlein Co., 1937-1939.

State of Michigan. *Report of the State Welfare Department of the State of Michigan.* Lansing, 1938.

Supreme Court of the United States. *Resolutions.* March 6, 1951.

U.S. Congress. *Annual Report of the Governor General of the Philippine Islands, 1933.* (74th Cong., 1st sess.; H.R. Doc. 32, serial doc. no. 9914.)

——————. *Annual Report of the Governor General of the Philippine Islands, 1934.* (74th Cong., 2d sess.; H.R. Doc. 411, serial doc. no. 10027.)

——————. *Annual Report of the Governor General of the Philippine Islands, 1935.* (75th Cong., 1st sess.; H.R. Doc. 100, serial doc. no. 10114.)

U.S. *Congressional Record.* Vols. LXXIX-LXXXVI.

U.S. House of Representatives, Special Committee to Investigate Un-American Activities and Propaganda in the United States. *Hearings.* (75th Cong., 3rd sess., 1938.)

——————. Special Committee to Investigate Un-American Activities and Propaganda in the United States. *Investigation of Un-American Activities and Propaganda.* Report No. 2. (76th Cong., 1st sess., 1939.)

U.S. Senate, Committee on Education and Labor. *Report, Violations of Free Speech and Rights of Labor.* (76th Cong., 1st sess., 1939.)

——————. Sub-Committee of the Committee on the Judiciary. *Hearing, Nomination of Frank Murphy to be Attorney General of the United States.* (76th Cong., 1st sess., 1939.)

C. Books and Pamphlets

Alinsky, Saul. *John L. Lewis; An Unauthorized Biography.* New York: G. P. Putnam's Sons, 1949.

Arnold, Thurman W. *The Bottlenecks of Business.* New York: Reynal and Hitchcock, 1940.

Bald, F. Clever. *Michigan in Four Centuries.* New York: Harper & Bros., 1954.

Barnard, Harry. *Independent Man: The Life of Senator James Couzens.* New York: Charles Scribner's Sons, 1958.

Beasley, Norman. *Knudsen: A Biography.* New York: McGraw-Hill Book Co., 1947.

Biddle, Francis. *In Brief Authority.* New York: Doubleday and Co., Inc., 1962.

The Bill of Rights 150 Years After; the Story of Civil Liberty 1938-1939. New York: American Civil Liberties Union, 1939.

Buck, Arthur E. *The Reorganization of State Government in the United States.* New York: Columbia University Press, 1938.

Burns, James MacGregor. *Roosevelt: the Lion and the Fox.* New York: Harcourt, Brace and Co., 1956.

Coughlin, Charles E. *Eight Lectures on Labor, Capital, and Justice.* Royal Oak, Mich.: Radio League of the Little Flower, 1932.

Darrow, Clarence. *The Story of My Life.* New York: Charles Scribner's Sons, 1932.

Derber, Milton and Young, Edwin (eds.). *Labor and the New Deal.* Madison: University of Wisconsin Press, 1947.

Farley, James. *Jim Farley's Story: The Roosevelt Years.* New York: McGraw-Hill Book Co., 1948.

Fecher, Charles A. *The Philosophy of Jacques Maritain.* Westminster, Md.: Newman Press, 1953.

Freidel, Frank. *America in the Twentieth Century.* New York: Alfred A. Knopf, 1960.

Fuller, George N. *Michigan, A Centennial History of the State and Its People.* 5 vols. Chicago: Lewis Publishing Co., 1939.

Gerhart, Eugene C. *America's Advocate, Robert H. Jackson.* Indianapolis: Bobbs-Merrill Co., 1958.

Bibliography

Haldeman-Julius, Marcet. *Clarence Darrow's Two Great Trials*. Girard, Kans.: Haldeman-Julius Co., 1927.

Hayden, Joseph Ralston. *The Philippines, a Study in National Development*. New York: Macmillan Co., 1942.

Ickes, Harold L. *The Secret Diary of Harold L. Ickes*. 3 vols. New York: Simon and Shuster, Inc., 1953.

In the Shadow of War; the Story of Civil Liberty 1939-1940. New York: American Civil Liberties Union, 1940.

Kraus, Henry. *The Many and the Few: A Chronicle of the Dynamic Auto Workers*. Los Angeles: Plantin Press, 1947.

Levinson, Edward. *Labor on the March*. New York: University Books, Inc., 1956.

Malcolm, George A. *The Commonwealth of the Philippines*. New York: D. Appleton-Century Co., 1936.

Marquardt, Frederic S. *Before Bataan and After; a Personalized History of Our Philippine Experiment*. New York: Bobbs-Merrill Co., 1943.

Moley, Raymond. *After Seven Years*. New York: Harper & Bros., 1939.

Murphy, Frank. *Catholicism and the Crisis*. Washington, D.C.: American Council on Public Affairs, 1941.

——————. *In Defense of Democracy*. 3rd ed. Washington, D.C.: American Council on Public Affairs, 1940.

——————. *Lawyers and the Reign of Freedom*. New York: Contemporary Law Pamphlets, Ser. 1, no. 30, 1940.

——————. *Selected Addresses of Frank Murphy, Governor of Michigan—January 1, 1937, to September 30, 1938*. Lansing, 1938.

Ogden, August Raymond. *The Dies Committee; a Study of the Special House Committee for the Investigation of Un-American Activities 1938-1943*. Washington: Catholic University of America Press, 1943.

Perkins, Frances. *The Roosevelt I Knew.* New York: Viking Press, 1946.

Pritchett, C. Herman. *The Roosevelt Court; a Study in Politics and Values, 1937-1947.* New York: Macmillan Co., 1948.

Quezon, Manuel Luis. *The Good Fight.* New York: D. Appleton Century Co., 1946.

Roosevelt, Elliott (ed.). *F.D.R., His Personal Letters 1928-1945.* 4 vols. New York: Duell, Sloan and Pearce, 1950.

Schlesinger, Arthur M., Jr. *The Age of Roosevelt.* Vol. III: *The Politics of Upheaval.* Cambridge: Riverside Press, 1960.

Seidman, Joel. *"Sit-Down."* New York: League for Industrial Democracy, 1937.

Sloan, Alfred P., Jr. *The Story of the General Motors Strike.* New York: General Motors Corp., 1937.

Smith, Robert Aura. *Philippine Freedom, 1946-1958.* New York: Columbia University Press, 1958.

Stone, Irving, *Clarence Darrow for the Defense: a Biography.* Garden City, N.Y.: Doubleday and Co., Inc., 1943.

Sward, Keith. *The Legend of Henry Ford.* New York: Rinehart and Co., 1948.

Tebbel, John. *The Life and Good Times of William Randolph Hearst.* New York: E. P. Dutton and Co., Inc., 1952.

Tugwell, Rexford G. *The Democratic Roosevelt; a Biography of Franklin D. Roosevelt.* New York: Doubleday and Co., Inc., 1957.

Ward, Louis B. *Father Charles E. Coughlin: an Authorized Biography.* Detroit: Tower Publications, Inc., 1933.

Weinstone, William. *The Great Sit-Down Strike.* New York: Workers Library Publishers, Inc., 1937.

White, Leonard D. *Introduction to the Study of Public Administration.* New York: Macmillan Co., 1955.

Bibliography

Whitehead, Don. *The FBI Story; a Report to the People.* New York: Random House, 1956.

Wilson, Walter and Deutsch, Albert. *Call Out the Militia! A Survey of the Use of Troops in Strikes.* New York: American Civil Liberties Union, 1938.

D. Articles

Arnold, Thurman W. "Mr. Justice Murphy," *Harvard Law Review,* LXIII (December, 1949), 289-93.

Fellows, J. A. "Detroit's Crime Clinic," *The Nation,* CXXX (May 14, 1930), 568-70.

Hallgren, Mauritz A. "Detroit's Liberal Mayor," *The Nation,* CXXXII (May 13, 1931), 526-28.

Murphy, Frank. "Industrial Peace," *The Christian Front,* II (November, 1937), 156-58.

——————. "The Moral Law in Government," *The Commonweal,* XVIII (May 19, 1933), 63-64.

——————. "Politics," *The Christian Front,* IV (March, 1939), 38-39.

——————. "Progress in Democracy," *American Labor Legislation Review,* XXIX (June, 1939), 61.

Schweinhaut, Henry A. "The Civil Liberties Section of the Department of Justice," *The Bill of Rights Review,* I, No. 3 (Spring, 1941), 206-16.

Swisher, Carl Brent. "Civil Liberties in War Time," *Political Science Quarterly,* LV, No. 3 (September, 1940), 321-47.

E. Newspapers

Daily Mining Journal. October 22, 1932.

Detroit Free Press. October 30, 1938.

Detroit News, 1920-40.

257

Detroit Saturday Night. 1930-33.

Detroit Times. 1920-40.

Manila Daily Bulletin. 1933-36.

Manila Tribune. 1933-36.

New York Times. 1928-40; June 18, 1961.

Philippines Herald. 1933-36.

F. Unpublished Theses and Dissertations

Howard, J. Woodford, Jr. "Frank Murphy: A Liberal's Creed." Unpublished Ph.D. dissertation, Princeton University, 1959. Pp. 522.

Lunt, Richard D. "Agitators: Long, Townsend, and Coughlin Versus the New Deal—1932 through 1936." Unpublished Master's thesis, University of New Mexico, 1959. Pp. 166.

Roth, Ruth D. "Nightmare in February." Unpublished Master's thesis, Wayne State University, 1956. Pp. 83.

Sawkins, Penelope H. "Executive Leadership of Frank Murphy as Governor of Michigan." Unpublished Master's thesis, Wayne State University, 1950. Pp. 83.

Index

The manuscript was edited by Gene Tendler.
The book was designed by Sylvia Winter.
The type face used is Linotype Garamond
designed by Claude Garamond.
The book is printed on Warren's Olde Style Antique paper
and bound in Holliston Mills Zeppelin cloth.
Manufactured in the United States of America